The Lust to Kill

The Lust to Kill

A Feminist Investigation of Sexual Murder

Deborah Cameron
and
Elizabeth Frazer

Polity Press

First published 1987 by Polity Press
in association with Basil Blackwell
Reprinted 1988

Editorial Office:
Polity Press, Dales Brewery, Gwydir Street, Cambridge CB1 2LJ, UK

Basil Blackwell Ltd,
108 Cowley Road, Oxford OX4 1JF, UK

British Library Cataloguing in Publication Data

Cameron, Deborah
  The lust to kill : a feminist investigation
  of sexual murder.
  1. Murder   2. Sex crimes
  I. Title   II. Frazer, Elizabeth
  364.1'523'019   HV6515

  ISBN 0-7456-0335-1
  ISBN 0-7456-0336-X Pbk

Typeset in 10 on 12 pt Baskerline
by Pioneer Associates, Perthshire
**Printed and bound in Great Britain
by Billing & Sons Limited, Worcester.**

The Lust to Kill could not have been written without the inspiration of the Women's Liberation Movement in which we have both been active for a number of years. We dedicate our work to all our sisters in the fight against male violence: we hope they will see it as a worthy contribution to the struggle.

Contents

Preface

We would like to clear up a few points about the subject, purpose and approach of this book and to thank the many people who helped it on its way. We are especially keen to avoid misunderstandings about the assumptions we have made in writing it; and since we would prefer not to harp on issues of method in the text itself, we take this opportunity of clarifying them at what some readers may consider unnecessary length. For us as writers and researchers, methodology has been crucial: we have discussed it continuously throughout the process of composition, and we think our readers have a right to know what we think we are about.

To begin with, then, this is a book about male power and male violence, as expressed in what we call 'the lust to kill'. This expression plays deliberately on a historical peculiarity of the English word *lust*: originally meaning a desire or wish, it has narrowed so that in .everyday usage it applies to only two desires — sexual desire and the desire for blood ('blood-lust'). Our claim is that these two desires are systematically connected.

Our interest in the subject of murder came out of our involvement in political work on pornography and rape. Alongside our sisters in various groups, we had developed a radical feminist analysis of male violence, but we were still mystified by the brutal and irrational desires underlying it. Those desires seemed to be at their most overt — and by the same token, their most mysterious — in a type of violence feminists had written relatively little about: sadistic sexual murder.

The kind of murder we mean is everywhere, and women learn early to fear its nameless horrors. Girls are warned not to talk to strange men, in case — like Genette Tate[1] — they are never seen again. Young women are advised to mind how they go, lest some crazed sex maniac should rape and kill them. Prostitutes know to keep an eye on the punter, for he may be carrying a hammer, or a knife. (No one tells wives to keep an eye on their husbands, but their mutilated bodies turn up anyway.) During the years of the Yorkshire Ripper murders, wild rumours circulated about *what the killer did*. Horrified by the details (some of which later turned out to be true), many women asked: 'Why does he do it? What can he get out of it?' The conventional answer was, of course, sexual gratification; the Ripper and other killers act out desires that are also attested to in cultural products like snuff movies in which women are actually killed. But little is known, and less understood, of that strange conjunction of violence and sex. Where does it come from, what does it mean? These were the riddles we set out to solve.

We soon began to feel we were alone in our quest. In all the millions of words written about murder and the millions more about sexual desire, nothing we read seemed to answer the case. This suggested a further riddle: why has the problem of sadistic sexual murder been so massively neglected, or else so misleadingly stated? Our investigation had to broaden its scope, so that not only murder itself but also our culture's ways of thinking about murder, became of interest and significance to us.

The book which resulted from this widening of focus is rather more complicated than we originally thought it would be and consequently much more 'academic' in appearance. Nevertheless, we have tried to make it accessible and one of the aims of our preface is to explain what is in it and suggest some reading strategies.

If a researcher is going to be scrupulous in acknowledging her sources, discussing all her evidence and not over-simplifying complex facts and arguments, a certain amount of scholarly 'clutter' is unavoidable: notes, references, appendices and so on. In this book, however, the clutter has been kept as unobtrusive as possible. For example, it is feasible to read straight through the text, ignoring the notes, without missing anything crucial. Quotations are briefly attributed in the text and the notes in most cases merely give the exact source, without adding anything new to the argument. The bibliography contains a complete listing not only of the works we refer to, but also of other useful things we came across. Thus the reader who ignores the notes will not miss out on actual information, but if she wants to check our facts for herself, the details are to hand.

One piece of clutter is designed specifically to help those readers without an encyclopaedic knowledge of murder. The appendix consists of an alphabetical listing of all the sex-murderers referred to in the text, with brief details of the facts of their cases. Many readers will want to refer to these accounts as they encounter unfamiliar names in the text. It is also useful to have them all together as a dreadful reminder of the *scale* of sexual killing. For although we do not intend to wallow in gory details, we believe that feminists should be more aware than most are of the appalling reality of sadistic murder — the sadistic rituals, tortures, mutilations, assaults and rapes both before and after death, which characterize not only well-known *causes célèbres*, but also the 'fish-and-chip killings' that occur week in, week out.

Everything we have said so far tends to emphasize the feminist orientation of our work. Our subject-matter, our reasons for writing, our desire to document as well as to explain — all these are marks of political commitment, of our self-conscious and unashamed position as feminists. Yet there are other obvious and less obvious signs of our politics in the way we have chosen to write this book and especially in the way we have approached our research. For instance — and most readers will find this familiar — we problematize gender and the relations of power between women and men. This differentiates us from most writers about sexual murder, who have (apparently) no conception that gender is so important. In bringing the issue of gender to the fore, we identify ourselves as having a feminist perspective. Less obvious, perhaps, is the link between our feminism and the way we conceptualize the process of research. In line with recent thinking about the nature of knowledge, we regard ourselves as seeking out not objective truth, but rather an alternative interpretation of the world. Although this point of view is not confined to feminists, it is particularly likely to appeal to feminists: we, after all, have had ample cause to notice how often so-called objective research has been sexist research, beginning from partisan, masculine assumptions and presenting its equally partisan conclusions as 'the truth'.

It is worth considering in a fair amount of detail what this view of the research process has meant to us in practice. Many previous researchers on the subject of sex murder have assumed that somewhere there is a kernel of truth about why it occurs; they have often made the further assumption that particular methods, say psychoanalysis or karyotyping, would systematically reveal that truth. Our own assumptions are very different and we are often challenged to justify them. A sceptical reader might argue as follows: *The Lust to Kill* is a text about murder: it is also a text about texts about murder. On some level, this alone must invalidate our work, since instead of going straight to the heart of the matter, we have merely produced a commentary on secondary material; for the most part, we have read what everyone reads, in one form or another; and what, after all, can possibly be learnt from such an indirect and parasitic procedure?

Yet it might be argued that there is no alternative. For what would constitute 'the heart of the matter'? Interviews with sex-murderers, perhaps? A detailed breakdown of factual details, culled from the records of psychiatrists and police? Even if these lines of enquiry were possible, we believe they would beg very fundamental questions. The accounts that policemen and psychiatrists give of killers, not to mention the accounts that killers give of themselves, are not 'the truth', they are yet more constructed texts: as such they depend, like biographies and news reports, on the codes of the culture to give them meaning. When the murderer writes a confession, a life story, he cannot do it outside the limits of his own understanding of what he has done and how it appears to others. Furthermore, this understanding is not miraculously given, a pristine and privileged insight into the killer's own mind; the killer who tells us 'I don't know what came over me', or 'I really loved her' or 'I was cleaning up the streets' is using a formula, a generic convention which he learned in society and which both he and others recognize as 'the sort of account someone might give of that sort of event'. It is these cultural codes that interest us: we have chosen to study them in and for themselves. The discourse by which sex-killing is made intelligible to us, whether it comes from the killer, a psychiatrist or *The Sun*, is not parasitic on some higher truth: it is the heart of the matter and the rest is silence.

There are many examples and case histories which suggest the close relationship of murder and discourse about murder, even for that supposedly 'irrational' creature, the murderer himself. One celebrated instance, widely known as a result of Michel Foucault's concern with it, is that of the Norman peasant Pierre Rivière, who was convicted in 1836 of a triple murder. His memoir, edited and published by Foucault, is titled '*I, Pierre Rivière, Having Slaughtered my Mother, my Sister and my Brother . . .*'. Although it is a confession, written after the killings, Rivière maintained it was 'written in my head' before the act. Commenting on this, one writer has observed,

The text did not *express* a desire, which was then *expressed* in action. Desire, text and action were indissolubly linked, because they were shaped, made possible, therefore in a sense *produced* by a particular 'discursive practice' made up of Bible stories and history learnt at school, famous murders commemorated in flysheets and broadsheets and, not least, the confessional autobiography.[2]

Rivière, in other words, could envisage his act of slaughter as meaningful and justifiable because he was familiar with various kinds of discourses, like broadsheets and true confessions, which were staple forms of popular literature in the nineteenth century. His reading gave him a context for his acts, a tradition to place himself in, even conventions for writing his confession later on. We are not suggesting that literature *caused* Rivière to kill; we do think, however, that human culture crucially involves processes of representation, and the representations available to Rivière shaped the form of his killing and the way he understood it.

The sense that one is part of a continuing tradition and that the role of murderer is an identity one takes on, is common among the mass-killers we have looked at and it seems to go with the same urge Rivière had, the urge to turn act into discourse (and vice versa). One thinks of Dennis Nilsen, with his obsessive accounts and drawings on such subjects as 'dismembering a body'; or of the sender of the Yorkshire Ripper tape, whose identity is still unknown, but who was sufficiently familiar with the case of Jack the Ripper a century earlier to set out deliberately to continue the tradition, imitating in more up-to-date form the letters to the police sent originally by 'Jack'. And there are many lesser-known examples which graphically illustrate the same point.

For instance, there is the case of Ronald Frank Cooper, a white South African who in 1976 wrote the following passage in one of several diaries he was keeping at the time:

I have decided that I think I should become a homosexual murderer and shall get hold of young boys and bring them here where I am staying and I shall rape them and kill them [there follows a very detailed list of methods]. . . . This does not apply to the four boys I have selected as possible human sacrifices. They will be killed by strangulation, after which I shall cut their

throats and drink part of their blood and cut off their private
parts and then cut it up. . . . I will not stop before I have killed at
least 30 boys. Most of them will be raped. It doesn't matter
whether I rape them before or after they're dead. . . . When I
have killed these 30 boys I will start a murder campaign against
women.[3]

Many things about this passage are striking (and they are common to
other murderers): the extraordinary detail, presumably highly
arousing to its author; the taking on of a deliberate persona ('I have
decided . . . I should become a homosexual murderer').

What is especially interesting about the case of Cooper is that when
he did finally commit a murder, the real experience did not measure
up to these carefully documented fantasy killings. Cooper was keeping
several separate diaries and the incident of the murder was recorded
in all of them. Each successive account is a more minutely detailed
description of the same events: it is as if the writer was trying to
exorcise reality and turn it into the imaginary again. The shortest
entry in the sequence went as follows: 'Today I strangled a 12 year old
boy. . . . When he was dead I tried to rape him but I simply couldn't do
it. I am really sorry I murdered him.'[4] Here, Cooper has produced yet
another account of himself, quite radically different from the one we
quoted earlier. One conventional approach to this difference would
be to say the two texts correspond, respectively, to 'fantasy' and
'reality': or in other words, that one of them is 'truer' than the other.
We do not accept this conventional view. Although they are
descriptions of a fantasy and a real event, they are nevertheless *both
descriptions*, i.e., constructed accounts, representations which are both
made possible by the prior existence of cultural codes. It is idle to ask
which diary entry is 'the truth': there is no truth, there are only these
accounts and that is why we approach the whole phenomenon of
murder in the way that we do, through discourse about it.

It follows that we do not claim to have produced, in this book, the
one true explanation of sexual murder. Rather, we have produced an
alternative account which makes criticisms of existing explanations.
We evaluate our account and expect others to evaluate it, not by its
degree of correspondence to the 'objective facts', since for us that
whole notion must always be in question; but rather by the usefulness
for feminist politics of having the concepts and categories we propose.

One further sign of our commitment to feminism is the consciously interdisciplinary focus of *The Lust to Kill* and the fact that we have felt able to venture into academic territory where we have no special claims to expertise. Feminists are notorious for not respecting the 'proper' boundaries of academic disciplines and in our opinion that is all to the good. Women trying to analyse and change things cannot afford to be deterred by their own apparent ignorance: we need to have confidence in our ability to read and interpret. Rather than believe in 'experts' who imply they know it all, we must look for the gaps and the hidden agendas. If knowledge and power go hand in hand, it is the responsibility of feminists both to acquire knowledge and to transform it.

That said, our own quest for knowledge was made immeasurably less arduous by the constant help and encouragement we received from other people. Some of these were professionals or 'insiders' whom we consulted about unfamiliar and specialist fields, or to get information that was otherwise unavailable. Particular thanks are due to Richard Dawkins, Gwen Hewitt, Nicola Lacey and Rachel Perkins for their guidance on aspects of biological science, criminal law and clinical psychology, and to the lawyers and criminologists who participated in a workshop on sex murder at the 1986 European Critical Legal Studies conference. We also acknowledge the kind co-operation of Dave Edwards and colleagues at *True Detective* and Julia Reddaway, formerly of Argus Publications Ltd. Mrs Flavell of the Bodleian Library's John Johnson collection helped us in locating broadsheet materials, while Jennifer Chibnall and Caroline Henton made valiant efforts to track down obscure references on both sides of the Atlantic. Crucial readings were suggested by Patricia Duncker (to whom we are indebted for very detailed discussion of chapter 2), Jo Garcia and Jocey Quinn. Last but not least, we are very grateful to all the other people who read the typescript at various stages in its composition and made helpful comments on it: Jill Bourne, Deborah Georgiou, Maree Gladwin, Emma Letley, Buffy Mullet, Zbigniew Pelczynski, Nicole Polonsky, Elizabeth Powell-Jones, Irené Ray-Crosby and Jenefer Sargent.

D. J. C.
E. J. F.

1

Introduction
In Search of the Murderer

It's just something that comes over me.

(Peter Sutcliffe, on being asked why he had stabbed one of his victims
through the breast.)

This book began from a simple observation: there has never been a
female Peter Sutcliffe. Women have committed very brutal murders;
they have killed repeatedly; they have killed at random. But in all the
annals of recorded crime, no woman has done what Peter Sutcliffe did
(or Jack the Ripper, or Christie, or the Boston Strangler). Only men,
it seems, are compulsive lone hunters, driven by the lust to kill — a
sexual desire which finds its outlet in murder.

If this initial observation is accurate, a number of questions suggest
themselves at once. Why do some men find killing erotic? Why never
women, but only men? Not unnaturally, we went in search of answers
to the extensive literature of modern criminology. But it seemed our
questions were not on the agenda: we found ourselves confronting a
void. From *True Detective* to the scholarly journals, from popular
biographies to clinical case histories, the absence of women in the
ranks of sex-killers was both *presupposed* and at the same time *obscured*.

In the chapters that follow, we survey all this literature and attempt
to explain why its gender-unawareness cannot be dismissed as a trivial
oversight. An account of sexual murder which does not address gender
is not merely incomplete, but systematically misleading.

But before we can embark on a detailed critique of the various
discourses about sexual murder, we must define our terms, establish
our facts and state more precisely where the problem lies. In this
introduction we want to begin by discussing the link between gender
and murder in general; only then will it be possible to consider how
far sexual murder, as we define it, should be regarded as a special
case.

RESEARCHING MURDER, PROBLEMS AND SOURCES

Certain facts about the incidence of murder are public property and common knowledge. The perennial fascination that violent death has for our culture ensures a steady output of material: encyclopaedias of case histories, books of famous trials, biographies of notorious killers, volumes of detectives' and pathologists' memoirs. To these we may add a mountain of ephemera, from printed broadsides and execution sermons to news reports and magazine features.

But although these sources contain much that is of interest (indeed we will be returning to them later) they provide little basis for generalization. Their coverage is always selective and piecemeal, and what they reveal are the preoccupations of an era, rather than what would turn out statistically to be its major social trends.

To us, for instance, it is very interesting that so much historical and contemporary material exists concerning women killers. Some of this material consists of serious studies of the social pressures which lead women to kill;[1] much of it consists of mere sensational accounts cashing in on the notoriety of cases involving women. It would certainly be wrong to deduce from the abundance of documentation that murders by women have been either frequent or typical; they were probably notable because they were neither, as well as inspiring a more prurient interest (to judge from the many popular accounts of women's executions, described in lingering detail).

Popular accounts of murder in general mislead by focusing only on sensational cases. A great deal of murder is extremely banal; yet as Terence Morris and Louis Blom-Cooper point out in their introduction to *A Calendar of Murder*, a useful volume which gives very brief outlines of every murder trial in England and Wales between 1957 and 1962, 'Any discussion about the nature of murder or the character of murderers must, if it is to be valid, take into account all instances of the crime, many of which are lacking in any newsworthy quality.'[2] If we wish to make generalizations about murder, we cannot confine ourselves to a few well-documented and grisly cases: we need to find out the full facts of murder from systematic and reliable sources — a task which can prove surprisingly difficult.

In writing this part of the book, we decided to concentrate on our own time and culture as a manageable case-study (though we do consider later on in this chapter how far our observations might be valid across cultures and particularly for the United States). The obvious place to seek information on murder in twentieth-century England is the Home Office, within whose sphere crime and punishment fall. The details it issues are minimal, however: a set of annual criminal statistics and occasional digests or reports based on them.[3] For the ordinary researcher without privileged access, little of a more detailed nature is available. It is therefore necessary to turn to court transcripts, or more usually, reports of court proceedings. Morris and Blom-Cooper employed three researchers to comb through newspapers ('frequently obscure and . . . excessively parochial'). The extent of Home Office co-operation with their work was to provide a list of persons indicted, which ensured the researchers would look up every case, but left them at the mercy of journalistic oversight and bias. We made extensive use of the *Calendar of Murder*, because it aspired to be exhaustive; but we were also obliged to use more haphazard sources, such as popular case-books, newspaper clippings and occasional state-sponsored research reports.[4]

Of course, we also used crime statistics, and these presented problems of their own. It comes very naturally to think of figures as essentially neutral and free from bias, but a moment's reflection shows that this is naive — compiling statistics involves making judgements and interpretations which are not above criticism. Somebody has to decide, for instance, what facts are important enough to record; someone must decide which cases are comparable and what the relevant criteria are. In making these decisions, implicit theories are at work and their assumptions may be highly questionable. In the case of statistics on the incidence of homicide, decisions about what to record and in what form depend very largely on legal provisions and specifically on the 1957 Homicide Act. Before a researcher can interpret Home Office figures, she needs to be conversant with the workings of the law.

Killing and the law, a beginner's guide

The definition of murder given in legal textbooks dates from the seventeenth century, when it was formulated in the following terms: 'Where a man of sound memory and the age of discretion unlawfully kills any reasonable creature in being, and under the King's peace, with malice aforethought, either express or implied by law, the death taking place within a year and a day'.

The important part of this is 'malice aforethought', that is, the intention to kill (or to commit grievous bodily harm). If someone kills by accident or through negligence, they are guilty of the lesser crime of *manslaughter*. It is also possible to have the offence reduced to manslaughter if the court accepts that there was provocation. The term *homicide* encompasses both murder and manslaughter.

What about killers who are mentally ill? A defence of insanity can be established if the case comes within the McNaghten rules, laid down in 1843: if 'the party accused was labouring under such defect of reason as not to know the nature and quality of the act he was doing, or if he did know it . . . he did not know what he was doing was wrong.' Killers whose cases fall within this definition are 'detained during Her Majesty's pleasure', which is to say, sent to a special hospital for the criminally insane.

Because most people prefer to avoid being sentenced to indefinite incarceration and also because the McNaghten criteria are so strict, insanity defences are rarely used now. Most mentally abnormal killers use section two of the 1957 Homicide Act, which provides for a defence of *diminished responsibility*. Section two states:

> Where a person kills or is a party to the killing of another, he shall not be convicted of murder if he was suffering from such abnormality of mind (whether arising from a condition of arrested or retarded development or any inherent causes or induced by disease or injury) as substantially impaired his mental responsibility for his acts and omissions in doing or being a party to the killing.

This defence allows a court to consider a much wider range of circumstances than the McNaghten rules. (For instance, an 'irresistible impulse' might be counted as diminished responsibility, whereas it would not be judged a form of insanity.) It also reduces the actual offence from murder to manslaughter ('section-two manslaughter').

The point of commuting one offence to another has more to do with punishment than crime. Murder committed by an adult carries a statutory penalty which judges cannot vary, namely life imprisonment (since 1965). Yet where a killer is mentally ill, there is no question of deterrence and should be none of retribution; an automatic life sentence is both callous and too rigid. The killer may be successfully treated, in which case further detention is unnecessary; or he may be a danger for the rest of his life, in which case the length of his sentence is irrelevant. Making the offence into manslaughter rather than murder allows the judge to vary the sentence. Judges can make Hospital Orders under the Mental Health Act, with or without restriction and for any length of time. They can put a person who has killed on probation, or conversely, hand out a stiff custodial sentence.

There are two defences which, if successful, reduce the offence from murder to manslaughter: diminished responsibility and provocation (a third rare defence is when murder is committed in pursuance of a suicide pact). Feminists must take careful note of these, since their consequence is that many crimes against women — many wife murders, attempted suicide-murders, sexual killings of women and girls — appear, ironically, in the *man*slaughter figures. Furthermore, the workings of these defences are of interest, since there is often a veiled double standard at work. For instance, what counts as provocation? In England and Wales in the first half of the 1980s there have been several cases of husbands successfully claiming provocation after killing a wife who had allegedly nagged, or been unfaithful, or sexually 'unorthodox'.[5]

Another major question about section-two defences is who decides that a killer is abnormal? Somewhat surprisingly, it is rare for that decision to be made by a jury of the killer's peers in open court. Usually the attribution of mental illness is a matter for the experts alone. If psychiatrists for both prosecution and defence agree that a defendant is abnormal, the court accepts a plea of guilty to manslaughter under section two. There is thus no need for a jury trial to take place. According to a recent report on the workings of section two, this is what happens in 80 per cent of cases where mental abnormality is at issue.[6] Trials where a jury consider psychiatric evidence normally only happen when the two sides are *not* in agreement — though the most celebrated recent example of such a trial, Peter Sutcliffe's, took place because the judge felt it would be in the public interest to have a jury trial. Counsel for both sides agreed that Sutcliffe was abnormal: when the evidence was aired, however, the jury said he was not. In the typical instance, though, the whole matter is thrashed out between lawyers and psychiatrists — members, it must be said, of two overwhelmingly patriarchal and male-dominated professions.

Categories of killing

The provisions of the 1957 Homicide Act give rise to seven categories of homicide which are used in compiling the criminal statistics. The seven officially recognized types are normal murder, insane murder, suicide-murder, section-two manslaughter, common-law manslaughter reduced from murder, other common-law manslaughter and infanticide. Insane murder, suicide-murder and section-two manslaughter are sometimes conflated into a more general category, 'abnormal homicide' (i.e., homicide committed by a mentally abnormal killer).

Before offering brief definitions of these categories, it is extremely important to point out that the assignment of any particular incident to one category rather than another is based not on the nature of the incident itself, but on the outcome of the judicial process, which in some respects can be very arbitrary. Three identical incidents of wife-strangling, say, could well show up as a normal murder, an insane murder and a section-two manslaughter respectively. The difference would lie not in who did what to whom, but in what counsel decided to plead and whether the court accepted it. Thus in many cases, the category in which a homicide is placed tells you very little of interest about it. The outrageous acts of a Peter Sutcliffe can be classified as 'normal' murder (since the court rejected his plea of diminished responsibility), while on the other hand, anyone who commits suicide after murder is automatically classed as an abnormal killer, whether impelled by mental illness, unbearable remorse, or simply a desire to avoid going to prison.

Although the essential uninformativeness of this classification cannot be overemphasized, in the interests of clarity we offer brief definitions.

Normal murder   Any homicide committed with malice aforethought by a person not subsequently found to have been mentally abnormal by reason of insanity, diminished responsibility or suicide. There is a statutory penalty of life imprisonment.

Insane murder   Homicide committed by someone who falls within the McNaghten rules, i.e., does not know the nature of their acts, or that they were wrong. Insane killers are detained during Her Majesty's pleasure in a special hospital.

Suicide-murder Homicide followed by successful suicide. If a killer tries to commit suicide and fails, the incident is classed by its outcome, as usual.

Section-two manslaughter Homicide committed by someone who successfully claims diminished responsibility under section two of the Homicide Act. The penalty is variable, but often involves a hospital order for psychiatric treatment under the Mental Health Act. This may be restricted (i.e., unrevocable without reference to the Home Secretary). Ordinary custodial sentences are also common.

Common-law manslaughter (*reduced from murder/other*) Homicide committed without malice aforethought (for example by accident or negligence) or where the killer was responding to provocation. The penalty is variable depending on the circumstances.

Infanticide Where a woman kills her child of less than one year because she is suffering from the effects of pregnancy or lactation. This is an offence men cannot commit (though they can kill infants and frequently do). The penalty tends to be light, since these women are seen as victims of their biology.

Interpreting figures based on these categories is tricky, because various factors tend to be conflated. On one hand, there are people's own beliefs about their motives and mental states, while on the other there are those implicitly embodied in the law. Even more complicated are the ways in which people present their actions in the light of their understanding of the beliefs of the courts.

An example may help to clarify this point. Take the crime of infanticide, which the law believes is caused by a temporary insanity rooted in female biology. Presumably there are infant-killers whose rationale is completely different: for instance, they never wanted the child and had no way of supporting it, so they killed it at birth. Nevertheless, they are likely to concur with the legal notion of what caused their actions; their lawyers are likely to encourage this, because it means that the sentence will be light. Consequently, we cannot assume that if ten women a year commit infanticide, they have all done the same thing and for the same reason.

Other problems of a similar kind present themselves in relation to gender differences. For instance, suppose we find that women killers are more often in the abnormal than the normal category. Does this mean that only mentally ill women kill, or does it mean that women who kill are likely to be labelled mentally ill automatically? Or suppose we find that large numbers of men plead diminished responsibility after killing their wives in a jealous rage. Does this mean that the individual killers are abnormal, or that sexual jealousy is regarded in our culture as a form of madness for which a man is not responsible? Or is the whole thing merely a charade, a cover for widespread beliefs in society that unfaithful women deserve to be punished, while their murderous husbands should be leniently treated? Bearing these various problems in mind, we turn to the statistics.

Homicide statistics for England and Wales

Homicide statistics never tell you quite as much as you think they will; as a source of information they have important limitations and we want to begin this discussion of them with the caveats painfully borne in upon us by hours of frustrating research.

The most obvious shortcoming of all crime statistics is that they probably underestimate the incidence of the crime in question. Criminologists believe that homicide is no exception and that published figures conceal a 'dark figure' of incidents which do not come to the attention of the authorities, either because they are passed off as natural deaths or because no body is recovered (thus a small but significant number of people — especially women and children — who disappear and are presumed to have been murdered are not actually recorded as homicide cases).

Other limitations have more to do with the way the Home Office and police classify incidents. From our point of view it is especially galling that so many of the categories used in homicide statistics systematically obscure gender differences. Figures are available on 'sex of offender' and 'sex of victim', so that numbers of male and female killers or victims may be compared; but when it comes to the relationship between killers and killed — for instance how many women are killed by men and vice versa — there is no information available at all. Even gender differences in marital and family killing are submerged by sex-neutral category labels like 'spouse' and 'parent'. Information on motive, which might conceivably shed some light on gender relationships, is itself very scanty and limited. The category of sexual murder, so important to us, is entirely absent from published statistics, even in its least controversial and most mechanical definition as homicide in the course of a sexual attack. The reason the Home Office gives for this omission (in an obscure but extremely instructive footnote) is that 'there is often insufficient detail available to determine whether any sexual contact was or was not with the consent of the victim.' [!]

Bearing in mind these shortcomings, what can be learnt from published homicide statistics? Some general conclusions can certainly be drawn and there is a certain amount of more detailed analysis available in secondary sources (such as Morris and Blom-Cooper's *Calendar of Murder* and the occasional research reports of Home Office statisticians on long-term trends in crime).

First of all, it is frequently noted that rates of homicide in England and Wales are fairly stable. From 1900 to 1960 the number of homicides per million of the population remained between 3.7 and 4.4, in contrast to other crimes of violence which showed a steady increase over the same period. The years since 1960 have seen some increase, but this has not been large enough to constitute a major upheaval.

It needs to be pointed out here that patterns of crime are culture-specific; there is no reason to expect every society to produce the same quantity or kind of homicide. Thus for instance it is obvious that a culture with a tradition of revenge killing, or one where hand-guns are routinely carried, will present a different profile from that of England and Wales. The type of homicide most prevalent in a given community will also reflect its traditions, leading to marked regional variations. For example, the anthropologist Henry Lundsgaarde investigated Houston, Texas, where rates of homicide are extremely high and a significant proportion result in acquittal. Lundsgaarde explains this with reference to the local concept of 'frontier justice', a historical hangover from the time when men were expected to protect family and property by shooting first and asking questions later.[7]

Compared with Houston, and with the United States generally, England and Wales have a low rate of homicide. Commentators have explained both the modesty and the stability of homicide rates with reference to the peculiar character of the English homicide: in this country, as Morris and Blom-Cooper put it, 'Murder is overwhelmingly a domestic crime, in which men kill their wives, mistresses and children, and women kill their children.'[8] In other words, England is different from societies like the United States in that homicidal violence is not primarily connected with an ever-expanding base of

organized crime, nor (as yet) with the brutalities of inner-city life;
rather, it is linked to those most basic and unchanging institutions,
heterosexuality and the nuclear family.

This observation immediately gives us a clue to the *gender*
composition of the English homicide figures. If murder is a function
of sexual and family relations, then given the imbalance of power
between the sexes, one would predict that so-called 'domestic' murder
would turn out, for the most part, to mean *men* killing *women*. The
remarks of Morris and Blom-Cooper suggest just this: on the subject
of domestic murder they write:

> Of the murder victims over the age of 16, seventy percent are
> female, and of these females nearly half are killed by their legal
> husbands and a quarter by other relations and lovers. . . . The
> commonest murders are that of a wife by her husband, a child by
> one of its parents or a woman by her lover.[9]

These comments were made in the early 1960s; more detailed
information on the whole decade comes from two research reports
compiled by Home Office statisticians. Both Gibson and Klein's report
Murder 1957—1968 and Gibson's later report *Homicide in England and
Wales*, which covers the years 1967—71, reveal a marked and consistent
tendency for killers to be male and murder victims female. To give
some idea just how marked this pattern was, we reproduce some of
Gibson and Klein's figures for sex of offender and sex of victim in
tables 1.1 and 1.2 (we have confined ourselves to normal murder and
the three categories of abnormal homicide, since manslaughter other
than section-two manslaughter includes many accidental killings and
infanticide, a female crime by definition, permits no comparison
between the two sexes).

The pattern revealed in table 1.1 for sex of offender is particularly
striking: there are very few women killers. Men outnumber them in
each category, every year and the imbalance is greatest in the normal
murder category. The picture for sex of victim is also fairly clear-cut,
leading Gibson and Klein to summarize it thus:

> The proportion of women among victims over sixteen was . . .
> high at about 80% for suicide murder and about 70% for insane
> murder and section two manslaughter. For all abnormal murder

Table 1.1   Male and female killers in four categories of homicide

	Normal murder		Insane murder		Suicide murder		Manslaughter S. 2	
	M	F	M	F	M	F	M	F
1957	34	2	14	6	26	14	15	4
1958	23	2	16	3	22	16	25	3
1959	44	—	22	3	25	10	16	4
1960	49	—	17	5	28	11	23	7
1961	38	2	15	5	25	9	18	10
1962	42	2	13	2	28	18	28	10
1963	35	1	10	2	22	14	45	7
1964	52	—	6	4	18	13	28	7
1965	49	2	7	1	29	11	38	8
1966	68	1	5	—	20	5	52	8
1967	64	1	8	1	26	9	33	14
1968	75	2	4	1	30	8	38	11

Source: Gibson and Klein (1969)

Table 1.2   Adult male and female victims in four categories of homicide

	Normal murder		Insane murder		Suicide-murder		Manslaughter S. 2	
	M	F	M	F	M	F	M	F
1957	21	23	2	10	3	20	1	10
1958	18	19	3	13	6	18	7	17
1959	19	27	4	19	1	17	3	13
1960	21	20	8	11	6	21	1	17
1961	18	24	7	11	4	18	6	14
1962	23	25	—	13	5	24	13	14
1963	11	29	3	10	5	15	13	20
1964	29	30	3	6	7	19	7	18
1965	26	35	3	4	6	23	11	25
1966	42	32	4	1	1	18	12	35
1967	37	35	3	4	6	25	8	28
1968	34	40	1	2	6	25	14	26

Source: Gibson and Klein (1969)

over the period, about three quarters of adult victims were women, in contrast to 'normal' murder in which men and women victims were about equal in number.[10]

In fact table 1.2 shows that there were only three years between 1957 and 1968 when men outnumbered women victims even in the normal murder category.

Would these generalizations still hold good for the 1970s and 1980s? Unfortunately, the Home Office has issued no reports comparable to Gibson and Klein's which cover the fifteen years since 1971; our information on this period is correspondingly less full. Nevertheless, it is clear from the annual statistics that something has happened to modify the pattern of the 1960s. Although male murderers still vastly outnumber females — just as in table 1.1 — it is no longer true that women make up the majority of victims. In every year since the mid-1970s, there have been more men killed overall than women. In 1984, for instance, the figures were 319 men to 244 women.

Interestingly enough, this change has recently been seized on and used by feminists for political purposes. In 1986, a young woman estate agent was abducted in London by a client and there was a wave of public anxiety about the safety of women at work; it was even suggested that they should not keep business appointments alone. Not surprisingly, a lot of feminists regarded this as a reactionary attack on their right to work. In an article for *Cosmopolitan* magazine, Anne Karpf argued strongly that the anxiety was misplaced, since the group most at risk of being murdered was *men*, and she cited the 1984 homicide figures to prove it.[11] She did not point out, however, that this was a fairly recent development, women having been more at risk for most of the century (albeit from their husbands and lovers rather than their business clients).

So exactly how is the change to be accounted for? Are women really less at risk than they used to be? Are the wives and mistresses fighting back? Limited information makes it hard to be sure, but we would argue that what is going on is not so much a shift away from domestic and sexual murder (also known as womanslaughter) as an accretion of all-male killings on top of it. Three factors in particular support this interpretation.

First and most obviously, there has not been a major decline in the numbers of women killed each year. Rather, the numbers of men have risen faster. This leads to the second, more general and theoretical point: it has been generally observed by criminologists that rising rates of homicide tend to correlate positively with rising numbers of male victims, and vice versa. That is, rather than involving a redistribution of victim roles across a constant number of homicides, changes in the gender composition of murder victims are a consequence of more homicide being committed. We have already seen that homicide rates have gone up somewhat since the 1960s. Thirdly, the rise in homicide seems to be an increase in normal murders rather than abnormal homicides (especially section-two manslaughter). We noted earlier that women victims predominate in the abnormal categories and we may presume that they have continued to do so; they have simply been overtaken by rising numbers of mostly male normal-murder victims. (On this point, of course, it would be useful to have more detailed information, since in theory the increase in normal murder might represent nothing more than a hardening of court practice to permit fewer successful diminished responsibility defences. However, it has been argued that whereas domestic and sexual crimes are apt to be classified as abnormal, typical 'male on male' killings, for example in quarrels or gang warfare, are poor candidates for defences of insanity or diminished responsibility.)

All in all, then, we would argue that although the English homicide is no longer as overwhelmingly domestic as it was, there is just as much killing of women going on as in the days when this showed up so strikingly in the figures. Nevertheless, the quantitative picture contains many crucial gaps, so that many questions remain unanswered. At this point it is useful to turn to more qualitative sources, and to look in more detail at specific types of murders in the hope of finding patterns not revealed by crime statistics.

Wife-killing

The killing of wives and mistresses is an obvious category to take if one is interested in homicide and gender differences. Data on the subject is particularly plentiful, since this was until recently the most common type of homicide in England and Wales. Clearly, it is more common statistically than husband-killing; indeed this has been true throughout the whole modern period. (J. S. Cockburn, the historian of crime, examined records of indictments before the courts of three counties from 1559 to 1625 and found that 'wives were the victims of almost three quarters of the instances of marital killing.'[12]) But apart from this numerical sexual asymmetry, it can also be shown using court reports that male and female 'marital killers' have different motives and are treated very differently.

Judicial treatment of marital killers has long been affected by a sexual double standard. For centuries this was written into the law: as late as 1789 in England, to kill one's husband was not murder but 'petty treason', for which the penalty was burning at the stake. Domestic violence against women, in contrast, was both more widespread and more leniently treated. Deplorably, this is still the case, though as a matter of practice rather than statute. English law does not permit a husband to kill his wife and her lover if he finds them together — as was legal until very recently in Italy and is still allowed in the Texas penal code — but if he *should* kill a wayward or adulterous wife, he will often be treated with considerable sympathy (see note 4). As the American lawyers Schneider and Jordan have written, 'The acts of men and women are subject to a different set of legal expectations and standards. The man's act, while not always legally condoned, is viewed sympathetically. He is not forgiven, but his motivation is understood by those sitting in judgement upon his act.'[13]

But what exactly *are* these 'acts of men and women'? To ensure we considered a reasonably typical selection of marital killings, we chose a year from the *Calendar of Murder* and examined every trial involving a spouse, cohabitant or lover. In the year we chose, 1961, there were forty-six examples of this type of trial, forty-one where the victim was female and only five where the victim was male.

The first reason why men murdered wives and mistresses was straightforward quarrelling over money, children and divorce. It accounted, however, for a mere eight cases — less than 20 per cent of the total wife-killings. There were ten cases where the motive was clearly jealousy because the woman had been seeing another man; and ten more where adultery was not a factor, but in which the man had been rejected by the woman and had killed her because of that. It seems that men resent independent women as much as unfaithful or promiscuous ones. John Airey, who stabbed his wife Patricia, explained, 'I thought if she was going to live away on her own, life would not be worth living, so I thought I would kill her and I would get hung and we would both go together.'

Airey's perception of his wife as an extension of himself — 'If I go, she goes' — is very common in murders by husbands and especially in suicide-murders. Since by definition the killer in a suicide-murder is dead and no trial is possible, there are no examples in the *Calendar of Murder*. Nevertheless, they are often reported in newspapers, euphemistically referred to as 'family tragedies'. In some cases a would-be suicide survives and the resulting trials are well worth examining, since they reveal extraordinary judicial attitudes to the man whose desire to kill himself 'naturally' extends to his wife and family. Take the following case, reported in 1981:

A pensioner who mistakenly thought he had cancer killed his 71-year old wife and then attempted suicide by running in front of a lorry. Mr G. pleaded not guilty to murdering his wife Agnes but admitted manslaughter on the grounds of diminished responsibility. Mr Justice Woolf said, 'I regard this as a sad case. I am satisfied you were deeply devoted to your wife.' The prosecution said that Mr G. was suffering from a severe depressive illness, and by October 1980 he had decided to kill himself. But he was very worried about what would happen to his wife if he died. On January 12 he attacked his wife with a hammer on the head and neck, then went out and ran under a passing lorry. He was seriously injured but did not die. The QC for Mr G. said, 'This was a long, happy and secure marriage.'[14]

It seems almost incredible to us that anyone could utter such sentiments without irony, and the court's acceptance that the pair were 'devoted' is if anything more extraordinary than Mr G.'s own act. Psychiatrists believe that suicide-murderers do genuinely regard their victims as extensions of themselves — their acts, in other words, are essentially *self*-destructive. What remains to be explained if that is really the case is why men regard their wives in this light, whereas women suicide-murderers usually kill only their children. It seems plausible to speculate that this pattern has a power dimension: family members feel entitled to kill only those in relation to whom they are dominant.

Thirteen cases of wife murder which came to court in 1961 were strikingly lacking in any motive whatsoever. The killers themselves found their acts inexplicable: Frederick York, having hit his wife Louise with an axe, told police, 'I had a feeling come over me.'

Something also 'came over' Arthur Weston, who battered his wife to death with a washing-machine roller (the jury rejected a defence of sleep-walking). Robert James strangled his terminally ill wife, not to end her misery but 'in a fit of frenzy', while Geoffrey Gooch, 'happily married' to Florence, one day hit her with a chisel for no apparent reason and subsequently strangled her. Richard Bryant also strangled his wife, Mary, with a dressing-gown cord; while Albert Hall tried (and failed) to gas himself after meting out similar treatment to his wife Mabel. With the exception of the Yorks, all these couples were described in reports as 'happy' and 'devoted'.

The question is surely not whether these men were all insane: it is why so many men's madness takes this specific form. For this is an affliction peculiar to men: apart from Irene Duke, who shot her husband after hearing 'noises in my head' and was found guilty but insane under the McNaghten rules, the women who killed their husbands in 1961 (four, apart from Mrs Duke) were battered wives, who had suffered years of abuse so appalling that in one case, the judge actually congratulated the killer.

It seems that wife murder has a number of meanings, from an extension of habitual domestic violence to an expression of pathological possessiveness or jealousy. Some of it appears to be random brutality, which if taken at face value is completely inexplicable. Women are butchered, apparently on impulse, by previously gentle and 'devoted' men. Husband-killing is a great deal less common, and is almost always done in self-defence.

Both in the courts and in criminological literature, an assumption is made about marital killing that it arises from couples' individual circumstances: the strains and problems of cohabitation, the stress and frustration of sexual passion. Yet if marital killing is caused by these purely 'personal' factors, why the gross difference between women and men? Either partner in a marriage can feel stress or frustration, but it seems it is husbands who murder their wives. One common-sense explanation is that men are simply more violent and more given to using violence to solve personal problems. But the case histories we have cited indicate something more complex. Many wife murders are different in *motive* from husband murders — the difference is one of kind, rather than degree. What is strikingly absent from most killings by women is a close connection between violence and sexual desire, the idea that 'you always hurt the one you love.' There is something mysterious about this idea and it seems to be connected with another phenomenon which both experts and laypeople find even more deeply puzzling. We mean the phenomenon of 'sexual murder', in which the urge to kill is compulsive and depersonalized, but the motifs of desire and irrationality are expressed in a form both mysterious and grotesque. Even more obviously than spouse murder, sexual murder is the province of men: and this is what we shall be concerned with in the remainder of this chapter and the rest of the book.

SEXUAL MURDER

'Sexual murder' is much more difficult than marital killing to define precisely. Although the term is often used in the specialist literature (along with 'lust murder' and sometimes 'serial murder') its range of reference is not always clear. The narrowest and therefore the simplest definition is murder following rape or sexual assault: despite its clarity we find this problematic, because it excludes so many crimes we would intuitively want to describe as 'sexual'. Among notorious mass-murderers Christie, for example, was a necrophiliac rather than a rapist; Sutcliffe raped only one of his thirteen victims, but his habit of stabbing their genitals and breasts, as well as the fact that his targets were prostitutes, leaves little doubt of a sexual motive.

An alternative definition is suggested by some writers who maintain that for certain men, killing is *itself a sexual act*. Morris and Blom-Cooper explain the point as follows:

> In the cases of murder following a rape, it is generally assumed that the killing is committed for the very reason that it will remove all evidence of the rape . . . [However] studies of the psychopathology of sexual violence would suggest that both the acts of coitus and of killing represent a psychic unity and indeed the rapist may achieve orgasm only during the act of killing itself.[15]

The case of Peter Sutcliffe illustrates that coitus itself may not even be necessary: as the compilers of the *Encyclopaedia of Modern Murder* comment, 'Sutcliffe never admitted to having orgasms as he stabbed his victims; but anyone acquainted with the psychology of sexual criminals would take it for granted that this occurred.'[16]

It is not only criminologists and other 'experts' who have put forward the bizarre and unpalatable idea that sexual pleasure may be derived from acts of killing and mutilation. On the contrary, this point has been made quite regularly by killers themselves in confessions and other remarks. The nineteenth-century sexologist Richard von Krafft-Ebing cites a case reported by the great Italian criminologist Lombroso in 1873, in which a man named Vincent Verzeni throttled, then mutilated and disembowelled (and possibly cannibalized) several women. In his confession, Verzeni remarked, 'I had an unspeakable delight in strangling women, experiencing during the act erections and real sexual pleasure . . . much greater than that which I experienced while masturbating.'[17] Similarly unambiguous statements have been made by other murderers, notably by Peter Kürten, the 'monster of Düsseldorf'.

It seems that rape and sexual assault are neither necessary nor sufficient to make a murder 'sexual'. What is important is the eroticization of the act of killing in and for itself. Bearing this in mind, we shall define sexual murder as including all cases where the killer was motivated by sadistic sexual impulses — 'the lust to kill'. Of course, this leaves open the question of what these impulses are and what is sexual or erotic about them. That is one of the problems we examine and no simple answer is possible at this stage.

We would certainly argue that sexual murder is a *fuzzy* category with unclear boundaries. Whether some killer derived sexual satisfaction from a particular act of murder is obviously not a straightforward question to answer, unless one operates with a wholly mechanical definition of sexual gratification. For example, who is to say that the sort of domestic killing we have cited in our discussion of marital murder never originates in sexual impulses, never affords a sexual *frisson*? It has also been argued that killings which take place in religious or occult rituals, or extreme social circumstances (like Nazi concentration camps and torture chambers) have an underlying sexual significance. In the course of our analysis we will have to explore more fully the affinities which seem to exist between sexuality, power and purification.

In the meantime, we plan to start with the 'clear cases', the ones everybody would regard as sexual murders because whatever their status in science or law, they constitute a cultural category or *genre*, the genre of the 'sex beast' or 'fiend'. (We discuss the construction of this popular figure in chapter 2, 'The Murderer as Hero'.) The clear cases typically concern individuals (not participants in mass rituals or functionaries of the state) who kill compulsively and without having any specific grudge against the particular individuals who become their victims. These individuals are often selected because they are of a certain type: prostitutes, young girls or boys, elderly people, blondes. But the killings are not for gain, or jealousy, or revenge, they are animated by desire for that kind of sexual object. For us, the 'canon' of clear cases would include a number of well-documented mass-killings: those of Jack the Ripper, Kürten, the Boston Strangler, Christie, Sutcliffe and Dennis Nilsen (whose victims were of course men: we do not claim that the killing of *women* defines sex murder, but rather that the victim is a sexual object for the killer). Two things are especially striking about this list. In the first place, it contains not a single woman; and secondly, none of the cases on it occurred any earlier than 1888. In short, it implies that our category 'sexual murder' is both distinctively modern and exclusively male. Both these suggestions need further discussion.

The history of sex-killing: is it a modern phenomenon?

Although various writers make historical points in passing, there are few works which set out to give a detailed historical account of sex crime in general and sex murder in particular. The exceptions to this rule are certain of Colin Wilson's essays — especially his preface to the *Encyclopaedia of Modern Murder* — and a popular work, now out of print and hard to get hold of, by the American authors Masters and Lea. This book, promisingly entitled *Sex Crimes in History: Evolving Concepts of Sadism, Lust Murder and Necrophilia from Ancient to Modern Times*, was published in 1963: it is far from satisfactory on a number of counts, being racist, sexist and extraordinarily credulous (for instance, it recycles as 'facts' details culled from such dubious sources as confessions extracted under torture), but it is the most sustained attempt at a history we have been able to discover. We will take it both as a convenient starting-point and as a model of the kind of historical interpretation we have tried to avoid in our own analysis.

For Masters and Lea, sadism, lust murder and necrophilia are aberrations of human nature and sexuality which have always existed and always will exist — because, it is implied, they stem from organic psychosexual disorders. In the late nineteenth century this began to be recognized and dealt with in clinical or scientific terms; previously, such terms had not been available and other, mistaken explanations of sadism had therefore prevailed (for instance, sadistic acts were thought to indicate demonic possession or involvement in witchcraft). For Masters and Lea, however, it is an obvious truth that the many killers accused of being witches, satanists, vampires or werewolves were 'really' sexual deviants in the sense we understand that concept: the age they lived in just did not know it. We moderns, luckily, are more enlightened; advances in scientific knowledge allow us to see the 'correct' pattern in history. Thus Masters and Lea present an unbroken chronological account of sex crime and sadistic murder beginning with the Caesars, moving on to the fifteenth-century French mass-killer Gilles de Rais, taking in the sixteenth-century Hungarian Elizabeth Bathory, who had young women murdered apparently in and for occult and magical rites, then the various werewolves who roamed sixteenth-century Europe, the Rippers and Stabbers of the 1880s, ending up in 1930 with the inevitable Peter Kürten. Despite the great disparities of time, place and practice in these case histories (for surely there is little enough resemblance between the Emperor Tiberius, a werewolf and Jack the Ripper), they supposedly illustrate a single category of mental disorder, manifesting itself in what we now refer to as 'sadism'.

In our view, this kind of account begs crucial questions. Even if we accepted that all the case histories cited did manifest some essence of 'sadism', we would surely want to ask why this had taken such different forms at different times and in different places. Why, for instance, was the sixteenth century overrun with werewolves who have apparently since become extinct? Why was there a plague of Rippers in the 1880s? The most plausible answer, put simply, must be that the varying forms of sexual desire and practice, as well as the varying forms of violence and crime, are intimately connected to the forms of the wider culture — what societies believe, how they define things, what they do about them. Thus it is not surprising to find that werewolves have disappeared: we no longer have the sort of belief system to support the idea of lycanthropy (even in delusions: it is important to note that the delusions of the mentally ill reflect, albeit distortedly, what is culturally salient, so that psychotics still imagine they are God, or the devil, but not on the whole that they are transformed into wolves).

The point we are trying to make here is this: cultures change quite radically in the course of their history and it is therefore very difficult to argue for the existence of unchanging qualities like Masters and Lea's 'sadism', simply on the basis that particular behaviours (for example 'mass-killing') recur. We need to know not just what was done, but what it *meant*: the same act does not always have the same significance and to interpret the events of the past through the categories of the present is to make the error of historical anachronism.

Sexual killing actually illustrates this argument very well, since if one reads contemporary accounts of, say, werewolves, it is striking that neither they nor the communities they terrorized regarded their crimes as peculiarly 'sexual'. Indeed the idea of a killer being motivated by deviant sexual urges, familiar and obvious as it may appear to us, was regarded by many people as recently as the late nineteenth century with astonishment, distaste and often outright disbelief. Colin Wilson points out that the case of Jack the Ripper occurred at what now seems like a point of transition. The Ripper killings were explained by some commentators as the work of a 'sex maniac', demonstrating that the category did exist at the time; but this explanation was not universally accepted, with many other hypotheses being seriously suggested.[18] Nowadays by contrast it is very unlikely that the repeated murder and mutilation of prostitutes would be explained as anything other than a sexual crime.

This illustrates the massive shift that has taken place in our definitions of the sexual itself: we are able to ascribe sexual meanings to actions and events which did not have those meanings for the original participants and commentators. Arguably, this is a tendency we need to beware of, since it leads to unwarranted, anachronistic interpretations. For instance, take a case cited by the historian J. S. Cockburn in his study of the assize courts in three English counties: 'In 1589 two Penshurst labourers attacked a local woman, stabbed her then slit open her stomach, from which they took an unborn child.'[19] To us as moderns, this suggests a possible sexual motive: if someone did it now, we would suspect precisely that. But Cockburn more cautiously calls it 'inexplicable brutality', implicitly making the point that we do not know how it was regarded in 1589. Would it make sense to call this incident 'sexual murder'? We think the answer is *no*. Between the Elizabethans and ourselves lie a number of highly influential discourses — psychiatry, sexology, criminology and so on

...ave redefined our notions of sexuality and crime. It is these
...alking and conceptualizing that enable us to think of murders
...ial'; they were not available to people in 1589.

...find it especially interesting that most of the discourses we have
mentioned as important factors in the creation of a category of sex
murder date from the mid-nineteenth century to the early twentieth
— that is to say, from the very period which marked the recognition of
sex-killing and the start of its distinctive canon of case histories. One
might say that it was the existence of a certain theoretical framework, a
certain set of controlling discourses, that allowed the new category to
come into being. And it was only when this category *had* come into
being that earlier killers like Gilles de Rais and the werewolves could
start to be seen as exemplars of the same phenomenon. Such cases
were integrated into the canon retrospectively (not to say misleadingly)
and made to exemplify something which had not existed when they
were originally documented. The case of Gilles de Rais is a particularly
obvious example; far from 'hanging around' for centuries as a puzzling
anomaly, it seems to have been suddenly revived during the nineteenth
century — i.e., exactly when it could be fitted into a new category of
crime, some 400 years after Gilles had been executed.

As well as allowing the production of a history, the emergence of a
recognized category of sex-killing provided a self-conscious identity
or role for individuals to take up and define their acts by. By the turn
of the century a man could set out to be, or be seen as, a 'sex maniac' in
a way that would have been impossible fifty years earlier. The coming
of a category thus brought with it the possibility of creating a *tradition*,
which established itself in practice both by expanding to encompass
the killers of the past and (as we pointed out in the preface) by offering
a label to those of the future.

So although killing for sexual pleasure existed as a form of behaviour
well before Jack the Ripper, with sporadic reports going back at least
to the fifteenth century, sexual murder as a distinctive category with a
meaning for experts and lay members of the culture is a product of the
mid- to late nineteenth century and was not completely established in
its present form until the early years of this century. We will argue
later that this chronology reflects not only scientific advances and
changes in clinical practice, but also philosophical and aesthetic
developments associated with the construction of 'modern' sensibility.
To that extent, then, sexual murder *is* a 'modern' phenomenon.

Gender and sex-killing: is it an all-male preserve?

We began this book with the claim that sexual murder, as we define it, is invariably committed by men and not women. Our evidence for saying this is almost entirely negative: we just have not been able to find any women who fit our concept of a sex-killer, despite the existence, which we pointed out earlier, of a disproportionate volume of material about murders committed through the ages by women.

The literature on women killers contains endless discussions of what are referred to as 'female sadists'. The pantheon of these sadists can be divided into two main groups, neither of which conform to our terms of reference. First, there are the famous and powerful women of history or legend, who are reported to have indulged voracious appetites for both sex and cruelty: Cleopatra, Messalina, Zingua of Angola, Catherine the Great, etc., enthusiasts of witchcraft like Countess Bathory, who bathed in the blood of her eighty-odd girl victims, and high priestesses of sadistic cults involving bizarre sexual rituals and (sometimes) human sacrifice. This group of women certainly did perpetrate and/or participate in appalling bloodshed, but in no case could this be called sex murder without the sort of anachronism we have already warned against.

The second group, by contrast, consists of fairly ordinary killers who seem to have been labelled sadists simply because they were women — a woman who kills, be her methods never so mild by male standards of brutality, is sadistic by definition in the eyes of many writers. Thus one finds blood-curdling recitals of male violence (bludgeonings, stabbings, stranglings) in which the word 'sadism' is never so much as mentioned; yet many women are classed as sadistic for putting arsenic in their husband's coffee. We are forced to conclude that the 'female sadists' are mere projections of a sexual double standard, which judges women not by 'objective' criteria but by an idealized stereotype of feminine gentleness.

This is not to say, of course, that women are *never* sadistic in the sense of enjoying inflicting pain on others. There are plenty of cases on record of women participating in sadistic rituals and in various forms of torture — of their children, servants, apprentices and prisoners, many of whom have indubitably died as a result of female sadistic abuse. And just as in the cases we alluded to earlier, the male concentration-camp guard and the orgiast, it is not impossible that such women derived sexual pleasure from this kind of sadism. Yet it cannot be denied that the sex-killers' canon contains only one woman at the very most — Myra Hindley, and even she did not act alone, but as her boyfriend's accomplice, which renders her motives much less clear-cut. In the great tradition of sadistic sexual murder, it seems that women are virtually non-existent. And this immediately begs the question, *why?*

Some people have suggested to us that the absence of women sex murderers is an artefact: we do not want to think that women have similar violent sexual proclivities to men, so when they do something similarly violent, their actions are deliberately read as being quite different from those of male sadists. This analysis — that a double standard of judgement applies to the behaviour of the two sexes — has much to recommend it in many cases (for instance, we have already pointed out that women are labelled 'sadistic' much more readily than men are). Nevertheless it does not seem to hold for the issues we are concerned with here. For example, we have examined cases where women attacked men and mutilated their genitals. Were these female versions of the classic 'Ripper'? We had to conclude that they were totally different, because their motive was never sexual gratification. Invariably, the attacks were directed against a specific individual, and motivated by jealousy or the desire for revenge (including revenge on violent men, as in the occasional cases of castration by feminist vigilantes). We have already remarked that 'true' sex-killers attack generic objects and not particular persons.

However, it is certainly the case that when women mutilate men's genitals this act is given a meaning by the culture quite different from the meaning that attaches to mutilation of women by men. We found a startling example of this in our reading of nineteenth-century broadsheets about crime (broadsheets were a form of popular literature). One of the texts we came across concerned the case of Ann Crampton in 1814. The long-standing girlfriend of one Robert Jordon, she reacted very badly to the news that he planned to marry another woman: 'Determined that his intended wife should not be the better for him . . . she procured a large knife . . . cut and mutilated him in a manner too shocking to express.' What interested us about this broadsheet was the way it diverged from the standard conventions for talking about violent crime. Male sex beasts in the nineteenth century were discussed in sensational and moralistic terms; Ann Crampton is treated as something of a joke. The verse which accompanies her story is doggerel laced with innuendo:

> Mrs Cutcock's come to gaol,
> Keep her wolf and do not fail . . .
> Keep her upon bread and water
> This audacious mother's daughter [etc.]

There is apparently something ridiculous about a woman cutting off a man's genitals: it is merely aberrant and not really threatening.

The other side of this particular coin, though, is the hysterical vilification of women involved in sadistic crimes. If they are not to be ridiculed, they are to be painted as much more wicked than any man. A pertinent contemporary example is the moors murderer Myra Hindley, convicted jointly with her lover Ian Brady. More and more, she is depicted as the arch-female sadist — even by writers who doubt that she herself killed the pair's victims. As one popular source has it, 'It remains open to speculation whether Hindley's perverted pleasure lay in witnessing Brady perform his odd homosexual acts . . . or in watching the act of murder itself.'[20] Few male sexual killers — whose pleasure lies not in watching, but in doing — attract the virulent hatred Myra Hindley does (even Brady is not so viciously and constantly reviled). Whatever other crimes she may have committed, Myra Hindley has offended against standards of femininity and has been punished accordingly. We discuss her case further in chapter 4.

If women do derive sexual satisfaction from killing, this fact is not manifested in their choice of victims or in the kind of death they choose to inflict. Whereas male murderers may kill prostitutes or young girls obsessively, we have no record of comparable obsessions among women; and whereas rape, sexual assault, necrophilia, breast and genital mutilation are the commonplaces of male sexual killing, these are for the most part practices quite alien to women. The 'psychology of sexual criminals', which permits a Peter Sutcliffe to climax while stabbing, is evidently a type of masculine psychology: sexual murder is a distinctively male crime.

Once again, this is borne out when we examine the murder trials of 1961. The *Calendar of Murder* lists eleven killings which we would classify as sexual, all committed by men. Two cases were murders of young men by homosexuals, while the rest were. heterosexually motivated. Two of the female victims were prostitutes and two were young girls, aged six and twelve. One incident was a double murder, in which a young couple were killed and dismembered. Parts of their bodies were later used to satisfy what were referred to mysteriously as the 'pervert instincts' of the killer, Edwin Sims.

Sims was convicted of section-two manslaughter, as were Charles Kinley, a 'psychopath' who stripped and strangled a teacher, and Anthony Collop, who killed a thirteen-year-old boy. Other sexual killers were not found abnormal — or possibly, were not allowed to get away with pleading diminished responsibility, so great was the repugnance generated by what they did. Arthur Jones, who raped one Girl Guide before abducting, assaulting and strangling a second, did not even attempt a section-two defence. The other child-killer tried in 1961, Alan Wills, tried to plead subnormality under section two, but he was convicted of murder anyway. George Sutton, whom the judge described as a 'Jack the Ripper' killer after he had stabbed and strangled a prostitute was found guilty of murder though he too was a 'psychopath.' The other prostitute murder of the year was described by police as the work of 'a sex maniac' since the body was mutilated with a garden trowel. A man was tried, but his confession had been obtained under duress and so he was acquitted. Less understandably, so was Willis Boshears, who did not deny strangling a woman after having intercourse with her, but maintained he had been asleep at the time. Incredibly enough, the jury believed him.

Culture and sex-killing: is it universal?

We have already observed that patterns of homicide reflect the culture in which they occur and that these reflections are fairly complex (as in Lundsgaarde's account of 'frontier justice' in Houston). It may therefore be asked whether sexual murder as we have described it is a reflection of some particular culture or type of culture; whether it is recognizably present everywhere.

It is certainly true that sex-killing is associated in the popular imagination with particular types of societies — particularly with Anglo-Saxon and Protestant ways of life, in which sexuality is thought to be repressed with especial severity. (We will argue later that this is irrelevant, since repression *per se* is not the most important factor in sex murder.) This popular myth of the Calvinist sex-killer is not borne out by historical facts: sex murder is fairly common in England and West Germany, but has also been recorded frequently in France, Italy, the countries of the Soviet Union and Poland — very different societies, and none of them Protestant.

Once we move outside Europe, information is more difficult to get hold of — even in Europe we are dependent on case histories to categorize murder as sexual, since sex-killing is nowhere an official category in the collection of crime statistics, but qualitative sources are heavily biased to Western Europe. There is also quite a large amount of information on Australia, South Africa and the United States, all of which have some incidence of sex murder. North America in particular has produced many *causes célèbres* and these confirm the pattern that sex-killers are always men. None appear in Ann Jones's history of female killers in the United States; and in an article on so-called 'serial killing', the (as yet) specifically American phenomenon where killers travel up and down the country claiming victims in their dozens and even hundreds, the journalist Philip Jacobson has stated that 'So far, known serial killers have all been male, almost all white, often unusually intelligent or extremely cunning. . . . Most victims are female, usually young women whose death is frequently accompanied by violent sexual assault, sometimes by torture and mutilation. A number . . . have involved homosexuals.'[21] It is likely that sexual murder in the United States resembles the British and European phenomenon more closely than North American homicide figures in general resemble British or European ones.

Our knowledge of homicide patterns in Third World countries is fairly scant and unfortunately much of it comes from unreliable and racist sources, such as Masters and Lea's study, which includes an essay on 'Sexual Savagery in the East'. Although this was obviously written expressly to show 'how vicious' eastern peoples (especially Arabs) are, it notably fails to cite any outrage fitting our definition of sexual murder. We have heard of what appears to be a case of sex murder in Bombay (it was the target of feminist protest there and was claimed to be inspired by a Western-style film thriller).[22] But in general sexual murder seems to be associated (as yet) with Europeans and their settler descendants.

The last few pages have uncovered, we think, some significant patterns in relation to sex murder. It occurs in many cultures (but apparently not all); it emerged at a particular period of history; and above all, it is invariably committed by men, not by women. But so far we have only empirical findings based on observation and analysis of data. What we need is a broader, explanatory *theory* which puts the pattern into some kind of perspective. Without a theory we are in the position of asserting that gender is related to murder, but not being able to say precisely *how*. At this point, therefore, we must turn our attention to the crucial problem of explaining murder.

EXPLANATIONS OF MURDER: THE TRADITIONAL APPROACH

Social behaviour in developed societies is the object of both scholarly and popular discourses. Popular explanations pass for 'common sense' whereas scholarly versions have the status of 'theory' or 'science'. In fact, the two things are interdependent: on one hand, theories are popularized and enter into our everyday language, while on the other, academics are heavily influenced by whatever is the popular wisdom of the moment. (The feminist Christine Delphy has argued that we should not be dazzled by academic writing, for most of it 'does nothing other than paraphrase and reiterate the dominant ideology'.[23] We found her comment depressingly accurate as we ploughed through the literature of modern criminology.) There are both popular and scholarly explanations of murder and unsurprisingly they have a good deal in common.

Many popular accounts of murder have a tendency to be journalistic: they concentrate on *what* killers do and often have little to say about *why*. Reviewing a best-selling biography of Peter Sutcliffe, Patricia Highsmith said of the author, Gordon Burn, that he 'gives us no comment of his own on the story he has to tell — just the facts: no speculation as to why Peter Sutcliffe behaved as he did, just the events, the family life, anecdotes that may or may not be pertinent, the pubs and their atmosphere'.[24] This description illustrates another general feature of popular accounts: that if explanation is attempted at all, it will begin and end with the individual killer, his background, relationships and personality. Sociological facts are brought in *ad hoc* to assist in an essentially biographical account.

But this emphasis on the individual is not confined to popular journalism. It is also typical of expert discourses and particularly of criminology. Although there are many different 'schools' of criminology, including feminist and Marxist ones, most of the work which has been done on sexual murder has been done in a framework that is highly *asocial*. Sociological studies of homicide in particular areas (such as Wolfgang's book on Philadelphia and Lundsgaarde's on Houston) are strong on ethnicity, class and culture but typically ignore the whole issue of gender; feminist criminology, on the other hand, has concentrated on the criminalization of women, which has meant effectively ignoring murder precisely because women so rarely commit it.[25] All in all, where murder is concerned, and especially sexual or abnormal murder, the field has been left to the traditionalists with their individualistic, often clinical approach. We discuss their work in much more detail later, but it is useful to pick out some of its main features here.

The traditional emphasis in mainstream criminology is on explaining the crime through the person who commits it. This has often involved investigating measurable personal characteristics: in a hundred years criminologists have progressed from calculating the size of convicts' skulls to testing their chromosomes, hormones and brainwaves, or alternatively constructing sociological indices (memorably dismissed by Ann Jones as 'turning their attention only from the criminal's eyebrows to his neighbourhood').[26] The theory underlying all these procedures is that criminals are somehow quite different from non-criminals and commit their crimes because of inherent defects or at the very least, individual pathologies. In the case of violent crimes like murder, this notion is also popular wisdom. It is expressed in a host of well-known stereotypes: the 'sex beast' beloved of tabloid reporting, the 'split personality' and the 'psychopath'.

Recently the exclusive focus on criminals has been supplemented by a new interest in victims. 'Victimology', as this approach is known, stresses that in many cases there may be a relationship between criminal and victim and the dynamics of the relationship may explain why a killing occurs. Victimologists recommend looking closely at the behaviour of victims in their final encounters: homicide may be 'victim precipitated', i.e., directly provoked by the victim's actions.

What these approaches have in common is a highly individualistic outlook. The behaviour of both killers and victims is to be understood as arising from their individual circumstances: family tensions, mental instability, sexual jealousy, the desire for revenge. (At the same time, emotions like jealousy and anger are held to be part of a shared 'human nature'.) From our point of view this is quite inadequate, since it implies what we know is by no means the case, that the two positions of 'killer' and 'victim' may be occupied indifferently by any individual. In fact, there are various social constraints on who is a killer and who gets killed. One of these is, quite simply, gender: killers are mostly male, victims mostly female.

Criminology can provide no explanation for this within its framework of thoroughgoing individualism, for in a universe full of autonomous subjects with individual passions and personal relationships, there is no reason at all why one social group should be prototypical killers, while their victims cluster in another social group. Criminology seeks to explain why *this* individual kills *that* one; yet the facts suggest there is a prior question, why members of some *groups* kill members of others. To answer that question it is surely necessary to connect acts of killing (and the motives behind them) with social structures and power differentials. But this is something which most criminologists seem either unable or unwilling to do, at least where the sexual power hierarchy is concerned. As we noted earlier, much of the literature both presupposes and obscures gender difference in murder.

Criminology's selective unawareness of gender is strikingly evident even from its language. Thus one of the most common types of homicides there is, men killing their wives, becomes 'domestic crime'; repeated sexual murders of women are sometimes reported as 'random' killings; and suicide-murders, more than two-thirds male-committed, are known euphemistically as 'family tragedies'. Other gender differences are ignored or concealed. The fact that sexual killers are without exception male has attracted no sustained discussion that we are aware of. Some writers manage to leave it out completely, while others, implicitly recognizing it, nevertheless treat it as totally natural and unproblematic. For a feminist, of course, it is neither of those things. It is a fact about our culture that cries out for explanation.

Why, in the morass of confused emotions that characterize family and sexual relations, is it usually men who are driven to kill women, and only very rarely that women kill men? Why are there no female sadistic sex-killers and why are there so many men of this type? What is the connection between murder and the erotic? What is the difference between 'normal' men and killers? To ask these questions, it seems to us, is to ask something about men — or more precisely, about the construction of masculine sexuality in our culture. Yet throughout the literature this line of enquiry is systematically turned on its head. Not content with sins of omission in failing to ask why sex-killers are men, many writers go one step further and attempt to erase men altogether. Inevitably then, they focus on *women*: what do women do to get themselves murdered? How do we provoke the lust to kill?

The answer, of course, is that women represent the sexual: and to the degree we flaunt it, we're asking for it. The callous treatment of prostitute murder victims, which excuses — or rather, *erases* — male sadism, recurred in practically every source we looked at. It is at its crudest in popular writing, as for example in this anecdote from the memoirs of a leading pathologist: 'When I lectured to medical students, at Guy's or Oxford, I would often fasten their attention by saying casually, "Now, I've had a number of prostitutes over the years". A burst of cheering from the students, then I'd smile thinly and get into my subject.'[27] His subject, of course, was the sadistic abuse to which 'these wretched girls' are frequently subjected: a sadism which finds its parallel in his own cheap joke and the cheering of the students.

But (proving Christine Delphy's point once again) we find similar attitudes in academic discourse. Morris and Blom-Cooper concur with our pathologist in pointing out that prostitutes 'know the risks'. Their remarks on the subject are worth quoting at some length, since they provide a particularly clear example of how male responsibility for murder is erased.

> Some women may *contribute to their own deaths* by running the risks *associated with prostitution*, of which violent death is *an occupational hazard*. . . . The prostitute, whose client is unknown to her, may be murdered *simply* because she represents a readily accessible sexual object to her killer, to whom anonymity in his victim may be important. More commonly, prostitutes are the only women *prepared to co-operate* in the sado-masochistic perversions which form, for the killer, an integral part of the homicidal drive.[28] [Emphases added]

It is hard to know where to begin with this, so skilful is its language in rendering sadism invisible. Not only is there no sign of male desire here, male power is also unaccountably absent. Anyone reading this would gather that prostitutes are in the game of their own free will and possibly even for sexual thrills ('prepared to co-operate . . .'). And yet it is only the sexual power hierarchy that explains the existence of their risky occupation.

Morris and Blom-Cooper show how victimology can easily turn into victim-blaming, especially when the victim concerned is a woman. It seems from their comments that women are to blame for most of the terrible fates that attend them: women who hitch-hike and get sexually assaulted, women who resist rape and provoke the rapist further, women who panic and force burglars to hit them, 'masochistic' women who pick up sadists and get murdered. Even little girls need blame no one but themselves if they are killed, since according to Morris and Blom-Cooper, 'the child victims of sexual killing may in fact be children at a stage of psycho-sexual development in which they deliberately involve themselves with men in a quasi-seductive role.'[29]

Yet this kind of argument ignores one crucial question, namely why do men *want* to hurt and kill the objects of their desire? All the risk-taking, all the masochism, all the seductive behaviour in the world could not put in jeopardy a single woman's or child's safety if there were no violent or sadistic men.

The fact that male violence *is* endemic in our culture has long been recognized in feminist analyses. Many feminists have argued that violence against women, exemplified in practices like rape and incest, is not just a collection of randomly vindictive acts, but a social institution which is crucial in reproducing male power by keeping women in a state of fear and unfreedom. This view gains credence when we look at the ways in which violence against women is covertly condoned: rape victims find their own morals on trial, battered women cannot trust police to protect them, social workers respond to incest with a concern for 'the family' which may entail a girl risking further abuse within it, men who bludgeon their wives to death are praised for their 'devotion' . . . Is the violence really aberrant, or is it somehow in tune with the workings of our society?

And what of sexual murder? Can this analysis be applied in the case of a Sutcliffe or Boston Strangler? The wife-killer is easily seen as a wife-batterer gone to extremes, but the mass sexual killer is quite radically 'Other', treated by civilized society as an incomprehensible monster of depravity. Nevertheless, during Peter Sutcliffe's long reign of terror, feminist voices were heard asserting that the Ripper phenomenon was no aberration. It was pointed out, for instance, that the police and the killer made the same distinction between 'respectable' women and prostitutes. There were also protests against the police line that women should turn to other men for protection (an argument which assumes you can recognize a sex beast). Many women reported casual comments from men that implied they shared the Ripper's pleasure in female fear. In Leeds, football crowds adopted 'Jack' as a folk hero and chanted at one stage 'Ripper eleven, police nil'. Hundreds of women co-operated in the enquiry by turning in their husbands, boyfriends and brothers. By doing this, they underlined the point that he was not necessarily 'Other': he could have been anyone, must have been someone. As Gordon Burn was later to put it, this was 'somebody's husband, somebody's son'.[30]

The case of Sutcliffe familiarized feminist analyses of sexual violence to an unprecedented degree; it could never again be enough to say that sexual killers are 'madmen' or 'psychopaths', to go along with the mainstream criminological emphasis on the individual in order to explain why sexual killers behave as they do. What was needed — it still is needed — was an approach that would recognize that although the murderer is by no means typical, he is a product of his social order; though few men could do what Sutcliffe did, many men share some of Sutcliffe's desires. (In this connection it is clearly essential to have an analysis of violence against women; though it is also important to retain some notion of the *specificity* of sexual murder, both as a type of murder and as a type of male violence.)

Our ultimate goal here is to offer an approach of the kind we are recommending: a socially and politically informed account of this particular type of murder which will illuminate the facts we have uncovered in this introductory section. At the very least, we offer some tentative frameworks for making sense of the sex-murder phenomenon. But in order to do this, it seems to us necessary that we first examine existing frameworks and put old approaches in some kind of perspective. The central part of this book is therefore devoted to a critical discussion of the discourses of murder.

We have chosen to divide this discussion into three major chapters, 'The Murderer as Hero', 'The Murderer as Deviant' and 'The Murderer Personified'. Of these chapters, the first and second are concerned with tracing what we consider the two most important themes in our culture's treatment of sexual murder. The 'hero' theme

— where the murderer is the main protagonist in a fiction, assuming the dimensions of a mythical archetype — can be traced in both high art and popular culture: street ballads, tabloid journalism, Gothic literature and so on. These genres represent killers as sub- or superhuman: monstrous individuals who inspire a horrible fascination. The other main theme is that of the 'deviant', the diseased or otherwise abnormal individual to be examined dispassionately and objectively by science. This theme is expressed in the discourse of 'experts' purporting to study and explain the sexual killer: criminologists, psychiatrists, psychoanalysts, social theorists and social anthropologists. In our third main chapter, 'The Murderer Personified', we discuss in detail a number of specific cases and show how they exemplify both 'hero' and 'deviant'.

In each of these chapters, our primary interest is in the way that murder and murderers are explained. We will aim to make explicit certain covert assumptions about the nature of gender, sexuality and power. In our final section, 'The Murderer as Misogynist?' we turn to the concepts and debates of modern feminism in an attempt to define our own position.

A famous dictum of criminology is that 'society gets the crimes it deserves.' We believe sexual murder is no exception; its roots deep in modern patriarchal society are what we intend to expose.

2

The Murderer as Hero

*I imagined him to be an ugly hunchback with boils all over his face,
somebody who couldn't get women and resented them for that. Somebody
with totally nothing going for him.*

(Carl Sutcliffe, on being told his brother was
the Yorkshire Ripper.)

Carl Sutcliffe's inaccurate characterization of the man who killed and
mutilated thirteen women between 1975 and 1980 is highly significant
inasmuch as it invokes an enormously powerful popular stereotype. It
is in the tradition which explains sexual murder as the act of 'maniacs',
'beasts', 'fiends' and 'monsters'. The sex beast is either someone
outwardly repulsive (in Carl Sutcliffe's account, interestingly, the
traditional significance of physical deformity as a visible sign of
inward and spiritual wickedness has been overlaid by a layer of
popular psychology: the ugly 'can't get women' and their frustration
leads to violence) or else he is a latter-day Jekyll and Hyde, concealing
his depravity beneath a facade of respectability and even charm. (We
shall have occasion to come back to the Jekyll and Hyde story, which
was a hit, as it happens, on the London stage in the same autumn that
the original Jack the Ripper was terrorizing Whitechapel.)

In this chapter, we want to examine the popular myth of the
murdering sex beast and to argue that it is still an important means by
which the extraordinary acts of sexual killers can be slotted into our
culture's scheme of things. In tracing the history and current forms of
the myth, we want to show how it has profoundly affected our responses
to cases of sexual murder. We want to show, too, that the concept of the
beast is like other explanations to be dealt with here: it does not
address the issue of gender and therefore it obscures the phenomenon
it appears to be explaining. The beast is not only (as his name implies)
subhuman; he is also, mysteriously, a *male* subhuman.

Our calling the chapter 'The Murderer as Hero' may at first seem bizarre, since there is nothing heroic in the acts of a Christie, a Sutcliffe or Nilsen. Yet one meaning of *hero* in contemporary usage is 'chief male character in a book or play' and this is exactly the role of the murderer in popular discourse, whether his exploits are celebrated or reviled (or both at once). In popular fictions, biographies and in journalism, the figure of the killer is mythologized in various ways. There is a difference between the lone man in the dock, whose inadequacy is documented in clinical case histories, and the 'Yorkshire Ripper' or 'Monster of Düsseldorf' whose mythic persona strikes terror into millions. It is primarily the folk-devil we are seeking in this chapter: how is he constructed, by whom and for what purpose?

One obvious approach to these questions is historical: where does the tradition of the sex beast begin? In the introduction we put forward the theory that sex-killing itself, as a fully realized concept or category, did not become established until the turn of the century, because its categorization was heavily dependent on the development of discourses on sexual pathology, 'scientific' criminology and so on. If this argument is correct, does it also imply that the sex beast is a distinctively modern creation?

In this case we believe things are rather more complex, for the sex beast is not only the popular reflex of theories filtered down from the academy and the clinic (certainly these theories have been integrated with the myth; but then again, as we shall see, they have made use of it themselves). Rather, he represents an extraordinary patchwork of ideas and cultural forms from different historical traditions. Today's sex beast has many different faces, all of them highly recognizable to our culture: the Sadeian libertine, Mr Hyde, the Gothic villain, the monster, the hunchback; or on the other hand, the social/mental deviant: the madman, the psychopath, the existential rebel.

It is possible to isolate a number of important influences on the development of the sex beast as we now understand him. One is certainly the very old tradition of 'true crime' literature, from which we inherit certain conventions of the genre: the narrative form of the criminal case history and its sensational yet moralistic (Christian) tone. A second, more recent influence is the Gothic genre and indeed the Romantic movement of which it was a part. From this development of the late eighteenth and nineteenth centuries we get a characteristic ambience: a fascination with terror, with the evil and repulsive, and a persistent conjuncture of transgression, sex and death which is associated in particular with the Marquis de Sade. Carl Sutcliffe's image of sex-killers as pock-marked hunchbacks (or more generally as physically repellent men) is a Gothic convention which lives on, with many others, in the popular imagination of Western culture. The third main influence on the development of the sex beast is the clinical model of the social/sexual deviant. We deal with this in detail in the next chapter, but it is so intertwined with other strands that we shall refer to it where appropriate in our analysis of popular and literary representations.

The interaction of these different traditions sets up problems and contradictions whose repercussions can still be felt in contemporary debates — it is not the case, however much we might like to think so, that the older ways of thinking have been simply displaced by a 'scientific' model. This chapter will demonstrate the enduring strength of more metaphysical and Gothic modes of interpretation. For example, what should be our response to sex-killing? Moral condemn- ation, as in the 'true crime' tradition? Appalled fascination, as in Gothic writing? Scientific curiosity, perhaps, as in the clinical model? It is clear that most contemporary discussions on the subject contain overt elements of all three responses. Indeed, the development of the sex beast from the nineteenth century on is a history of unresolved struggle between them. Even now, questions of whether killers are mad or bad, whether they are society's constructs, its casualties or its rebels, continue to reverberate through our conversations (and our courts). How this state of affairs has come to be, how its strands have developed and interrelated in the way sexual murder is culturally represented, will be our main concerns in this part of our analysis.

THE MYTH OF THE SEX BEAST FROM BROADSIDE TO TABLOID

We have pointed out already that an important historical source for the sex beast is that form of popular literature whose subject is crime and whose protagonist is a criminal or 'rogue'. One long-lived and popular true-crime genre, which provides a great deal of informative material, is the *broadside*, a single printed sheet, which was sold, before the advent of mass-circulation newspapers, on the street, at fairs and other public gatherings. From their beginnings in the sixteenth century to their eventual demise, broadsides dealt (among other subjects) with true-crime material, which was perennially popular.

The kind of crime which was recorded in broadsides and also in other forms of popular literature, was not necessarily or mainly murder. For instance, if one turns to the *Newgate Calendar*, a popular collection of true-crime material, it is striking to a modern person that the dominant figures are not rapists and killers but rogues and vagabonds, pirates, footpads, highwaymen and thieves. This presumably reflects the fact that in early modern England, the major crime threat was perceived as being from attacks on property by the rootless poor and later from the professional criminals of the cities. Many broadsides focused on executions and some were written in the form of confessions from the scaffold. Among these, accounts of murders were well represented, but so too were other capital crimes, like coining and horse-stealing. The twentieth-century commonplace that murder dominates the popular imagination because it is somehow peculiarly heinous appears then to mark quite a recent shift of attitude.

During our research, we examined crime broadsides from the late eighteenth and nineteenth centuries.[1] Most of them dealt with notorious killings (many of them very far from topical or fresh: hoary old favourites like the 'Murder in the Red Barn' were endlessly reworked in innumerable broadsides) and in them it was possible to discern key elements of the outlook which still dominates the popular press today.

Take the following headlines, for instance, which illustrate the sort of killing people found newsworthy:

The Full Account and latest Particulars of the Awful, inhuman and barbarous Murder of a female by cutting off her head, arms and legs and burning them.

A true and concise Account of a barbarous Murder committed by Samuel Wood on the body of his Wife by cruelly knocking out her brains with a coal-pick at Nottingham on Wednesday November 16 1825.

Alexander Gibson, hanged and HUNG IN CHAINS at Speyside in Inverness-shire on Nov. 14 1810 for a RAPE on the Person of

Elspet Land (10 years) whom he afterwards most cruelly and barbarously murdered by breaking her Skull in pieces.

These accounts were often illustrated with line-drawings and typically contained verse narratives in addition to the prose account (since the audience for broadsides contained many illiterates, verses intended for recitation from memory were used to ensure the gist could be transmitted orally). A strong, traditional ballad element is present in the verses with their predictable formulas:

> Of all the dreadful deeds of blood that stain the page of crime
> This one exceeds in horror the crimes of any time
> A murder so atrocious, so frightful to unfold
> The bare narration of the same will make your blood run cold

Verses often ended on a moralistic note (the evils of drink being frequently canvassed, especially in nineteenth-century broadsides) and a prurient interest was normally taken in the criminal's demeanour as s/he faced her/his death.

From our point of view, the most interesting question concerns the treatment of sex crimes in pre-modern broadsides. Although it is clear that no comprehensive theory of sexual deviance *explicitly* informs this popular tradition, it is equally evident that some notion of sex crime, including the mythical figure of the sex beast, was in place from the early nineteenth century on. One especially interesting piece of evidence for this comes from an account of the trial of a well-known street harasser, charged with cutting and tearing a woman's 'cloak, gown and petticoats' in the public street. It is headed 'A Full, true and particular account of the trial of Renwick Williams commonly called The MONSTER. Who had infested the public streets of London for some Months back and had been a Terror to all the Female Race.' The interesting point here is the use of the label *monster* for a sexual deviant: as we shall see, this is still a keyword in the lexicon of the sex beast.

Broadsides dealing with rapes, child-killings, murders of prostitutes and 'good-time girls', implicitly if somewhat erratically recognize a sexual component in the crime they are describing. For example, in relating the murder of a nine-year-old girl, Euphenia Couper, the writer asserts of her seventy-two-year-old killer, 'He had long been in the habit of indecently assaulting the female sex when ever an opportunity offered.' The relatively minor crimes are linked to the killing in a way that reminds us of modern clinical discourses.

What is missing, however, is any account of the killer's motivation, either social or psychological — a reader today feels very acutely the lack of any developed psychopathology. Instead we have an account in crude moral terms, as for instance in the case of William Biggs, who raped and then murdered a servant maid. 'During the whole of the trial this man conducted himself in the most hardened manner, and after his conviction he expressed his sorrow for not having added more victims to his brutal lusts.' The following confession is also attributed to the 'hardened' Biggs: 'In my fifteenth year I stopped a female coming from Market, where on attempting to violate her person she resisted me with such courage, that I was unable to effect my purpose, which so exasperated me, that I instantly shot the poor girl, who fell dead at my feet.' Here we have a recognizable sex beast, his behaviour 'explained' in terms of various clichés. 'Brutal lusts' (i.e., animal rather than human impulses) are adduced as the motive for Biggs's acts, while his lack of remorse serves its usual purpose of indicating innate, incorrigible depravity. The underlying model is of sin, not sickness, of personal evil, not social *malaise*. As a broadside writer pontificated apropos of Daniel Reay, who in 1824 killed a woman with a butcher's knife:

> It is a heart rending reflection, to look back and consider over the occurrences of this nature which happen daily, and likely to continue to happen, by men suffering themselves to be carried away, by the violence of their evil passions, and to be led to commit the most dreadful and distressing outrages on society, which have forever rendered their lives miserable, or otherwise been the cause of their ending their days upon the gallows.

This tradition is of course very old and its invocation here should not surprise us. What *is* surprising is to see how these clichés, rooted in an age without psychopathology (and one which preserved the equation between sexuality and sin) have only been codified and not really changed, by the popular representations of today. We, after all, have various alternatives to the rhetoric of inherent 'evil passions' and these do impinge to some extent on public debate. But while the popular press pays lip-service to expert 'scientific' accounts of the sexual killer, in essence the language journalists use is almost identical to the language of the broadside.

Thus animal brutality and lack of remorse continue to function as marks of the beast: *The Sun*, for instance, said of a recent child-killer that he possessed 'no particle of the compassion and conscience that raise human beings above wild beasts'.[2] There has also developed a distinctive vocabulary reinforcing this picture of the sex-killer as a subhuman, lust-crazed demon: its keywords are *maniac, beast, fiend* and *monster*, all remote from the secular discourse of deviance. This lexicon is used without apparent awkwardness, despite its anachronistic whiff of fire and brimstone:

HORROR AS SOBBING TOT SEES
MANIAC MURDER MUM

A young mum was brutally attacked and then strangled in front of her sobbing baby girl. The fiend pounced while the 21-year old Indian-born mother was asleep in bed cradling the tot in her arms.[3]

It seems that 'maniac' and 'fiend' are interchangeable: they will do as descriptions of exactly the same man, which suggests that sickness has simply been added to sin as part of the repertoire of easy explanations; the two are not seen as mutually exclusive. (It is interesting, though, that the term *maniac* hovers on the boundary between 'mad' and 'bad'; it certainly implies some mental disturbance, but is barely clinical by comparison with, say, *schizophrenic* or *psychopath*. In its way, the term *maniac* is as archaic as *fiend* — modern psychiatrists no longer treat 'mania' any more than they refer to their patients as 'lunatics'.)

In popular discourse, it actually serves the same purpose to label a killer either sinful or sick: it distances him from the mass of 'normal' men. Ideologically, this distance is crucial and it is also created in various other ways by popular representations of murder. Since the demise of the broadside and the rise of popular mass-circulation newspapers and magazines, coverage of killers, especially multiple killers, has become essentially a coverage of the hunt, with police and other hunters as major figures in the story.[4] This approach permits —

indeed it *requires* — that the journalist construct an identity for the killer before his actual identity is known. Thus the beast is relentlessly personalized: when he commits a crime, or a series of crimes, the press is on hand to provide him with a name — the M4 Rapist, the Beast of Belgravia, the Fox, the Ripper — and a matching persona. The power of this myth helps resolve the contradiction that arises when a killer is finally caught: his real identity and characteristics can be separated off from the constructed persona.

This is, however, a separation which can never be complete or unproblematic, as we see from the fact that the most enduring sex beast myth has been that of Jack the Ripper, whose true identity remains unknown. In most cases, the beast will eventually be revealed not as a monster, but as the man next door. The journalist must then deal somehow with the glaring fact that sex-killers are rarely, in Carl Sutcliffe's phrase, 'ugly hunchbacks with boils all over their faces'; they are more likely to fall within the journalistic category 'happily married father of two'. The usual response to this conflict of images is to invoke another myth, that of the secret life or 'dual personality'. Family and friends of the killer are called upon to express their ritual horror and total disbelief. There is even a minor genre of books by women who have had a casual friendship or sexual encounter with a man who is subsequently revealed to be a multiple rapist and murderer![5] If this kind of narrative has any point at all, it is to demonstrate that the average sex beast is really no different from anyone else — at least, that is, no different on the outside. For the underlying postulate of the dual personality is not the absence of evil, but rather its concealment.

The major modern reference point for this line of thought is a work of Gothic fiction: Robert Louis Stevenson's 1886 story, 'The Strange Case of Doctor Jekyll and Mr Hyde'. In the story, a highly respectable physician develops, through chemical experimentation, an *alter ego* who is totally evil:

There was something strange in my sensations, something indescribably new and, from its very novelty, incredibly sweet. I felt younger, lighter, happier in body; within I was conscious of a heady recklessness, a current of disordered sensual images running like a mill-race in my fancy, a solution of the bonds of obligation, an unknown but not an innocent freedom of the soul.

I knew myself, at the first breath of that new life, to be more
wicked, tenfold more wicked, sold a slave to my original evil;
and the thought, in that moment, braced and delighted me like
wine.[6]

The most important idea here is still that of original sin, which is held
in check by the social 'bonds of obligation'. In a sense, then, all of us
have dual personalities, for 'original evil' is latent even in the most
admirable and respectable persons. Furthermore, that evil has a very
strong appeal — it may enslave, but the thought of it also 'braces' and
'delights'.

Few writers nowadays would care to admit to an explicit belief in
original sin. But Stevenson's vision nevertheless survives, for we
believe that in everyone there is potential for evil which lies beneath
even apparently respectable surfaces. Today, of course, we are able to
put a Freudian gloss on this supposition. According to a psychoanalytic
account, in our unconscious minds we all lead secret lives and it does
not require Dr Jekyll's fiendish powers to transform evil impulses
from fantasy into fact.

When the sex beast turns out to be a man after all, the 'Jekyll and
Hyde' model may be invoked, but in post-Freudian rather than
Calvinist terms. Thus Colin Wilson explains that mass sexual killers
like the Yorkshire Ripper

are not necessarily human monsters, creatures of nightmare,
driven by a craving for violence. Sutcliffe was a basically normal
person, who slipped into murder as gently and gradually as a
child slips into a swimming pool at the shallow end. . . . The
mystery, of course, is what peculiar pressures turned this quiet
man into a maniac who stole up behind women in the dark,
smashed in their skulls with blows from a ball-headed hammer,
then pulled up their skirts and blouses and carefully inflicted
dozens of wounds with a specially sharpened screwdriver.[7]

This kind of commentary opens the way for a more sociological or
clinical case history in which the analyst elucidates those 'peculiar
pressures' that gradually transform an ordinary person into a killer:
we will look at some studies of that type later on. Meanwhile, it is very
important to point out that the premisses even serious writers work on

are heavily influenced by popular stereotypes: what Colin Wilson takes entirely for granted (apart from Sutcliffe's gender, glossed over in the phrase 'a basically normal *person*') is that when he 'stole up behind women in the dark', Sutcliffe could properly be defined as a 'maniac'. In other words, he fails to challenge the division between 'normal' men and 'maniacs'; however we account for Jack the Ripper, he is qualitatively different from Jack the Lad.

To label sex-murderers mentally abnormal and leave it at that is in at least one respect no better than declaring they are fiends and monsters possessed by the devil. To acquiesce in either supposition is to render the acts of sex-murderers meaningless and thus to deny the possibility of an account which goes deeper than mere reportage and sensation.

In fact, the archaic formulas of tabloid journalism have just this mystifying effect: the pages of *The Sun* and the *News of the World* are apparently still stalked by motiveless 'fiends' whose 'brutal lusts' remain for ever unspecified, their connection with masculinity somehow obvious, yet unexplained. There is no room here for any kind of analysis other than the most conventional: the focus is rather on the horror of the act and also, increasingly, the thrill of the chase.

Both these aspects of sexual murder — the killing itself and the hunt for the killer — are given new objectivity and precision in a genre which is arguably the pinnacle of true-crime literature, to wit, the specialist crime magazines such as *True Detective, True Crime* and *Master Detective*. Like broadsides and tabloids, these magazines are ephemeral, but they provide more scope for extended treatment of similar themes and are addressed to a narrower, more knowledgeable audience. In effect, they are a rather bizarre form of soft pornography, and this is something we shall have more to say about when we come to consider the 'Gothic' strand in the sex beast tradition. Meanwhile, we must describe detective magazines in more detail, paying particular attention to the strange 'implied reader' constructed in their pages. This reader is a man who is obsessed — and titillated — by murder, especially sexual murder.

'Exotic murder': the true-crime monthlies

True-crime monthly magazines[8] have been part of popular culture in a number of countries for several decades. The British edition of *True*

Detective was launched in 1952 and has continued to appear without a break ever since; its publishers also produce two other titles, *Master Detective* and *True Crime* (that the latter was started as recently as 1982 may be taken as evidence for a continuing demand). Their combined readership is estimated at over 195,000. There is a close relationship with American true-crime magazines, since the British titles have always carried a proportion of syndicated American material. The various editions and titles also share a format which has hardly altered since the 1950s: it consists for the most part of detailed narrative case histories, together with readers' letters, cartoons and brief editorials.

But if the format has been relatively stable, the tone and content have changed considerably. In early issues, *True Detective* contained a mixture of different types of cases, from spying and confidence tricks to drugs and gang warfare. Its verbal and visual style was evidently influenced by the Raymond Chandler, 'hard-boiled' school of American crime fiction. More recently, however, and especially since the late 1960s, the magazine has come to be dominated by murders, with a significant proportion being sexual murders in our sense, or else murders of other kinds with a sexual angle. The writing now recalls tabloid journalism, while the visual iconography, especially on the cover, is derived from sado-masochistic pornography, featuring leather, bondage, screaming or terrified women and scantily-clad women holding knives or guns. The prototypical concerns of today's *True Detective* are summed up in a headline of 1976: 'exotic birds, exotic sex, exotic murder'. (Asked about this shift of emphasis, the editor expressed an opinion to the effect that 'people are more worldly-wise nowadays' and alluded to the implicit criteria of public taste which had caused his predecessors to leave out certain details. Given that the shift occurred most markedly in the late 1960s, it would appear to be part of the general 'sexualization' of popular culture which has taken place since then. The acceptance that soft porno-graphic images may be publicly displayed is only one part of this process.)

Where should we locate the current form of the true-crime magazine in relation to the genres we have dealt with already, the broadsides and tabloids with their characteristic themes? To begin with, there is a certain continuity of material: all the magazines quite often carry 'classic' stories culled from sources like the *Newgate Calendar*, which must certainly have been the subject of earlier street literature. 'Classic' cases — whether of eighteenth-century or World War Two vintage — are used to propound a concept of crime as a timeless, fixed essence in human life. A recent issue of *True Detective* retold a story of a mother and daughter who beat apprentice girls to death. The narrative opens in the following way: 'If you should be thinking that today we must live in an age when murder, rape and crime in general have never been more prevalent, callous and gruesome, think again! For, compared to some of the dark deeds perpetrated in London in the 1750s, many crimes of today pale into insignificance!'9 There is an absolute failure to acknowledge here that the murders and rapes of today are committed in very different circumstances and for very different reasons from apprentice murders in the eighteenth century. The writer merely invokes a common brutality, a 'gruesome and callous' quality which appears in every age. On the other hand, *True Detective* frequently deplores an assumed rise in crime rates and decline in moral standards. Such contradictory, deeply conservative and completely unilluminating pronouncements on crime are reminiscent of other genres, especially of contemporary tabloid reporting.

In fact *True Detective* shares many concerns and more generally an outlook, with the *News of the World*. There is the same concern with sensation, for instance, and the same kind of breathless, attention-grabbing prose: 'Vampire drank victim's blood!', 'Blonde was cooked alive in a sauna!' proclaim the captions on the cover. Inside, the narrative style is equally wide-eyed, a relentless build-up of macabre details. 'Large spikes stuck out from the rafters, the idea being that Douglas would hang victims from them and then dismember them while a camera recorded their torture deaths!'

It is also evident that the monthlies resemble the tabloids in viewing crime as the product of sin and not of sickness or social factors. In fact, this position is more explicit and aggressive in the specialist titles than it is in the tabloids: *True Crime* and *True Detective* rarely miss an opportunity for sniping at the 'softness' of psychiatric experts. Speaking of a child sex-killer, one contributor concludes: 'Psychologists will no doubt have some fancy words to describe the state of such a person's mind, but such descriptions are of little solace to the parents of dear little children so wickedly murdered.'10 The need for retributive punishment, including the death penalty, is constantly harped on throughout this type of literature.

One area where the true-crime magazines differ from the tabloids is

in the influence modern crime *fiction* has had on them. Although most
true-crime literature from street ballads on has taken a recognizably
narrative form, the monthly magazines were originally part of a
fashion for a certain type of American crime novel, and they retain a
number of the conventions of that genre: vivid description; fast cutting
between scenes; and most notably, the dialogue given to characters in
the story as a means of advancing the movement of the plot. Thus in
True Detective, all the characters have dialogue; policemen, witnesses,
even the victims ('"Please help me!" begged the woman as she tried to
hold her intestines inside her body.') Since all this apparatus of
character and dialogue must be invented (despite the boast that the
narratives are 'compiled from police records', in fact they are mainly
researched using newspaper cuttings) the magazines hover on the
uncertain boundary between factual reporting and imaginative
literature.

   To judge by the letters received at *True Detective*, there are many
people who appreciate being able to obtain the complementary
pleasures of well-made fiction and authentic fact in a single genre:
'Since I started to read *True Detective*', enthuses one reader, 'I have lost
my taste for detective fiction.' Both readers' letters and editorial
content generally make it clear that true-crime magazines offer their
readers some highly specific and unusual pleasures. Again, this marks
a definite divergence between the popular press and more specialist
literature: inasmuch as the pleasures *True Detective* provides combine
voyeurism and the thrill of the forbidden (in the form of 'gory details'
and explicit photographs), it is more akin to pornographic magazines
and the reader to whom it is apparently addressed resembles the
solitary punter at a peep-show.

   The reader who is constructed in the pages of *True Detective* is not
just an averagely curious or voyeuristic individual: that much is
proved by the fact that he has gone out and bought a title (or perhaps
even three) which concerns itself with nothing other than murder. We
might describe him as a *murder buff*, in the same way as others might
be film buffs or wine buffs. (We imagine the murder buff as a man, by
the way, because obsessive enthusiasts of all kinds are typically male
and because the visual content of true-crime magazines is so clearly
directed to the male gaze. However, many or most actual readers of
the magazines are women — a fact which surprised us, and which we
shall have more to say about later on.)

   So what, exactly, *is* a murder buff? Like all enthusiasts, he has made it his business to inform himself minutely on all aspects of murder (statistical, procedural, forensic, etc.) — and he prizes the unusual or interesting case, as well as the familiar (which serves to reassure him that he is indeed an expert). Yet the murder buff *is* rather different from the wine buff or film buff, or the dedicated hobbyist (the train-spotter or pigeon fancier), since his interest is in something which cannot, without irony, be described as a 'hobby'; which might, indeed, strike many people as utterly repellent. There is something strange about a murder buff: he appears to take the ghoulish tendencies many of us exhibit on occasion to extremes and is thus constantly susceptible to the charge of prurience. The true vocation of *True Detective* has therefore to be a dual one and this is of the greatest interest: not only must it cater to the murder buff's tastes, it must also provide some defence or justification of them. Hence the magazines' peculiar mix of salacious details and moralistic rant.

The dilemma has occasionally been recognized by correspondents like the man who wrote to *True Detective* as follows: 'Many writers to this page have condemned (and rightly so) the conduct of some criminals as deplorable. They seldom, however, finish a letter without making it clear that they consider the reading in your magazine entertaining.'[11] The letter goes on to ask 'whether there is something lacking when one condemns crime and violence, yet considers the same on film and TV or magazines "entertaining"?'. This very pertinent question cannot, of course, be resolved within the imaginative world of the true-crime monthly: to challenge the basis for its pleasures of voyeurism coupled with a feeling of moral superiority would threaten to destroy the foundations of the genre.

Murder buffs, however, have other forms of pleasure besides voyeurism and sensation (which are also on offer elsewhere, albeit in less detail). They bring to their reading the sensibilities of the connoisseur, someone who rejects the banal or inauthentic and whose enjoyment may be heightened by the smallest nuance.

Authenticity is a crucial concept in our interpretation of true-crime magazines and our understanding of the pleasures they offer. It is the feature most often singled out for praise by the writers of letters to the magazines' editor. In one sense, of course, this is quite paradoxical, since the very details that give an authentic 'feel' — the atmospheric dialogue and characterization — are precisely inauthentic, complete fabrications. But it is important to readers that the narratives are 'true'

(*True Crime* is billed as 'the great no fiction magazine') and that they contain a wealth of explicit detail. Any lack of explicitness draws complaints and even praise is tempered by the desire for more detail: 'I thought your article "Eliciting the truth: from cruelty to cunning" was first rate. It is only a pity that you did not have more room for a fuller account, especially involving the more ancient methods of gaining the required truth.'[12]

The detailed information given in case histories has another function besides ensuring authenticity: it gives the reader the pleasant illusion that s/he possesses expert knowledge and is involved in the fight against crime. Thus authors are careful to use technical terms which assume that forensic matters are intelligible to readers and editorials cite *causes célèbres* in a way which implies that we are all familiar with them and with their place in the canon of crime.

Yet although this repetition of the familiar is important, so is the introduction of novel material. A murder buff needs to be constantly stimulated by reading about cases he has not come across elsewhere (thus although most material in the monthlies is American or British, Australian and European sources are also used). He particularly likes the bizarre and grotesque, as opposed to the humdrum or common-place killing (bland material also brings letters of complaint). Cases involving unusual modes of death (for example boiling alive), the dismemberment of corpses or the execution of the killer are perennial favourites, while a historical analysis also reveals more short-lived obsessions (such as Nazi atrocities in the 1960s, gay sex-murders in the late 1970s and recently several cases involving private snuff-movies). New cases are explicitly presented and judged in terms of the established canon of murder and how well they fit into it. A recent editorial in *True Detective* commends a case to the reader as follows:

> Crime in California often tends to be larger than life. One thinks of the likes of Manson, the Black Dahlia killings, Stephen Nash — all with claims to everlasting notoriety on America's West coast. There are lesser-known sadists, too, almost daily committing murders every bit as weird. Such a killer is the subject of Jack G. Heise's detailed report. . . . It is a real cracker![13]

This illustrates exactly what is most distasteful about the true-crime monthlies and their murder-buff readers. We are back to the category of 'exotic murder' and to the judgement of a crime by quasi-aesthetic criteria of originality and nastiness ('larger than life . . . a real cracker'). With crime in general, and particularly murder, dismissed as an eternal manifestation of human wickedness, no explanation or analysis of why it occurs is required (and unsurprisingly, none is attempted). Thus the reader is reduced to the prurient and voyeuristic pursuit of gory details for their own sake.

Who are the actual, as opposed to the implied, readers of true-crime magazines? The British titles are not included in the National Readership Survey, but during 1984 a small survey was conducted via a questionnaire placed in all three magazines. Of the 1,200 readers who responded, over 85 per cent were women and most respondents were aged between forty-four and fifty-four.

In so far as this survey accurately reflects the whole readership — and it is telling that our informant at Argus Publications said it confirmed her previous conviction that the typical reader was 'a C2DE woman aged 45+' — it seems to raise two rather puzzling questions. First, why do middle-aged women enjoy reading this kind of literature, against all the stereotypes? And secondly, given their awareness that the magazines are read mainly by women, why do the producers so consistently address their visual and verbal content to *men*? We put both these questions to the editor and to the publishers, but they were either unable or unwilling to give any opinion.

Our own account, though it must be rather tentative, would focus on women's complex and rather ambiguous relation to the pleasures and dangers of transgression, represented in our culture by sex and violence. Femininity, as our society constructs it, is incompatible with transgressive behaviour, so that women are denied opportunities for transgression and severely punished if they do indulge (feminist criminologists have documented this process very fully; it is fundamental to the criminalization of women). On the other hand, a great deal of transgressive male behaviour is frighteningly alien to women's experience — is directed against women, or contains misogynist elements — so that women's attraction to violent transgression cannot be unmixed with anxiety and distaste. It could be argued that true-crime literature offers a way of resolving this contradiction, or rather, a way of satisfying both sides. The woman consumer of *True Detective* can read about depraved and revolting behaviour, but in a framework which emphasizes moral condemnation and which makes her appear as merely an eavesdropper on a dialogue really intended for men. This solution accommodates the desire for 'thrills' alongside the feeling that one ought not to desire them and it also allows for ambivalent feelings about the *kinds* of thrills which the magazines present.

As various people have suggested to us, there may be an analogy here with the scenes that take place when a sex-murderer — especially a child-killer — comes to court. On these occasions, women turn out in force and often indulge in both verbal and physical violence (shouting, catcalling, throwing eggs and fruit). This behaviour is permitted, not to say approved, by society because it can be seen as confirming women's role as protectors of children and guardians of morality. What it means to the women who participate is rarely if ever probed; in our view this is a complex topic which would certainly repay sociological investigation. In any case, the analysis of true-crime literature indicates that simplistic accounts in terms of either sexual arousal or straight moral outrage will not do: one does not subscribe to a monthly magazine simply to be outraged, though this is an integral part of the appeal.

Although we have analysed true-crime magazines as a species of that type of popular literature which also includes older genres like ballads and broadsides, their concern with exoticism and horror for the sake of it also links them with a different, less ancient tradition, which stresses the *pleasures* of transgression and cruelty instead of the *dangers* attendant on sin. The onset of this tradition has often been placed at the end of the eighteenth century. According to Foucault, the old forms of crime literature such as broadsides

> disappeared as a whole new literature of crime developed; a literature in which crime is glorified, because it is one of the fine arts, because it can only be the work of exceptional natures, because it reveals the monstrousness of the strong and powerful, because villainy is yet another mode of privilege: from the adventure story to de Quincey, or from the *Castle of Otranto* to Baudelaire, there is a whole aesthetic rewriting of crime.[14]

One outcome of this process was detective fiction; another, more salient from our point of view, was the 'Gothic' literature of sensation and cruelty (*The Castle of Otranto* was an early example). Apart from producing new representations of sadistic killers, this literature also had explicit connections with a type of discursive and philosophical writing that exalted the murderer as a hero and a rebel. Our modern conception of a sexual killer owes more than a little to this strand of thought and literature, which transforms the beast, the 'less than human', into his precise opposite, the Superman, and provides a bridge whereby murder can become a concern not only of popular genres but of high art and culture.

DEATH AND TRANSGRESSION: FROM MONSTER TO REBEL

In our society, the taste for horror is well developed: significant sections of the leisure industry are given over to maintaining it. Thus we have horror movies, from the arty to the low-budget kitsch (and not forgetting the latest variation, produced by new technology, the 'video nasty'); we have horror comics, paperback thrillers and the Chamber of Horrors at Madame Tussauds.

A certain weakness for this kind of thing, an appreciation of the *frisson* that horror produces, is not considered outlandish or abnormal, any more than it used to be considered abnormal to take family parties to a public hanging, though in fact the hanging had a function for the collectivity that is absent from the modern experience of horror. Horror today belongs to the domain of the aesthetic, and consists ideally of pure sensation. Thus people who rush to the scene of a disaster for the pleasure of witnessing actual death and destruction are deemed to have acted inappropriately precisely because they have derived from reality a thrill which we think should be confined to the realms of fiction.

One of things we noticed early on in our research was the extraordinary way in which discourse about sexual murder seems to blur the boundaries between fact and fiction. On one hand, we find the exploits of sexual murderers being represented exactly as if they were fictions: it is hardly a metaphor to speak of 'the murderer as hero' when Jack the Ripper has starred in so many films and been treated exactly like Dracula or Frankenstein, that is to say, as a Gothic stock character; or when a quasi-documentary film like *Ten Rillington Place*, with Richard Attenborough as Christie, uses all the techniques of the well-crafted thriller. Yet on the other hand, we find fictions being treated exactly as if they were flesh-and-blood realities: Norman

Bates in *Psycho* becomes a reference point in public discussion of the Boston Strangler; Raskolnikov and Othello are dealt with in forensic textbooks. Every major killing becomes a lurid paperback or movie; many murderers turn out to be avid consumers of the literature which celebrates the pleasures of (imaginary) horror. In more and more cases, according to one expert, the killer is motivated partly by the desire to become famous, to appear on television and on the front page of the newspaper.[15] He wants to be a hero in the Great Tradition of murder. The experts will collude with him in realizing this aim by constructing a profile and an account of his behaviour in terms of the existing 'conventions of the genre' (he has a grudge against his mother; he is a latent homosexual). If, as a forensic psychiatrist recently observed, 'It is very difficult to give a thumbnail sketch of someone who goes around killing old people', that is probably only because no one has yet got round to making a film about it![16]

The tendency to view sexual murder in terms of fictional stereotypes — sinister hunchbacks, diabolic dwarves, vampiric seducers, ineffectual clerks who turn into homicidal maniacs, cruel sensualists, libertines and devil-worshippers, secret transvestites with a grudge against their mothers, primitive monsters and degenerate monks — goes just as deeply into popular consciousness as the sex beast rhetoric of tabloid reporting: in fact the two sets of stereotypes are connected in fairly obvious ways. The generic characters of horror fiction function in just the same way as the tabloid 'fiend': they provide convenient stock explanations in terms of an inherent, but unnatural and subhuman wickedness; they also drive a wedge between the murderer and the man in the street by depicting killers in stylized, one-dimensional ways.

But horror fictions actually go beyond this. For instance, it is striking that unlike the tabloids, they tend to obliterate the victim completely. In a news report, the murdered person will often be sentimentalized, but at least she is a presence of some weight and significance, along with her angry and grieving relatives. In the book and the film she will be, at best, a shadow, obscured by the dazzling wickedness of her killer and by the horror of his acts which acquire a central importance of their own. The primacy of the *thrill* in this type of representation marks its greatest divergence from true-crime literature. It transmutes crime not just into sensation, but into an experience which can be appreciated *aesthetically*. That we are able to respond to a murder in this way is a result of the existence of a particular discourse on the beauty of the Horrid and the pleasure of cruel acts. Not only does this discourse affect our reading of sexual murder today, it was also, arguably, an important factor in the original emergence of this kind of crime.

It is evident that what is considered beautiful or significant will vary across cultures and change through time. During the eighteenth century in Europe, an aesthetic theory was gradually elaborated which stressed the attractions of what was called 'the Horrid'. Essays were published with titles such as, 'On the Pleasure Derived from Objects of Terror' and 'Enquiry into those Kinds of Distress which Excite Agreeable Sensations'.[17] The devotee of Horrid beauty was struck by such phenomena as rugged landscapes, dark forests, caves, ruined castles, graveyards and thunderstorms. 'Tainted' or 'corrupt' forms of female beauty (hunchbacks, consumptives, dead bodies, etc.) were much admired by the great writers of the Romantic period: in 1846 Edgar Allen Poe wrote, 'the death of a beautiful woman is, unquestionably, the most poetical topic in the world.'[18] In a great deal of literature from the late eighteenth and the nineteenth century, this enthusiasm for horror may be discerned, along with a strain of eroticism which is frequently sadistic or necrophiliac.

The sado-masochistic tendencies of the period were evidenced in particular by the Gothic 'tales of terror' which arose in England in the 1790s, enjoying considerable popularity which soon spread throughout western Europe. These fictions — the forerunners of Victorian penny dreadfuls, 'bodice rippers' and the Hammer House of Horror — predate the sex-murderer by almost a century, but they provide many of the codes by which he has come to be read. Set most often in suitably Horrid locations, such as castles, forests, graveyards and monasteries, their plots turn on torture, incest and murder, which are often described with lingering, voyeuristic pleasure:

A St Bartholomew, flayed, with his skin hanging about him in graceful display — a St Laurence, broiled on a gridiron and exhibiting his finely-formed anatomy on its bars, while naked slaves were blowing the coals beneath it — even those were inferior to the form half veiled, half disclosed by the moonlight as it lay.[19]

This was written in 1820, since when the annals of sex-killing have provided many edifying examples of men who found the flaying off of someone's skin exciting, not to mention those who agreed to the proposition that one's sexual objects look most alluring when dead.

What underlay the development of an aesthetic whereby, in the words of Burke, 'Whatever is fitted in any sort to excite the ideas of pain, that is to say, what is in any sort terrible . . . is a source of the sublime'?[20] According to most commentators it was connected to a number of developments in other fields of knowledge; especially the theory advanced in psychology by Novalis that painful and pleasurable sensations were closely related in the nervous system and that desire and cruelty were thus very similar, and the dissemination of details from quasi-anthropological studies of 'primitive' peoples and their 'cruel' customs. A further factor in producing new visions and articulations of desire was the major social upheaval which was taking place in Europe at the time, most obviously in the French Revolution of 1789.

It was just this social upheaval which produced a writer whose visions of desire have profoundly influenced our modern notions of the erotic. Awareness of these visions is part of our capacity to make any sense at all of the phenomenon of sexual murder. We are referring, of course, to the Marquis de Sade, hailed as 'one of the greatest inspirers of the moderns' and certainly an obvious and explicit forerunner of the modern tendency to associate sex, transgression, cruelty and death.

Philosophy in the charnel-house: the Marquis de Sade

If Donatien-Alphonse-François, Marquis de Sade (1740—1814) had not existed, the history of sex murder might well have been quite different. Sade's influence on our cultural conception of sex-killers, the extent to which he underwrites 'the murderer as hero', is almost impossible to overestimate, while as far as the clinical approach is concerned, his founding presence in the literature of sexual deviance is attested in the category we call by his name — *sadism*, of which murder (according to the experts) is an extreme, but in some sense archetypal manifestation.[21]

As far as we know, Sade himself was not a murderer: his many hagiographers hasten to assure us that he was sickened by the smell of blood from the guillotine. He did, however, commit serious sexual assaults; and he was the elaborator of a philosophy which spoke of the pleasures — erotic, aesthetic, intellectual and moral — attendant on humiliation, torture and murder. He created a solipsistic sexual universe ('Do not all passions require victims?' he asked, explaining how sexuality must consume its objects totally) and a perception of the sadist as a rebel and martyr which continues to glamorize transgressors even now. In short, the ideas associated with Sade's life and work so influenced and changed the Western cultural climate, they must be regarded as preparing the way for the later emergence of the sexual killer and the myths which surround him. In the words of Michel Foucault:

> Sadism is not a name finally given to a practice as old as Eros; it is a massive cultural fact which appeared precisely at the end of the eighteenth century, and which constitutes one of the greatest conversions of Western imagination: unreason transformed into delirium of the heart, madness of desire, the insane dialogue of love and death in the limitless presumption of appetite.[22]

Even allowing for the historical hyperbole always evident in Foucault, it can hardly be denied that the 'madness of Sade's desire' stands as a model, implicitly or explicitly, for every sex-murderer of the modern age. We shall see later on in this book how it served as a reference point for discussions of Jack the Ripper in the late nineteenth century and also how Ian Brady, child-killer of the 1960s, self-consciously defined himself as a follower of Sade. For the moment, however, we must outline the ideas which make the 'divine marquis' a prophet of sexual murder.

Sade's thinking, unsurprisingly, given the age in which he lived, reflects the general scientific and philosophical preoccupations of the French Enlightenment of the eighteenth century (the complete works of whose great luminaries, Rousseau and Voltaire, were among his effects at Charenton when he died). He did not invent the character of the 'libertine', the rational free-thinker and sensualist who lives outside social and sexual convention, but in the pornographic fictions which constitute his *oeuvre*, he took libertinage to new extremes.

We do not intend to recapitulate in any detail the actual contents of Sade's major works (*Justine, or the Misfortunes of Virtue*; *Juliette, or the*

Prosperities of Vice; *The 120 Days of Sodom*; *Philosophy in the Boudoir*): many writings on Sade give full accounts.[23] Our own concern is with the premiss that informs all these fictions, namely that cruelty and domination, represented most graphically by actual annihilation, are the true mainsprings of erotic pleasure. Sade approaches this insight in two rather contradictory ways.

First, he continually emphasizes how the pleasures of cruelty are entirely *natural*, that is, in accordance with the dictates of nature. In a typically materialist account, he explains (in terms that echo Novalis and would later be echoed by the sexologist Krafft-Ebing) that sexual pleasure is a matter of nerve sensations and that as far as producing these sensations is concerned, lust and cruelty are very similar stimuli. Our physiology itself produces pleasure out of sadism. But at a more exalted level, furthermore, we may see cruelty and destruction as ordained by nature, which is itself cruel and destructive: 'Who doubts that murder is one of nature's most precious laws? What is her purpose in creation? Is it not to see her work destroyed soon after? If destruction is one of nature's laws, the person who destroys is simply obeying her!'[24] It follows that the 'monstrous' killers of the past, such as Gilles de Rais (whom Sade explicitly mentions) were natural phenomena and not aberrations: 'Fools object to me, "But these were monsters!" Yes, according to our morals and our way of thinking; but in the sight of nature above us, they were only instruments of her designs; it was to fulfil her laws that she bestowed on them their fierce and bloody natures.'[25] It is only a short step from declaring murder natural to proclaiming it admirable, as Sade does continually. The world he creates in all his fictions is one where vice is 'naturally' triumphant and where virtue is not only not rewarded, it is actually punished by suffering and death (to underline the connivance of nature in this, Sade has his virtuous heroine Justine killed by a thunderbolt).

But the pleasure of murder is not to be found merely in 'doing what comes naturally'. If killing is justifiable because it obeys the laws of nature, it is *pleasurable* because it does *not* obey man-made laws: it flouts the morality of society and religion and it is this element of overt transgression that commends the act of murder to the true libertine: 'Oh! what action so voluptuous as destruction . . . there is no ecstasy like the one we taste in giving ourselves up to that divine infamy.'[26] Murder in Sade (and in post-Sadeian writing) is the symbol of transgression and of sexual pleasure, which thereby come to be inextricably intertwined. They are also made to stand for what Simone de Beauvoir, one of Sade's modern intellectual apologists, saw as a central theme of the human condition: the 'dramatic confrontation' between 'man-as-transcendence and man-as-object'.[27] The aspect of Sade's life and work which has converted the Western imagination is the idea that the individual who transgresses is a rebel, in search of a freedom and pleasure — a 'transcendence' — which society, in its ignorance and repressiveness, denies him. Thus the way is paved for the sexual murderer to become the quintessential modern hero.

This process has been completed in the modern age: the intellectual status we assign Sade as an apostle of transgression and freedom is startlingly different from the status his own contemporaries gave him. The change is mirrored in a whole range of cultural developments. The aesthetic movement of which Sade formed part has gone from strength to strength, with Gothic becoming part of the repertoire of 'high art', revered by intellectuals (as is Sade-inspired pornography, for instance that of Georges Bataille). The surrealist current of the early twentieth century held that the ultimate surreal (aesthetic) act would be to go into a crowd with a revolver and fire it indiscriminately. With their cult of 'convulsive beauty' (a notable strand in which was the admiration of women who murdered) the surrealists took over many of the motifs of the Horrid and of romantic sado-masochism.[28] The idea of the murderer as hero was thus well established by the mid-twentieth century, and has only gained in influence since; a glance at the best-seller lists demonstrates that the murderer is quite often the literal hero of contemporary literary productions, for instance.[29]

As in the eighteenth century, twentieth-century fictions of murder as trangression/transcendence have their underpinnings in philosophical discourse. The importance of the theme is most clearly reflected in the thought of existentialist philosophers, whose debt to Sade — as we shall see — is no small one.

The murderer as rebel: existentialism

'Existentialism' is concerned with the philosophy of the meaning of existence, and the nature of man's condition — especially the ways in which men are prevented from being free and the ways in which they can struggle to be free. Existentialist philosophers take it that man has no 'essence' which transcends his concrete mode of existence: that is, there is nothing corresponding to a universal, timeless and unchanging 'soul'. Instead, man *is* his material and social being. For the philosophers we are most concerned with here, Jean-Paul Sartre, Simone de Beauvoir, their mentors and followers, man's situation is tragic. A crucial aspect of his material being is his *subjectivity*: he is not an object, that which is experienced, but an experiencer; not that which is acted upon, but an actor. He is a potentially free being, *but* he is trapped in a tight cocoon of body, conventions and meanings, so that the moments of being and experiencing are fleeting. Even when he feels himself to be acting freely, he is acting in accordance with the norms of the society; even as he looks at someone, he is also being looked at and thus objectified, made not-subject. This is the tragedy.

Our use of masculine pronouns in the last paragraph is quite deliberate. As with philosophy generally, existentialism does not deal with all humankind, as though men and women were philosophically equivalent. To use neutral or feminized language when discussing this literature would be to conceal this very salient fact about it. It is only if we bear the masculinity of the subject in philosophy firmly in mind that we can pay attention to all its implications. For we will go on to argue that women cannot merely be 'written back in' to discussions about 'man's' struggle for transcendence.

Sartre and de Beauvoir were perennially interested in murder. They had been persuaded of its peculiar philosophical significance by the surrealists and by André Gide, who convinced them that 'in every person there lurks . . . an indestructible kernel of darkness, something that cannot break up social conventions or the common currency of human speech, but does, now and then, burst out in a particularly scandalous fashion.'[30] What 'bursts out' is subjectivity in its struggle to act freely, against social and material constraints. The act of murder is by definition an act which transgresses life itself and thereby breaks down the conditions — bodily, psychological and social — which keep man's free will in chains. André Gide's celebration of murder as 'the culminating *acte gratuite* that liberates man from the determinism of the material universe . . . the point at which — irremediably — man opts for his own freedom' encapsulates this view.[31]

In the work of Jean Genet, the theme of murder as an ultimate act of freedom and defiance of determinism is worked out again and again. Murder is 'the absolute dividing line between material and transcendental, profane and sacred. Once crossed, the past no longer has any relevant existence, time ceases; the future is an open choice, and the necessity for choice has itself been freely chosen.'[32] Having murdered, the murderer is 'left alive, without identity and therefore free' because he has burst the bounds of socialization, has ceased to be the social being he was brought up to be.[33] He has also destroyed the law of God and God himself, thereby *becoming* God. He has crashed through into a realm of pure being.

In Genet, as well as this celebration of murder as a straightforward transgression for the sake of freedom, we find a motif of transgression as inherently erotic. Murder can then be seen as a symbol of *erotic* violence. The critic Richard Coe explains this in terms of timeless and fundamental meanings that are indivisible from the human condition: 'In all intense and primitive eroticism the sexual act is associated with the dissolution of life . . . sex and death are hedged about with the same taboos, rape and murder offer the same types of temptation.'[34] It is obvious, of course, that Coe's 'human condition' here is actually a *masculine* condition. Rape seems to offer little temptation to women, for whom sex is associated not only (not at all?) with the dissolution of life, but also with its creation.

If sex and death are connected in existentialist thought, an associated idea is that of the near identity of hate and love. In love, the Self tries to escape from itself, and into the Other; but because the Other necessarily excludes the Self by virtue of its Otherness, love can easily turn to loathing and desire to destruction. In these coincidences of transgression and eroticism, sex and death, love and hate — and finally, therefore, freedom and death — we can see the possibilities for an existentialist account of sex murderers as the ultimate rebels, the ultimate actors-out of eroticism in its purest form.

There are, however, two major problems with the existentialist account of (and celebration of) the murderer. To begin with, in a certain sense it is incoherent: the transformation of love into hatred and death is seen as a means by which individuals break free of stifling social convention, but arguably this transformation is itself conventional. It is a possibility firmly encoded, since the eighteenth century, in our culture, and certainly not a novel move on the part of any particular individual. But if sexual murder is not an authentic and gratuitous expression of individual will, but rather a possibility defined by the culture, it can hardly represent the triumph of free will in defiance of determinism. Put another way, antisocial acts are not always *a*social acts: they are frequently underpinned by already existing social meanings. The existentialists seem to us to have glossed over this important point, and a massive question mark must therefore hang over their central idea that the Self can transcend its objectified condition by acts of will.

The fact that existentialists' so-called 'freedom' is actually determined by social and cultural convention becomes even more obvious when one considers examples of allegedly daring and transgressive acts from life and literature. For example, in the work of Sade there is a motif of cross-dressing which is meant to illustrate the willed overstepping of conventional gender boundaries. In *Juliette*, the heroine and her companion play a game of cross-dressing whose intention and effect is to profane the rite of marriage. Yet even here, as Angela Carter points out, the male instigator is careful to omit 'certain elaborations which would truly suggest an anarchy of the sexes — that, for example, Juliette as a man should marry he himself as a woman; not for one moment, even in fantasy, could he allow Juliette to act out that kind of class dominance over himself.'[35] We think this example illustrates the principle that what is thought of as 'freedom' actually operates within rather strict constraints. It is a form of play which is seldom if ever permitted to offer serious challenge to the realities of power.

Intellectuals, unfortunately, have frequently imagined that the structures of power were about to crumble because some individual committed a gratuitous act of violence. For de Beauvoir and Sartre, for instance, one attraction of murder was that it could often be interpreted as satisfyingly anti-bourgeois. They enjoyed *causes célèbres* like that of the Papin sisters, who brutally murdered their bourgeoise mistress (their story is the basis for Genet's play *The Maids*), though de Beauvoir correctly observes that this action could not in the end be read as simple rising against class oppression, still less as a conscious revolutionary act. In fact, it is always difficult to postulate murders like those of the Papin sisters as genuinely or ultimately free acts. At best they are acts of relative freedom, in so far as the killer flouts the social conventions and relationships which are normally treated as sacred. Nevertheless it is with this kind of act that men struggle, however vainly, for pure transcendent subjectivity in the existential scheme of things.

We begin to perceive a reason in all this for Simone de Beauvoir's advocacy of Sade. His life-style and writings flouted bourgeois convention in quite a conscious way and should therefore be celebrated. But in the same way that Sade could not take the step of making his fictional game a true 'anarchy of the sexes', so we find in existentialist thought a similar obfuscation of the actual gender of those people who transcend the social and material conditions of life.

This is the second major problem with the existentialist celebration of murder. Who murders whom? The first chapter of our book suggested that, overwhelmingly, it is men who murder; very often, it is women whom they murder. But Sade is the feminist's friend, according to Angela Carter, because he hints that this need not be eternally the case. Sade says that women too can murder: the Juliettes of the world can also be victors in the struggle for transcendence.

Recently this general issue — whether anyone can take up the dominant or central position of Subject — has been explored by very influential theorists working in the tradition of French existentialism and especially by feminists influenced by Lacanian psychoanalysis. But what it tends to come down to is that to become a Subject you have to become masculine (this current of thought is 'anti-essentialist' and does not equate masculinity and femininity with biological male or femaleness). To become masculine however is to reject and revile the feminine. It is hard to escape the metaphysical/metaphorical opposition that Angela Carter detects in Sade, whereby he 'regularly subsumes women to the general class of the weak and therefore the exploited, and so he sees femininity as a mode of experience that transcends gender. Feminine impotence is a quality of the poor, regardless of sex.'[36]

Sartre and de Beauvoir fudge this issue. For Sartre, of all the loathsome objectified stuff which suffocates man and ties him to his materiality, the female body represents the most vile. The existentialist idea of transcendence is above all transcendence *of* the feminine, of what Genevieve Lloyd refers to as 'the holes and slime which threaten to engulf free subjecthood'.[37] In her critical discussion of existentialist philosophy, Lloyd draws attention to the resulting contradiction in the idea of a feminine attainment of transcendence. The subject of history is, and in political thought always has been, masculine. For the male, transcendence of the bodily, the material and the social means breaking away from that within him which is feminine and leaving it firmly behind. For the female, however, there is 'no such realm that she can both leave, and leave intact'.[38] Transcendence for women is self-destruction, since to transcend the feminine is to destroy herself.

Neither Sartre nor de Beauvoir fully acknowledge these fatal barriers to women's freedom and their successors, including feminists, in the French tradition, have been rather uncritical of the existentialist legacy. There has been little criticism of the whole notion of transcendence, yet as Genevieve Lloyd asks, 'Should we really want to be transcendent selves, leaping about in triumphant assertions of will?'[39] This question is nowhere more pertinent than in relation to existentialist ideas about murder, for to make of murder a metaphor for freedom is to overlook the inescapable fact that it must also entail a massive *deprivation* of freedom. If freedom equals transcendence, to be achieved only at the expense of an Other, we do not feel it is a suitable basis for a feminist politics, now or in future. Nor is this point invalidated by the ideas of those feminists who assert that our ultimate goal must be the elimination of the categories 'masculine' and 'feminine' themselves (so that transcendence will not be, by definition, transcendence of the feminine). In general we are quite sympathetic to this line of thought, but we hardly think the glorification of sexual killing will have a deconstructive effect. Feminist theorists who sanctify Sade are so dazzled by the prospect of transcending femininity, they do not seem to realize that 'freedom' as it is usually defined is the reflex of a commonplace, unreconstructed masculinity. One must surely deconstruct both sides of an opposition.

Once again then, we ask 'Who murders whom?' If in fact there are no barriers to feminine transcendence — except perhaps women's own pusillanimity — we are still left with the question of why sex-murderers are male. The fact that they *are* male — and that murders of the powerful by the powerless are in general so rare — makes us dubious about the whole existentialist argument. It suggests that murder is not the ultimate free act, available to everyone, but a function of patriarchal and other power structures.

One existentialist-influenced writer who has faced rather more squarely up to the facts of gender, and the close relation of masculinity and maleness, is Colin Wilson. Wilson is a self-styled existentialist, the author of novels, literary criticism and innumerable studies of cultural phenomena. He is more or less completely ignored by academics, either literary or scientific, but anyone interested in the cultural study of murder will find it impossible to avoid citing his work. Its quantity and obsessiveness make it highly salient.

Wilson is deeply interested in murder, for typically existentialist reasons:

> Murder is the meaninglessness of life become dynamic, a dramatisation of the hidden futility of life. It is the human act, with all its inherent values, placed upon the microscope slide where it cannot dissolve into the featureless landscape of all other human acts. The study of murder is not the study of abnormal human nature; it is the study of human nature stained by an act that makes it visible on the microscope slide.[40]

Man's tragedy for Wilson is that he knows freedom is an illusion: but paradoxically, his subjectivity forces him to choose — there are no timeless and enduring values. The murderer is different from other human beings only in degree and not in kind. We all know our values are only makeshift, but the killer goes further than we do in substituting his own convenience for a commitment to what the culture pretends are 'absolute' values.[41] The murderer emerges once again as a rebel who refuses to join in the futile make-believe of conventional social life.

This account of the murderer dates from 1961, since when Wilson has become less and less inclined to celebrate murder as something heroic. Instead, he has become more and more appalled at the varieties of sadism endemic in Western culture. In 1972 he introduced the concept of the 'assassin', the killer who feels he has some kind of right to murder — Charles Manson and Ian Brady are mentioned as examples.[42] Such killers are to be distinguished from, for example, women who kill in self-defence. They require an analysis of 'what has gone wrong'.

The analysis Wilson provides of assassins is still an existential one, but the search for transcendence is seen in their cases as having gone too far, got out of hand as it were. Wilson concentrates on sex murder, rape and other sadistic acts as manifestations of Nietzsche's *Will to Power*. Violence defies the law and social norms, it is an assertion of the actor's right to dominate, and of his lack of guilt.[43] The point of this defiance is preservation of Self, of an intact, unviolated subjectivity. The increase in bizarre sadistic acts through the twentieth century is analysed as a cultural phenomenon: a peculiarly modern obsession with freedom and an understanding of the individual as oppressed by a generalized, collective 'Other': society itself. By 1983, Wilson is analysing these writings as the product of the ideas of Rousseau and Marx — thinkers whom he holds pretty much responsible for the atrocious degeneracy of contemporary societies![44]

Wilson has an Anglo-Saxon impulse to empiricism wrapped up with his existentialism, however, and this leads him to ground his cultural analysis and existential categories in a framework of biologistic 'drives' and 'causes'. A model which is very important to Wilson is Maslow's 'hierarchy of needs'. This suggests that the first needs people have are for food, shelter, human and sexual relationships. When these have been satisfied by the society people live in, the need arises for self-esteem and respect, then for self-actualization and creativity. The hierarchy is related by Wilson to the history of crime. Whereas 200 years ago most crime was committed for food, and 100 years ago we saw the emergence of sex crime, now we are witnessing the onset of a type of crime which is 'inexplicable' and appalling: exemplified by Brady, Manson, Sutcliffe and Nilsen, this is a crime committed 'for' self-esteem.[45]

We have said that it is a virtue of Colin Wilson that he does not blur the fact that it is men who commit these crimes, that men are sadists and sexual killers, that women never exhibit, let alone act out, the lust to kill which is now so common. On the contrary, Wilson's relentless empiricism, if nothing else, forces him to expose the actual, concrete acts which are overlain and codified by the fantasies of Sade and his apologists, the surrealists, the existentialists. The will to power might be an aspect of the human condition, but it is men who warp it, in whose hands it goes so appallingly wrong. The sexual drive is a biological drive, and therefore it shapes women's lives too — but it is men who indulge in violence that goes beyond sex, that becomes loathing and hatred, that turns a life force into something stagnant and poisonous.[46]

Nowhere, though, does Wilson seriously attempt to throw light on this issue. Why do men, and not women, find self-esteem such a problem? Wilson also uses various quasi-scientific concepts like 'frustration', 'aggression' and 'sexual perversion' which engender more heat than light, taking it utterly for granted that women are just not likely to suffer these things. This ultimate resort to biological explanation makes Wilson a rather 'transitional' figure between the existentialists and the scientists we consider in the next chapter.

CONCLUSION

Our examination of 'the murderer as hero' has revealed a complex and varied picture. In particular, there seem to be two *kinds* of heroes: first, the 'fiend', 'beast', 'monster' or whatever, whose terrible desires put him outside the pale of society and reduce him instead to the status of an animal, or as the father of Tessa Howden said of her killer, 'He's a creature masquerading as a human being!'[47] To refer to this subhuman as a 'hero' is to purge the word of any positive connotations. The second type is the libertine or rebel, whose desires are also outside social norms, but only because society is so repressive and constricting. This is the 'Outsider', the Nietzschian 'Superman', admired so relentlessly by intellectuals (though he also has his more popular side, in the Gothic fictions of mass entertainment).

Have these two versions of the murderer as hero anything important in common at all? Obviously, they could be seen as contrasting responses to the same basic phenomenon, 'evil': one version reacts to it with moral condemnation, the other with fascination and even delight. We find a different balance between the two responses at different historical periods and in different social strata; thus there was an upsurge in fascination with evil in the 1790s and its strongest effect was on the intellectual classes (even now, it is in that least intellectual genre, tabloid journalism, that moral outrage retains its firmest hold). But both responses are always 'there', available in the culture to be drawn on as required.

But we would argue there is another connection between our versions of the hero. They seem to be not just contrasting responses to evil, but variations on the theme of the 'state of nature'. The idea of a state of nature is derived from political philosophy of the seventeenth and eighteenth centuries. It is a kind of myth, a concept describing what human existence would be like without, or prior to, the formation of civilized society. In the years since the idea was put forward, it has generated conflicting attitudes. Originally, the state of nature was considered a very bad thing and the formation of the state with its coercive powers was justified on the grounds that without such measures we would revert to the horrors of a 'brutish' existence. But later thinkers, such as the eighteenth-century philosopher Jean-Jacques Rousseau, used the state-of-nature myth to criticize society. There was an idealization of the 'Noble Savage', the 'uncivilized' man who nevertheless lives a life more virtuous, more in harmony with Nature, than his alienated counterpart in Western society.

The murderer as hero in both his versions is essentially a man in a state of nature — unsocialized, uncivilized, outside conventional morality. In the sex beast stereotype of true-crime literature, the state of nature represents what it did for early liberal political theorists: anarchy, brutality, chaos, horror. The sexual murderer heralds the breakdown of civilized society and society must therefore respond immediately with unambiguous condemnation and the harshest punitive sanctions. The 'rebel' stereotype, in contrast, represents the idealization of the state of nature. The sexual murderer challenges society and offers us a wisdom, a 'natural' morality, a freedom which we have long since lost.

Thus the two versions of the hero are opposed in their view of the merits of the state of nature. But if we consider them from a slightly different angle, we may begin to suspect they are not so dissimilar: both versions implicitly reassure us that sexual killers are a breed apart. Put another way, by placing the killer in a state of nature, both lines of thought deny he could be in a 'state of culture'; that is, a product of society, not an outcast or a freak.

But this assumption is severely disrupted when we introduce questions of gender and power, in the context of a social and cultural analysis. The account of the construction of the murderer as hero which we have put forward in this part of the book provides plenty of evidence against the 'state of nature' view: it points to the 'culturalness' of sexual murder and its connections with cultural ideas of sexuality and gender.

For instance, our analysis reveals that sex murder is too historically specific a phenomenon to be sensibly treated as a periodic upsurge of animal impulses that would normally be 'tamed' by socialization. Why did man's eternal beastliness not erupt in this form before the late nineteenth century?

It also reveals how the potential for sex murder is embedded in western European culture and has been ever since the eighteenth century. The eroticizing of domination, cruelty and death is by no means *natural*: once again, it arose at a specific point in history. But it is also not confined to a few abnormal men: its imaginary forms are ubiquitous in the West, pervading both highbrow and popular culture, contributing to a taken-for-granted stereotype of masculine sexuality as intrinsically sadistic, intrinsically desiring to take the Other by force. In a culture which thus conflates sex, power and death, the sexual killer is hardly an exile.

We will take up this theme in much more detail when we reach our final chapter 'The Murderer as Misogynist?'. Meanwhile, we must turn to an alternative set of discourses which contribute something to the figure of the murderer. Our chapter on the 'hero' came to a close at the ideas of the existential writer Colin Wilson and we pointed out that by resting so much explanatory weight on biological notions like 'need' and 'aggression', Wilson was already beginning to nudge the murderer off his plinth and push him into the scientific laboratory. In the next chapter, therefore, we continue the process and focus our attention on those scientific approaches which, far from celebrating the murderer as a hero, deplore his behaviour as 'pathological' or 'deviant'.

3

The Murderer as Deviant

Will someone please explain pedophilia in geneticists' terms? Or shoe fetishism as the product of a brain mechanism constant through evolutionary development? Or penile exhibitionism as a hormonal defect? Or the need to rape old women as the effect of conditioning? Or necrophilia as merely a statistic at the outer reaches of a bell-curve?

(Robert Stoller, *Perversion, the Erotic Form of Hatred* [1976].)

In 1970, Dr Robert Brittain published, in the journal *Medicine, Science and the Law*, a composite portrait of 'the sadistic murderer'.[1] This picture was constructed, he claimed, not on the basis of any theory, but only from his own twenty years of observing such cases at first hand. According to Brittain, the ideal-typical sadistic murderer is introspective and withdrawn; obsessional; possibly a pseudo-intellectual; mild and generally non-violent; narcissistic and egocentric; prim and prudish in sexual matters; a hypochondriac; someone who may appear effeminate to others; highly intelligent; punitive in his attitude to other sex murderers; a day-dreamer with a rich fantasy life, tending to dwell on atrocity and horror. His interests may include Nazism, the occult, dinosaurs and other monsters. In a private room belonging to him, Brittain goes on to say,

> there could be a hood, possibly of the Ku Klux Klan type, or a mask, oriental-type clothing, a child's doll, a life-sized model of a woman, a rubber diving-suit, a scarf or towel, a semen-impregnated handkerchief, a cylindrical object of some kind, anaesthetics, carbon tetrachloride, petrol, glue or other volatile substances, a bed-frame or some similar construction.

In case this baffling inventory is not specific enough, Dr Brittain adds:

There might be a history of inordinate interest in underwater swimming or of the practice of seeing for how long the suspect could hold his breath under water, or of running through the deserted countryside wearing only a rubber mackintosh, or of offences in churches, or of desecration of vaults or of graves or graveyards. There might be a desire to use explosives to blow up, for example, public buildings, dockyards or penal institutions.

For Dr Brittain, these bizarre manifestations are linked because they constitute a *syndrome*, that is, a characteristic combination of symptoms contributing to a recognized condition (in this case, 'sadistic murder'). Brittain, then, is in agreement with us that sexual killing is a distinctive and meaningful category, but his reasons for holding that opinion and the account he gives of it exemplify a typically 'scientific' approach, of which we would be critical on a number of grounds. Let us briefly outline the points where we take issue with the current of thought represented by Brittain.

To begin with, scientific work of this sort makes certain assumptions about the centrality and fixity of the *individual*, who is to be systematically categorized in terms of the essential and invariant characteristics belonging to him or her. Secondly, these characteristics themselves are taken to stand in a certain, *causal* relationship with any *acts* the individual may commit: the sex-murderer murders because he is introspective, obsessed with dinosaurs, an underwater swimmer, etc. Or possibly, Dr Brittain might hold that there is some other factor — an unknown 'x' — which causes the introspection, the underwater swimming *and* the tendency to commit sexual murder. His calling sadistic murder a *syndrome* acknowledges the possibility of multiple aetiology, i.e., a number of causes. But it also asserts that this is a pathological condition of individuals, which must therefore be caused in each case by *something*.

Thirdly, the characteristics and concepts Brittain puts forward are raken as self-evident, objective scientific data: like most scientists, Dr Brittain appears not to recognize the ways in which his own concepts and categories, which derive from the culture in which he lives and learns, inform the way he interprets phenomena. Evidence for this can be found in the fact that Dr Brittain's portrait of the sex-murderer strikingly resembles the stereotypes we discussed in the last section, which are circulated in horror films and literature aimed at 'murder buffs'. It is not a clear-cut issue which account is parasitic on which; but there is obviously a certain degree of reciprocal influence, such that the 'hero' and the 'deviant' are not altogether distinct. If we take it that scientists are bound to be steeped in culture, there is nothing very surprising in this: however, it is part of 'doing science' to refuse to acknowledge it, or consider the implications.

Our fourth criticism concerns the data itself, a large proportion of which consists of sex-murderers' *accounts of* themselves, elicited over the years by Brittain. These accounts are persistently treated as if they were simple facts: unproblematic, unmediated reflections of the patient's experience and/or inner disturbance. We believe, by contrast, that such accounts are both more and less than reflections. They are representations, often consciously constructed, which draw on cultural as opposed to individual resources. The fact that sexual killers couch their accounts in the language of horror films, or use an imagery drawn from Nazism, testifies to the availability of 'scripts' which people can use if they are asked to give an account of themselves by someone like Dr Brittain.

The fifth question raised for us by Dr Brittain's paper concerns the concepts he uses to describe what sex-killers are like — 'narcissistic', 'deep aggression', 'high intelligence' and so on. These are theory-laden notions from the outset and we cannot accept they are ontologically self-evident, as Brittain implies. The claim to write without reference to theory is therefore unfounded; the implication that there *are* theory-free facts, to which scientists have access via observation, is to say the least, naive.

Dr Brittain does not proceed from describing his 'syndrome' to explaining *why* sadistic murderers are as they are. This is unusual in scientific discourse, as the process of science generally does take the step from conceptualization to causal explanation; science aims eventually to formulate law-like generalizations which will enable us to predict precisely and accurately, as well as accounting for observed occurrences. This again raises problems for us, and we will consider them further (together with the questions we have raised so far) as we analyse in detail the treatment of sex murder in the scientific discourses on crime, disease and deviance. We begin by giving a brief general account of how the scientific investigation of crime and criminals has developed since the eighteenth century.

CRIMINOLOGY: THE 'SCIENCE OF CRIME'

It is difficult for us to conceive of 'crime' without 'the criminal' — the two seem logically interdependent. Yet prior to the work of the classical criminologist Beccaria, author of the famous dictum 'the punishment should fit the crime', there were only two categories: crime and punishment.[2] The 'criminal' emerged along with the human individual who became the general object of the social sciences. In early accounts, criminals were viewed as free agents, responsible by definition for their criminal acts, then gradually it was recognized that not all individuals are equally free — some are mentally ill, or starving, or too young to take full responsibility.

The scientific study of crime then split into two main projects, both taking the criminal and his acts as their focus and trying to construct a causal chain to explain why the criminal committed such acts. One project was undertaken by the school of scientific criminology, which looked at the way in which social variables like sex, age, geographical location, etc., might affect the tendency of any individual to become a criminal. The other was pursued by the positivistic school, which began in the late nineteenth century with Cesare Lombroso's criminal anthropology, examining how features of the individual organism, such as body shape or skull configuration, might predispose people to crime.[3]

Lombroso's heirs continue to examine human biology to explain crime, while psychologists and psychiatrists concentrate on the 'criminal mind'. Other sociologists continue the old concern with *social* variables. But in the second half of the twentieth century, there has been a new development. The 'sociology of deviance' shifts the focus away from the individual criminal to the processes by which some acts or classes of acts come to be labelled 'criminal'. It examines both how people come to adhere to social norms and how and why they flout them; it analyses the processes by which norms are constructed and enforced. Marxist and other radical criminologists have then put the sociology of deviance into a class framework, emphasizing the ways in which policing and other forms of control (such as definitions of crime and deviance) uphold the class structure. Feminists have carried out a similar analysis for patriarchal social relations.

As we shall see, the radical criminologies find the sex-murderer a difficult phenomenon to deal with and have little or nothing to say on the subject. Thus the vast majority of scientific investigations into sex murder, or even murder in general, are firmly committed to a thoroughgoing individualism. The sexual killer is the ultimate social deviant, and the reason why this is so lies somewhere in his biology.

In fact, it is difficult even in mainstream criminology to find material which deals expressly with *sexual* murder. Sex-murderers are such a small population, statistically satisfactory research cannot be done on them (which means that the most directly relevant literature is to be found in the least positivistic kinds of discourse — psychoanalytically oriented writing, for example). They tend to be treated in most books or articles as a subset of all 'violent criminals' or all 'sex offenders' or all 'psychopaths' and thus the specificity of what they have done is always being lost sight of, subsumed into some vague notion of aggression; or worse still, into a generalized and meaningless 'criminality': astonishing as it may seem, great swathes of the literature are capable of lumping all convicted criminals, from murderers to juvenile delinquents to drunken drivers, into one undifferentiated analytic category.

In our discussion of the literature, we will be careful to make it clear just what kind of crime or criminal is under discussion. Most of the approaches and concepts we examine are not explicitly addressed to our problem and our concern must therefore be with the possible utility (and possible drawbacks) of applying them to the explanation of sexual murder *per se*. We begin with the 'biogenetic' approach which has dominated thinking about crime for so long.

BIOGENETIC EXPLANATIONS OF SEX MURDER

In 1901 H. Havelock Ellis's *The Criminal*, which he had written ten years previously, was published in a new edition in the Walter Scott Contemporary Science Series, which was obviously intended to introduce scientific and technical subjects to the lay reader (other titles in the series included *Volcanoes, Past and Present* by Prof. Edward Hall, and *The Germ Plasm: A Theory of Heredity* by August Weisman). In this book, Ellis is a popular exponent of the positivist school's individualistic criminology, although in his first chapter he commits

himself to a multi-causal account of crime in a hedging-about proviso
familiar to us from contemporary criminology texts:

> It is impossible to overestimate the importance of the social
> factor in crime. To some extent it even embraces the others and
> cannot be made to regulate or neutralise them. . . . [However]
> We cannot deal wisely with the social factor of crime, nor estimate
> the vast importance of social influences in the production or
> prevention of crime unless we know something of the biology of
> crime, of the criminal's anatomical, physiological and psycho-
> logical nature.[4]

Ellis is committed to the theory that criminals are born — they are of a
certain biological type. The direction of causality is clear: it goes from
'inside' the criminal to the acts he commits, though social conditions
can exacerbate or attenuate his criminal tendencies.

The criminologist Ellis took to be the most important of his time
was Cesare Lombroso, the criminological anthropologist whose
influential book *Crime, its Causes and Remedies* had been published in
the original Italian in 1899.[5] Lombroso was committed to a positivistic
method which demands that the scientist collect and classify those
facts which are given to observation. Lombroso, wanting to study 'the
criminal' and discover his essential characteristics, set about collecting
the indisputable 'facts' about criminals — that is, physical characteristics like length of ear-lobe, jaw-bone dimensions etc. in prison
populations. This work is an extreme example of how what seem to be
simple facts appear, from a different perspective, as clear theoretical
constructs, and impossibly biased ones at that: nearly a century later,
it is generally recognized that not everyone in prison falls *ipso facto*
into the category 'criminal' (indeed in Lombroso's time, the nineteenth
century, prisons contained an even larger proportion of the disabled
and destitute than is the case now). Furthermore, it is far from self-
evident to modern understanding that social scientists ought to be
concerned with measuring ear-lobes and jaw-bones. For this activity
to make sense, we have to be aware of the common sense of Lombroso's
day: the powerful and in many cases taken-for-granted assumption of
'social Darwinism'. This doctrine put the races of the world into a
hierarchy (white Europeans at the top). Some races and their physical
characteristics were considered more 'advanced' than others, just as

mammals are more advanced, from an evolutionary perspective, than fish.

The relevance of Darwinist ideas to criminology was this: according to Lombroso, born criminals were 'atavistic' — 'throw-backs' to a lower form of life (as represented also by the non-white European races). He also linked crime with epilepsy, speculating that such conditions could change a normal constitution into one similar to that of the born criminal. Psychic factors being difficult to measure, Lombroso concentrated on things like the shape of the jaw-bone, the length of the arms, body weight and shape, distance between the eyes, etc. These do admit of accurate measurement and of precise statistical analysis based on large numbers of subjects. The point of such detailed work on physical measurements was to associate certain 'atavistic' characteristics with criminality and to show that the latter was hereditary. Ellis tells us Lombroso drew on work suggesting that rogue elephants, undisciplined or untrainable horses and other 'criminals' of the animal world suffered from inherited characteristics; he also referred to insectivorous plants as 'the criminals of the botanical world'.[6]

Ellis is dissatisfied with the implication in Lombroso's work that all non-European societies are populated entirely by born criminals and he therefore discusses the problem of relativism. It is clear, as he says, that what counts as criminal behaviour varies from culture to culture. For instance, of the ten Hebraic crimes recorded as punishable by stoning, only one was a crime in Ellis's day — rape, which had altered dramatically from being a crime of property to one against the person. Criminality in general, therefore 'consists in a failure to live up to the standard recognised as binding by the community. The criminal is an individual whose organisation makes it difficult or impossible for him to live in accordance with this standard, and easy to risk the penalties of acting anti-socially.'[7] According to contemporary convictions about the progress of evolution from lower to higher forms of life and the assignation of non-Europeans to a lower point on the scale, it followed that Black people *would* find it hard to live up to the standards of 'civilized' communities and thus we find racist convictions and stereotypes are constantly invoked in relation to criminality: 'Our survey of the physical characteristics of criminals showed that they constantly reproduce the features of the savage character — want of forethought, inaptitude for sustained labour, love of orgy.'[8]

In the twentieth century, with its discrediting of the theory of 'higher' and 'lower' races, research into the atavism of criminals was dropped. There were also methodological problems with the work of Lombroso and his followers: that their subjects were not a homogeneous sample, and that they did not set up proper controls by carrying out similar research on the population at large. Lombroso also found, of course, that many people he examined did not have the atavistic characteristics he expected. In his later work he therefore had to back-pedal on his strong theory, and introduce new categories of criminals: the criminal by passion, who is driven by circumstance to commit an illegal act that is essentially out of character; and the criminaloid, whose crime is precipitated by environmental and social factors and by opportunity. Ellis refined this typology further. The *political criminal* can be a saint, martyr or hero; the *criminal by passion* seeks to redress injustice and will not be a recidivist; there are *insane criminals* who suffer from a recognizable mental illness and *instinctive criminals* who were labelled 'morally insane' (a term disliked by Ellis). *Habitual criminals* are created by the penal system and other social conditions.[9]

Of these classes, the instinctive criminals are the most interesting to Ellis, since social causes and rational motives seem to be absent from their behaviour. It is in this group, therefore, if anywhere, that we might find a criminality determined entirely by biology. However, attempts to find biologically based characteristics common to all, or even a significant number of those who commit such 'motiveless' crimes have proved notably unfruitful. To demonstrate this we will briefly review several ideas put forward during this century, which link criminality to biogenetic factors — bearing in mind that whether it is specifically mentioned or not, sexual murder is frequently regarded as a motiveless crime susceptible to just this kind of explanation.

Body type and criminality

Earnest Hooton had argued in 1939 that body shape and behaviour are related. This does not mean the latter is entirely determined by the former, but Hooton insists, 'I deem human [physical] deterioration to be ultimately responsible for crime.'[10] He claims that a physically degenerate individual will have a tendency to crime, though other factors may intervene to prevent his indulging it. In 1940, William Sheldon introduced the concept of three different body types, the ectomorph (a tall, thin body), the endomorph (a short, fat body) and the mesomorph (an athletic, muscular body).[11] The type of body a person has is determined at the embryo stage. Sheldon investigated the link between body type and criminality. From an original sample of 400 delinquent boys he selected a sub-sample of 200, and found there were far more mesomorphs in this group than would be expected in the general population.[12]

At first, Sheldon's association between mesomorphs and crime seemed promising: Glueck and Glueck followed up his research and found 'twice as many mesomorphs and less than half as many ectomorphs among the offenders' in a controlled study.[13] However, another study conducted by McCanless et al. found no association between body type and crime in either convicted or self-reported offenders from a random sample of 177 adolescent boys in a training school.[14]

Of course, even where a positive correlation between body type and crime is found, it hardly amounts to a causal explanation. Sheldon believed there was an intervening factor, in that body types correlated with specific sorts of temperaments. A follow-up study of his original 200 boys was done thirty years later by Hartl, Monelly and Elderkin, who claimed that body type did indeed correlate with personality type.[15] (The whole question of measuring personality is something to which we must return later in this chapter.) A correlation between three factors is more impressive than just two and might lead us to search for the causal mechanism behind all three with more energy and commitment. But on the other hand, everything said so far could be accounted for by a social theorist without recourse to any such mechanism. For example, it is possible that muscular and athletic juveniles attract more police attention than others and are watched and caught more. Given that the mesomorph theory has had considerable popular coverage, it may have become a self-fulfilling prophecy. It might be that big and strong boys are recruited into offending groups more commonly; peers assign the role of 'offender' to an individual. These and any number of other socio-cultural possibilities spoil the theory that it is biology *per se* which determines criminal behaviour. They turn our attention away from causal chains at the level of the organism, and focus on the cultural *meanings* in the light of which people act.

Criminality and the brain

Offenders of all types have had their brains examined. Hill and Pond, in 1952, found a higher proportion than expected of abnormal electroencephalograms (EEGs) in murderers who were clinically and legally irrational or insane, than in those labelled incidental, motivated or sexual.[16] This is an interesting finding for us, since it places sex-murderers firmly in the camp of the 'normal'. However, subsequent research does not associate EEG abnormality with disorders of behaviour. For example, Gibben et al. report a comparison between the criminal behaviour of a group of diagnosed psychopaths with normal EEGs and that of a group with abnormal EEGs over a ten-year period. They found no significant difference.[17]

Whatever the findings, the relationship between brain activity as measured on an EEG and behaviour is still obscure. Brain research has progressed in recent years: for instance, researchers can now stimulate 'anger' in a subject electrically, so that a person at the touch of a switch experiences feelings of anger.[18] It has been recorded, too, that pathological aggression can be caused in generally unaggressive individuals by brain tumours.[19] But this brings us no nearer to understanding what, in the absence of a scientist with an electrode, a brain tumour, etc., stimulates the brain to produce feelings of anger. After all, two people may face the same putative stimulus and feel quite different things: if someone tells them off, X may feel anger where Y feels humiliation; Y may feel amusement where X feels hatred. There are also well-documented cultural differences, both in what emotions are considered appropriate in particular social situations, and in what emotions are felt and how they are expressed.[20]

It is difficult for any materialist to quarrel with the biological proposition that for every event at the level of the whole human being — a feeling of anger or hostility, for instance — there is an event in the brain; we are not trying to dispute what we take to be obvious. But it is quite implausible to suppose that a murder is just a series of events in the brain which occur one after another on their own, without reference to what is going on outside. So for instance, we might well find a difference between the brain of a sex-murderer and that of a political assassin; but far from the brain-difference accounting for the fact that one person committed a sex murder and the other a political assassination, it might well be that the brain-difference is caused by the difference in the activity.

Chromosomes

The sex-chromosome pairs (a chromosome being a cluster of genes) are labelled XX in females and XY in males. In 1961 the presence of an extra Y chromosome in some males was described and this report was followed by others which linked the abnormality with aggressive or violent behaviour.[21] (As well as helping to explain aggression, therefore, it was thought the chromosome factor provided a plausible account of sex-differences in aggressive behaviour, specifically the association of aggression with maleness.)

A study of patients resident in Rampton and Moss Side special hospitals reported in 1971 by Casey et al. showed a rather more complex picture. Patients with XYY chromosomes were found to be significantly taller than normal, but this was the extent of their consistent physical abnormalities.[22] The sample also contained patients with other chromosomal abnormalities however: XXY and XXYY. Such people have pronounced physical abnormalities, known as 'Klinefelter's syndrome' — small testes, infertility and the development of breast tissue. But as far as 'aggression' was concerned, 'The behaviour pattern of patients with chromosome abnormality as indicated by their recorded criminal convictions show that they commit less offences against the person than controls.'[23]

Owen carried out a review of the entire literature on this subject and put forward a number of criticisms.[24] For example, the process of karotyping (analysing the characteristics of chromosomes) is not a straightforwardly objective proceeding, but involves subjective judgements. In addition, Owen suggests, the subjects in many experiments may have been karyotyped precisely because they were markedly taller than average and therefore suspected of having a chromosome abnormality (again this is a problem of controlling experiments properly). Furthermore, studies of newborn babies suggest that the distribution of chromosome types is 'not very different from that found in institutions', that is, there are just as many XYY males in the population at large as in the population of offenders or special hospital inmates. Thus to label XYY an abnormality in any pathological sense might beg the question. Owen also discusses the difficulty of measuring behaviour and assigning it to personality types — a topic we shall come to shortly.

Hormones

The literature on hormonally based sex-difference has often been cited in discussion of biogenetic theories of criminal behaviour.[25] Like chromosomes, hormones are felt to be an obvious explanatory candidate when scientists are investigating a behaviour — such as the commission of sexual offences — that exhibits marked sex-differences.

Once again, the actual link between hormones and criminality is assumed to lie in the intervening factor of aggression. For example, Gray and Baffery argue that there is a consistent pattern of behavioural sex-difference in all animals which originates in the higher levels of androgen to be found in males.[26] Castrated males, with less androgen, are uniformly less aggressive. In humans this natural difference is reinforced by the fact that women are more highly socialized. The socialized nature of women is associated with their superior verbal skills (which, it is implied, must be neurally based) and the sexual division of labour requiring aggression in the male and nurturance in the female. Gray and Baffery thus recognize the importance of socio-cultural influences, the valuing of male aggression and the concomitant disvaluing of female aggression, but they still regard biology as the fundamental explanation.

It is generally assumed, of course, that rapists and other violent sex offenders could be 'cured' of their behaviour by hormone treatment. One recent survey reported the majority of its respondents in favour of castration for rapists and there are reports occasionally on both surgical and chemical castration. But the popular belief that rape and other sexual violence results from uncontrollable urges which are themselves caused by excess androgen is not supported by logic or evidence.

To take logic first, it might well be true that castration prevents a man committing any further rapes. But this does not imply that his previous acts of rape were caused by the fact that he had *not* been castrated. Cutting off someone's hands would be an effective means of preventing them committing further pickpocketing offences; no one, however, would be silly enough to argue that pickpocketing is caused by the possession of hands.

Secondly, the scientific literature suggests that public faith in hormone treatment for violent sex offenders is misplaced.[27] The use of oestrogens, i.e., female hormones, to control deviant behaviour goes back thirty years, and in the 1960s artificial substances called 'anti-androgens' were developed. But reports on the use of oestrogens and anti-androgens are concerned with non-violent sexual deviants, like exhibitionists: there is no evidence that the therapy affects aggression in humans. Work like Gray and Baffery's, which does link androgen and aggression, depends on extrapolating from animal to human research, since most reported studies are on monkeys and rats.

A note on biological explanation

All the work we have considered so far shows a commitment to explaining events in the social world, or in the psychology of the individual, by reference to what is happening at the more 'fundamental' level of biology, or biochemistry. This notion of what constitutes a good explanation of human behaviour is widely accepted as common sense — biology must be the ultimate cause of everything — but we want to argue that common sense is misguided. However illuminating a biological account might be, it will never enlighten us about sexual murder.

'Sex murder' is not just a convenient label for a type of bodily act like 'shivering' or 'coughing', but a cultural category which represents an interpretation of behaviour. A biological explanation might be able to explain the bodily acts and events from which sex murder can be built up: it might tell us, for instance, what neurones fired in the murderer's brain at the crucial moment. But this will never be the same as explaining sexual murder as a meaningful act: an account of a murder in terms of neurone firings could in one sense be described as 'too true to be good'.[28]

To see this more clearly, consider the quite plausible idea that two acts of killing, one a sex murder and the other the killing of an enemy in hand-to-hand combat, might actually be underlain by exactly the same physiological events (for example arousal, levels of hormones, etc.). Yet there would be an enormous difference in the culturally ascribed meanings of these two killings: in everyday terms, they would not be analogous at all. The type and level of explanation that is needed is therefore at a higher level than 'which neurones fired', a level that can take account of differences in intention and interpretation.

This argument is the same one that crops up whenever comparisons are drawn between animals and humans. One influential argument contends that humans are conscious in a way 'lower' animals are not (of course there could be dispute about whether some species have consciousness in the same way as humans) and therefore human behaviour has a meaningful, intentional quality not susceptible to biological explanation. Against this position, some sociobiologists have argued that consciousness has emerged in the process of natural selection just like other human attributes, such as vision or hearing: in principle, therefore, conscious behaviour must be explicable in the same way as other aspects of the human organism. Social theorists counter this by saying that not only does conscious behaviour require alternative explanations, but the existence of self-consciousness compels us to look beyond biology when we consider in a human context behaviour that is typical of other animals too — mating and reproduction, home-building, group organization. In human culture these things acquire a kind of significance they do not have outside it and can no longer be conceived as being based purely on biology.

This means that explanation in the social sciences has to be a totally different thing from explanation in the natural sciences. In the natural sciences, traditionally, to explain is to discover the causal chain that brings events about. The objects of social science, however, are persons who are conscious and act in the light of their knowledge of their own desires and the meaning of those desires in the wider culture, with all its alternative meanings and norms. Social actors, in other words, orient themselves to social meanings, and their actions cannot be analysed causally. To explain social events and phenomena requires an understanding of the meanings which make them possible, and in the context of which social actors act. Sex murder is not a physiological event but a socially meaningful activity. It is therefore not to other physiological events that we look for an explanation of it, but rather to the social context which makes it possible and understandable.

PSYCHOLOGICAL EXPLANATIONS OF SEX MURDER

Psychology is usually thought of as a *social* science, aware of the kinds of issues about the explanation of human behaviour that we have just been discussing. Human behaviour might be biologically based, but nevertheless we need explanations at the level of psychological events. However, as it turns out, psychological explanations of crime and sex murder pose the same sort of philosophical problem as we encountered in the literature on biogenetic explanation: instead of seeing sexuality and social action as to do with *meaning* and *desire*, they are generally seen as being to do with *cause* or *drive*. Whereas desires are intentional and fixed on some object, so that the subject acts to fulfil desire, drives are pushed, so to speak, from behind. The individual is propelled along an inexorable chain of causes and effects. So if we want an explanation of an event, we must look to the past, to the chain of causes which, willy-nilly, brought about that effect. Desires have to be seen, by contrast, as belonging to the person in a way drives do not: to understand how and why a person acts in pursuit of desire, we need to look at the whole edifice of social meanings, which construct the object of desire for that person and sanction the ways in which it can or cannot be achieved.

Psychiatrists and psychologists study mental events and predispositions in order to explain criminal acts. Of course, it is possible to regard such events as themselves the outcome of a process of learning to behave in ways approved by society (or in the case of criminals, by those subcultures which value antisocial behaviour). Behavioural psychology stresses the way that rewarded behaviour may become automatic — a child who is rewarded for being good will in the end always be good even in the absence of a reward. If we take it that the type of behaviour that is rewarded depends on the norms of the culture, we will want to look closely at the culture to explain what counts as criminal within it (and whether there are enclaves in which criminal behaviour is, indeed, learned and rewarded). We deal with learning and subculture theories later in this chapter, under the heading of social explanations: here we examine psychological theories which see mental phenomena as manifestations of underlying biological phenomena, more or less, but it should be borne in mind that the more sophisticated investigators in this field would also have recourse to culturally informed learning theory.

Personality

A great deal of research has been done to test the hypothesis that people with certain types of personalities will commit criminal acts. By far the most influential figure in this area and in the project of personality measurement generally, is Hans Eysenck.[29]

Eysenck works with a model of personality which considers it presocial — that is, in the newborn infant the genetic factors which determine what her personality will be are already 'set'. Her ability to learn and be socialized is determined by her personality type, as are her probable responses to stimuli of various sorts (for example, whether she will hit back if someone hits her). This view differentiates Eysenck from the behaviourists, whose notion of personality includes much more plasticity. They think that if we know what a person or animal has learnt and how powerfully she has been trained to behave in a certain way, then given certain stimuli we can predict her reaction.

Eysenck's model of personality measures it along three dimensions: extraversion—intraversion, neuroticism and psychoticism. Eysenck himself holds that people who score highly on any of these dimensions are relatively more predisposed than others to criminality, and anyone who scores highly on two, or all three, is even more likely to commit criminal acts.

Personality tests are constructed painstakingly and empirically. The way this is done illustrates our point about the work of Robert Brittain, that scientific concepts are not just given by reality itself, but shaped by cultural and philosophical preconceptions.

Take for example the trait of 'sociability'. An item on a personality measurement questionnaire designed to measure sociability would normally be constructed using panels of ordinary people who are asked to judge whether certain behaviours, attitudes and reactions exemplify 'being sociable' or 'being unsociable'. For example, we might write down a number of possible items such as 'loves parties', 'would choose a job working with people', 'prefers to holiday alone'. Then we would ask a large number of judges to sort these into piles according to whether the responses indicated that the people who chose them were sociable or unsociable. When we looked at the way the sorters had divided the items, we would find that some items — 'loves parties' for example — had elicited a high degree of agreement that they indicated sociability; others might command far less consensus. Our final choice of items for the questionnaire would be taken exclusively from those which our sorters overwhelmingly agreed were good indicators of sociability. Almost inevitably, then, the questionnaire would consist of a series of cultural stereotypes.

In fact Eysenck's key dimension of extraversion results from the empirical finding that people who score high on measures of sociability have similarly high scores for 'activity', 'optimism' and 'outgoing and impulsive behaviour'. The covariation of scores on these traits led Eysenck to hypothesize that what was really being measured was an underlying trait of which the others were all just manifestations. He called this 'extraversion'.

In the process of conceptualizing extraversion in this way, many other possible traits will have been tried and discarded on various grounds. Perhaps because there was no consensus on how to measure them: it can readily be imagined that panels of sorters would have trouble agreeing on the indicators for, say, a 'happy—sad' scale. Some people might take 'laughs a lot' to indicate happiness; others might think that on the contrary it shows hysteria or mania and that therefore a person who laughs a lot is 'really' sad. Another factor which might cause Eysenck to discard certain traits is the finding that individuals' scores on them vary and change over time. When this happens, by definition the thing being measured is not a personality trait at all, since personality is characterized by invariance and fixity.

There are several things to notice about this. It is taken as axiomatic that personality is fixed. This is not determined independently and objectively, rather, any unreliable indicator (one which varies over time) is taken not to relate to personality proper. Since behaviour is believed, axiomatically, to be explained by personality, the changeable indicators are also assumed to be quite irrelevant in accounting for behaviour. But this raises puzzles in relation to well-known difficult cases such as Adolf Eichmann, who was responsible for the programme of extermination of Jewish people in Central Europe and was, at the same time, renowned for his tenderness towards children and animals and especially for his story-book performance as a father to his own children.[30] Can these wildly contrasting but contemporaneous behaviours be explained by reference to an Eysenckian fixed personality type? Or would it be preferable to say that Eichmann (and most other people) had a 'personality' which produced behavioural variations in different contexts?

Another point which needs to be made about personality measurement is that it does not measure anything directly, it elicits and measures *accounts of behaviour*. We have already made the same point about Brittain's description of the sadistic murderer, that it treats the subject's *accounts* as *facts*; in the case of a personality-measuring instrument the drawbacks with this procedure are even more severe, since the accounts are composed by the researcher rather than the subject: the latter can only agree or disagree with the suggestions printed on the questionnaire (for example 'loves parties'). Furthermore, the subject is bound to gauge her agreement and disagreement in terms of her knowledge of social norms and meanings (and possibly her sense of which ones the researcher is trying to probe). Someone who ticks 'the cinema' in preference to 'a party' when asked to name their favourite evening out has resorted, or been forced, to a cultural cliché which itself defines whether one is sociable or unsociable. A cultural theorist would be unimpressed by perfect correlations between 'sociability' and 'optimism' scores, since there is ample evidence that people have to learn how to label their experience, interpret it to others, etc.[31]

The empirical evidence from personality studies is not at all helpful in explaining why sex murder occurs and why only men commit it. Feldman reports that there is some support for the hypothesis that high extraversion is correlated with criminality in women, but not in men. There is some support for correlations between criminality and neuroticism and criminality and psychoticism. But most of this research suffers from the usual methodological defects and gender-unawareness.

Most experiments are not properly controlled: measurement is done on samples of convicted offenders, but not random samples of the population matched for age, sex, etc., simultaneously. It is therefore impossible to say whether the offenders differ significantly from the rest of the population. Furthermore, those people whose personalities are investigated are typically in prison, or some other institution and have suffered arrest, trial, sentencing and incarceration. It is obvious that responses to a questionnaire are informed by a person's experience, so the results are bound to reflect the effects of the stressful life-events prisoners have gone through, and especially those of institutionalization. Perhaps this very fact, that they are locked up, explains their extreme scores on, say, neuroticism. Or perhaps high scores indicate not a predisposition to crime, but a predisposition to getting caught!

We have come across no empirical evidence that throws any light on the gender-specificity of sex murder. Men and women can equally be neurotic, psychotic, extrovert, whatever, even though their actual behaviour can vary noticeably. Eysenck and his followers typically fall back on biogenetic explanations — hormones, chromosomes, etc. — when sex-differences are at issue. As Feldman remarks, all personality types are criminal and criminals are of all personality types.[32] Not all sexes are sex-murderers, however.

The psychopath

The notion of the psychopath is especially relevant to our concerns, since *psychopath* as a label has been applied indiscriminately in popular culture to the mass sexual killer. But although its current status is that of an all-purpose term of abuse, it nevertheless carries with it overtones of technicality, scientificity and therefore a weighty explanatory power to which it turns out not to have the remotest claim. The problem is one of relentless circularity: psychopaths are defined as the kind of people who commit horrifying and sadistic crimes and the reason why they commit those crimes is because they are psychopaths.

In some professional quarters, the imprecise popular usage of the term is deplored. Some psychiatrists themselves have argued that the concept amounts only to a 'dustbin' category, to which everything they are unable to explain or account for is consigned.[33] In the early 1960s there were moves to drop the term from legal and clinical terminology. But by then it had been enshrined in statute by the 1959 Mental Health Act for England and Wales, which represented a widespread feeling among British professionals that psychopathy is one end of a continuum of behavioural and personality disorders.[34] At the other end are people who might variously be described as having 'inadequate personalities', 'character disorders' and so on. The boundary between these and the much more serious 'psychopathic personality', 'aggressive, hysterical or schizoid psychopath' or 'sociopath' is fuzzy and indeterminate, though efforts were made, again during the 1960s, to tighten up the diagnostic criteria.

According to the British psychiatrist Michael Craft, a person should be diagnosed as psychopathic if they exhibit a combination of the following features, with the two primary positive features both being present and the negative features fulfilled.[35]

Positive features

1 A lack of feeling quality to other humans, described by some as affectionlessness and others as lovelessness. In extreme cases he may be without feeling sense.
2 A liability to act on impulse and without forethought (cf. the old legal phrase, *irresistible impulse*).

Secondary features (deriving from above)

3 A combination of the previous two, under suitable circumstances leading to aggression.
4 A lack of shame and remorse for what has been done.
5 An inability to profit by or use experience; which includes a lack of response to punishment. The antisocial quality of their actions may have been recorded in the past by way of conviction.
6 A lack of drive or motivation leading to a general inadequacy, so that the person does not use apparent abilities.

Additional

7 With the above, the presence of viciousness or wish to do damage to things or persons.

Negative features

1 Lack of psychosis, such as schizophrenia or depression, which are excluded on psychiatric examination.
2 Lack of pure intellectual deficit/mental ability less than half the average man, so that on testing he scores an IQ of under 50.
3 Lack of criminal motivation or planning of actions in the light of the risks at issue.

Interestingly, there is no international agreement on the diagnosis of psychopathy. In the United States, for instance, charm, vanity and social skills are emphasized; in West Germany it is emotional coldness that is looked for above all; and Craft in practice emphasizes impulsiveness and aggression.[36]

Emphasizing underlying personality traits allows the clinicians to avoid the circularities of behavioural definition. It also allows, of course, for the existence of law-abiding psychopaths in the community, and an American research project did indeed set out to see if there were such persons. The researchers advertised for 'charming aggressive carefree people who are impulsively irresponsible but are good at handling people and looking after number one'. The resulting sample of forty-five men and twenty-three women were given personality and other psychological tests which replicated previous research on incarcerated psychopaths: similarities between the two groups were found.[37]

However, we have already discussed the immense difficulties that exist in the concept of measuring personality and some researchers, such as Feldman, insist that any belief in 'the psychopath' is quite mistaken: there is only 'psychopathic behaviour'. To this observation we would have to add that what counts as psychopathic behaviour in actual legal/clinical practice has been highly variable, to a degree which confirms all fears to the effect that psychopathy is an infinitely elastic, catch-all category. According to West, since 1959 in Britain all sorts of young people who are delinquent but not neurotic have been labelled psychopathic. Under the 1959 Mental Health Act, men committed for indecent exposure, rape and pederasty have been labelled psychopathic simply by virtue of having committed those offences.[38] Peter Clyne even cites an American case where the medical witness pointed to the defendant's unkempt appearance, bitten nails and unhappy demeanour as indicative of psychopathy![39]

In short, the literature on 'psychopathy' is a minefield. Research papers are overwhelmingly of the 'measure psychopaths' brainwaves or personalities' variety, though some examine their social background, paying particular attention to their mothers. But these quests for the underlying cause of psychopathy not only fail to give any positive results, they are confounded in any case by the prevailing definitional confusion.

What, then, of that clear cultural category, the 'psychopathic sex-murderer'? None of the clinical definitions of psychopathy entails that psychopaths are especially prone to commit sexual murders and the scientific material does not suggest that this is what a large proportion of them have actually done. The literature does not problematize gender either — though it is taken for granted, curiously, that most psychopaths are men: 'As might be expected there is among psychopathic patients a marked preponderance of men over women, not to be found in other categories of mental disorder', remarks Kenneth Robinson.[40] Quite honestly, anyone perusing the literature could be forgiven for not expecting any such thing. None of the features that Craft uses in diagnosis and certainly not the American criteria of 'charm, high level of social skills and vanity' are obviously male attributes rather than female ones. Nevertheless, in 1962 there were five male psychopaths to every woman in the British special hospital population. Furthermore, case literature gives no clue at all to what women have to *do* to be labelled psychopathic. It is reasonable to assume that the same double standard operates here as for the label 'sadistic' for female killers, i.e., women have to do a lot *less*.

There is plenty of case literature on male psychopaths. For example, Michael Craft presents us with the following five examples which he adduces as typical.[41]

1 *John Straffen* was put on probation when he was eight, for stealing a purse, and his probation officer remarked that he had no ordinary understanding of right and wrong. At sixteen he threatened a thirteen-year-old girl with strangulation, and at eighteen killed Brenda Goddard, then Cecily Badstone, unconcernedly attending a film between the two offences. He escaped from Broadmoor, and during the five hours he was at liberty, strangled a small girl, Linda Bowyer.

2 *Neville Heath* was court martialled from the RAF and expelled from the British and South African armies. He became a 'bit of a confidence trickster'. At twenty-nine his impulses took a sadistic turn and he attacked a female lover (there was no prosecution). On one day he proposed marriage to and spent the night with one woman, the next night in the same room sadistically killing Margery Gardner. The next day he posed as an RAF group captain in another hotel where he casually met, killed and mutilated Doreen Marshall.

3 *Miles Gifford*, at age thirteen, was said to be the most abnormal boy the staff at his father's public boarding school had ever encountered,

being friendless, impulsive and a liar; in his twenties he was promiscuous and irresponsible, a heavy drinker who spent his own and his father's money. One night he killed his parents.

4 *Peter Rix* killed twelve-year-old Leslie Hobbs at her home. He was fifteen and had been difficult to control, although his authoritarian father had been able to manage him.

5 '*Alec*' had a miserable childhood in approved schools; he discharged himself from Michael Craft's unit, went to the flat of a chance female acquaintance and raped her sadistically (she got away before he could kill her, luckily).

Craft is committed to a multi-causal story of psychopathy and believes that psychopathic behaviour is probably *learned* (that is, he does not believe in an underlying biological or genetic cause). But he makes no comment whatsoever on the aspect of these men's and boy's careers which is so noticeable to us: that four out of five of them attacked and/or killed women or girls. Although everyone agrees that one crucial trait of psychopaths is their tendency to behave impulsively, giving in to violent desires without thought, it is not remarked that the desires which get them into trouble are hardly *random*. They often have a sexual component and are systematically misogynistic.

THE DIAGNOSIS AND TREATMENT OF PSYCHOSEXUAL ABNORMALITY: PSYCHIATRY, SEXOLOGY AND PSYCHOANALYSIS

It may seem strange to consider in one category the very different discourses of psychiatry, sexology and psychoanalysis, since in many respects they are not to be compared. As they relate to sexual murder, however, they do have a certain amount in common: together they represent what might be called a 'forensic' current in which scientific investigation of the deviant individual and medical notions of pathology or disease enter into the domain of the law and its proceedings, which determine whether criminals are responsible for their acts, and if not, what is wrong with them and how they should be managed.

Forensic psychiatry in cases of sexual murder is dependent not only on the clinical categories we have already mentioned, such as 'personality disorder' and 'psychopathy', but also on categories established elsewhere, in descriptive sexology and in psychoanalysis — discourses which have concerned themselves, to a degree to which psychiatry itself has not, with variety and deviance in sexual behaviour. Modern textbooks of 'psychosexual disorder' find no incongruity in placing Freudian ideas alongside the taxonomies of Ellis or Krafft-Ebing and the fruits of conventional scientific research (into chromosomes, say, or androgen levels). So although we will respect the divergence of aims and methods between traditional psychiatry, sexology and psychoanalysis, we must also emphasize the common purpose they have been made to serve in the diagnosis and treatment of psychosexual abnormality as manifested by violent sexual criminals, including the sex-murderers who will be the focus of our discussion.

Psychiatry: the medical and legal concept of madness

Law and psychiatry are often seen as being inextricably connected and this view is nowhere more justified than in cases of sexual and other 'abnormal' murder, where the question before the courts most often concerns the killer's responsibility for his crime and the potential explanation of his behaviour in terms of mental illness.

The interconnection of law and psychiatry was, however, developed through a historically specific process. In the course of the eighteenth century in Europe, the whole concept of madness increased in importance, both for society at large and more especially for the law, as it became possible to disqualify people from inheritance if they were suffering from conditions like 'imbecility' and 'dementia'. These terms were relatively unscientific, however: it did not take an expert to recognize 'dementia', which to all intents and purposes was a category of ordinary language. But in the nineteenth century, the situation changed. The emergent discipline of psychiatry developed and refined the notion of madness to include individuals who did not exhibit behaviour that either society or the courts would previously have described as mad.

In a paper 'About the Concept of the Dangerous Individual in Nineteenth Century Legal Psychiatry', Michel Foucault cites several cases which illustrate this change. He discusses, for instance, the following occurrence:

In Paris in 1827, Henriette Cornier, a servant, goes to the

neighbour of her employer and insists that the neighbour leave
her daughter with her for a time. The neighbour hesitates,
agrees, then, when she returns for the child, Henriette Cornier
has just killed her and has cut off her head which she has thrown
out of the window.[42]

Henriette Cornier and similar killers had no apparent reason for
doing what they did. Cornier was not jealous, vengeful or spiteful; she
could not have expected to make any form of profit from her crime.
Psychiatry constructed this type of murder as madness — a crime
which consisted entirely in insanity, an insanity which was manifested
by nothing but crime. Acts like Cornier's were so cruel and unnatural
as to be obviously mad: psychiatrists labelled their perpetrators as
sufferers from 'homicidal monomania'.

In its vagueness and circularity of definition, the concept of the
homicidal monomaniac is reminiscent of the modern concept of the
psychopath; and as in the case of the psychopathic killer, psychiatrists
had trouble persuading lawyers and the public that monomaniacs
really were mad and not just bad. By 1870 the label had been
abandoned and replaced by a concept of 'moral insanity'. This
depended on a further refinement of the definition of insanity, so that
one could be considered insane without necessarily displaying an
obvious disorder of cognition (for example hearing voices or being
unable to remember what one had done). Similar concerns with the
criminal's moral awareness can be seen in the English McNaghten
rules for defences of insanity: one criterion for insanity is not knowing
that your acts were *wrong*. The concept of diminished responsibility
more usually resorted to in cases of abnormal murder today represents
yet another stage, in which behaviour which is not insane may
nevertheless be defined as pathological. This whole process by which
criminal acts and pathological mental states are conflated has tended
to produce, as Foucault observes, 'a psychiatric and criminal
continuum'.[43] At its most thoroughgoing, the conflation goes so far as
to redefine criminality as intrinsically a psychiatric category.

Sex murder is among those crimes which are often perceived as
insane by definition (though as recent cases such as Sutcliffe's show,
not by the courts; psychiatric experts are still unable to convince
juries on this point, even when they use quite precise labels like
'paranoid schizophrenia'). We saw at the beginning of this chapter

how one psychiatrist, Robert Brittain, went so far as to construct a 'syndrome' from which sex-murderers were assumed to be suffering (with the automatic implication of abnormality). But while individual killers may be diagnosed as having mental disorders not exclusive to them (schizophrenia, psychopathy), the behaviour of sex-murderers *as a class* is usually taken as involving some specifically *sexual* deviance, commonly 'sadism' or 'sado-masochism'. At this point, forensic psychiatry meets up with the most important discourses on perverse sexuality, namely sexology and psychoanalysis.

Sexology

'Sexology' is the name given to the tradition of investigating the varieties of human sexual behaviour which begins around the turn of the century with the work of Krafft-Ebing, H. Havelock Ellis, August Forel and Magnus Hirschfeld, continuing down to more recent studies such as those of Alfred Kinsey and Masters and Johnson. Although in the course of its hundred-year history, sexology has changed radically in method and approach, it has always remained essentially a descriptive and classificatory enterprise, distinguishing itself both from the interpretive endeavours of psychoanalysis and the therapeutic or normative practices of 'sexual counsellors', etc. (though both the latter have of course become more and more dependent on the details furnished by descriptive sexology; and sex therapy is sometimes done by sexologists, for example Masters and Johnson). Sexual perversions, including sadism/sado-masochism, are a perennial concern of the sexological literature, though again we must stress the dramatic shifts that have taken place in the attitudes of researchers to these phenomena.

Of the early sexologists, the most interesting for our purposes is Richard von Krafft-Ebing, because of his avowedly forensic concern with aberrant sexualities and sexual crime. Krafft-Ebing, who entitled his great work *Psychopathia Sexualis, With Especial Reference to the Antipathetic Sexual Instinct: A Medico-Forensic Study*, was an enthusiastic reader of his contemporary, Lombroso, and thoroughly aware of the state of the art in nineteenth-century criminology and law. He wanted to bring home to the legal profession the *pathological* (as opposed to merely wicked) nature of sex crime and establish it as a properly medical concern; it was Krafft-Ebing who brought *sadism* into the clinical vocabulary and who did a great deal to crystallize the modern recognition of sexual murder as a distinctive type of crime.

Psychopathia Sexualis itself is a descriptive work which classifies sexual perversions in fine detail and exemplifies each with a selection of case histories. Between its first publication in German in 1886, and 1903, the book went through a large number of editions and new material was progressively added. Though Krafft-Ebing was pleased by the book's success, he never intended it to be read by the lay public and did his best (as his prefaces explicitly point out) to make sure that only professional experts could read it by using exceedingly technical language and translating the most obscene parts into Latin — an expedient to which he resorted more and more with each successive edition of the work.

Psychopathia Sexualis contains a good deal of material about sadism, which Krafft-Ebing defines as 'obtaining sexual pleasure by acts of cruelty'. He believed this perversion, and the concomitant crimes of rape and lust murder, to be ingrained in Christian and other cultures throughout history; he also felt that they were on the increase because of the 'degeneration of the race'. This was a commonplace idea in psychiatric thinking of the time: Kraepelin, the great clinical psychiatrist, for instance, declared sadism a 'congenital disease state' requiring 'an admixture of new stock'.[44]

In the case of sexual murder, or 'lust murder' as the German-speaking Krafft-Ebing called it, it is clear that *Psychopathia Sexualis* was instrumental in cementing this as a scientific concept and in providing the criteria for recognizing it:

> The presumption of a murder out of lust is always given when injuries of the genitals are found, the character and extent of which are not such as could be explained by merely a brutal attempt at coitus; and still more when the body has been opened and parts (intestines, genitals) torn out and wanting.[45]

The criteria seem to have been arrived at by induction from case histories collected from archives and other sources. In listing and analysing these it appears Krafft-Ebing emphasized aspects which had not necessarily been stressed in the original reports. Which is not, of course, to claim that his constructing a category of 'lust murder' came as a revelation to his colleagues. He was systematizing and publicizing ideas which were very much 'in the air'.

So much for description: what of explanation? Why does lust murder, or sadism generally, occur? Krafft-Ebing's views are in many ways typical of his age. He believed in 'moral degeneracy' and had rigid ideas about human nature and the innate qualities of women and men. Thus sadism to him was a timeless universal: he notes, for instance, the prevalence and persistence of a connection between cruelty, sex and religion, adducing as examples the lives of the saints, in which ecstasy and suffering are seldom far apart. But why this particular conjunction? In Krafft-Ebing's opinion (which reminds us of Novalis and Sade in the 1790s) it is because lust and rage are very similar emotions, with similar physiological effects of excitation and arousal. The conjunction itself becomes pathological when the arousal goes beyond certain limits, or when ordinary sadistic impulses do not meet with inhibition owing to 'defect of moral feeling' in the subject.

Krafft-Ebing is aware that sadistic impulses, especially those that would be counted pathological, are much less common in women than in men. To him, however, this seems perfectly natural, since men are the active and aggressive sex by nature. Women do not have strong sexual urges to get out of control, nor are they troubled by any innate desire for conquest. Indeed, it is women's instinctive coyness which fans men's sadism to fever pitch: 'It seems probable that this sadistic force is developed by the natural shyness and modesty of women.' Krafft-Ebing also makes the rather obscure observation that 'The obstacles which oppose the expression of this monstrous impulse, are, of course, much greater for woman than for man.'[46]

Psychopathia Sexualis does contain two case histories dealing with female sadism, but as usual a double standard is evident, and they are hardly to be compared with the murder and torture which is used to exemplify sadism in men. One of them concerns a woman who would have sex with her husband only if he cut his arm and allowed her to suck the blood; the other had bitten her husband until he bled. Apart from these accounts, Krafft-Ebing is reduced to citing fictional creations like Kleist's *Penthesilea*, so beloved of the sado-masochistic Romantics, in whom male sadism has been projected onto female figures.

The work of H. Havelock Ellis is less forensically oriented, though Ellis too was an enthusiast of positivistic criminology (and a popularizer of Lombroso, as we have already pointed out). It is notable, however, that Ellis fundamentally disagrees with Krafft-Ebing about the definition of sadism. Whereas in *Psychopathia Sexualis* sadism is defined as pleasure in cruelty, in Ellis's work it is associated with *pain* (for this reason, Ellis does not consider sadism and masochism to be fundamentally distinct and prefers the term *algolagnia* for both). According to this definition, as Ellis asserts, sadism is not cruelty but rather a form of love: 'Pain only and not cruelty is the essential in this group of manifestations [algolagnia] . . . the sadist desires to inflict pain, but in some cases, if not in most, he desires that it should be felt as love.'[47]

The question of what actually constitutes sadism is an important consideration if we are trying to determine whether sex-murderers ought to be defined as a subset of sadists; and whether or not we decide to define them thus, it is not without significance where their gratification lies. Certainly, there are various objections to Ellis's contention that 'pain . . . and not cruelty is the essential' in sado-masochism (S/M). Writers on S/M as a conscious practice, organized in the form of a 'subculture', have constantly reiterated that sado-masochists do not eroticize pain *per se*, but rather dominance — sub-mission relations, in which one partner is able to humiliate the other (the means used to do this can entail inflicting pain, but in many S/M scenes the amount of actual pain is negligible).[48] 'Cruelty' comes closer to recognizing what is erotic in S/M, since it includes some idea of pleasure in one's own power and others' fear.

Sexual murderers, however, do not carry on their activities under the aegis of any recognizable subculture, and there is thus little warrant for the assumption that their pleasures are the same as those of the 'Leather-man' or bondage enthusiast. We may pose the question of whether they are aroused by cruelty, pain or something which is neither. Some killers have talked about feeling rage and hatred for their victims ('Rippers', that is, prostitute-killers, are often of this type) while others have demonstrated a liking for psychological cruelty as well as the purely physical kind (for example the moors murderers). In the paper on the sadistic murderer (quoted earlier in this chapter), Brittain remarks on the preference many sex-killers have for strangulation and suggests that one factor in this is the feeling of power it gives them to be able to inflict such a lingering death — and indeed, to avert the victim's fate at any moment, if they wish. On the

other hand, some killers have spared their victims, not because they
wanted to play God but because they had reached climax before death
occurred. Both Kürten and Verzeni were aroused by throttling (Kürten
in addition was stimulated by a flow of blood), and both of them
occasionally stopped short of killing. This sort of thing seems more
akin to fetishism, and the death of the victim a merely contingent
means to sexual pleasure (as in the case of the Hungarian Sylvestre
Matuschka, who was aroused by the spectacle of trains colliding, and
therefore deliberately caused crashes in which people were — to him
irrelevantly — killed). It seems that the motivations of sex-killers are
varied and complex, in some ways similar to those of sado-masochists,
in other ways different.

Although they recognize the importance of pioneers like Ellis and
Krafft-Ebing, later sexologists have been critical of their work and
have turned away from their obsession with 'abnormality'. Kinsey, for
instance, whose book on male sexual behaviour was published in the
1940s, accused Krafft-Ebing of a lack of scientific rigour, pointing out
(not without justification) that his early work had produced 'scientific
classifications . . . nearly identical with theologic classifications and
with moral pronouncements of the English common law of the fifteenth
century'.[49] Kinsey here makes a point we have already mentioned,
namely that science may conceive of itself as ordering and explaining
a culture which it is outside, but in fact science must be a *part* of
culture, dependent on culture for the categories it starts with. It may
be less obvious, but this is as true of the present as of the past: for all
that Kinsey eschews 'moral pronouncements', he is still the prisoner of
his cultural assumptions about male aggression, female submission,
the irresistibility of desire, and so on.

Sexology from Kinsey to the present day has given up the arbitrary
use of case histories to illustrate taxonomies arrived at a priori, and
rather, has concerned itself with the sexual behaviour of a representative population of 'normal' individuals, researched using self-report
data and later, observation in the laboratory. Statistical evidence on
who does what to whom and how often has come to be the *sine qua non*
of all discussion, and the dictum that science is 'descriptive not
prescriptive' — that is, not in the business of judging morality or
appropriateness — has been rigidly adhered to, at least in principle.
In practice it has been the concern of post-war sexology not to
contribute to criminology, but rather to remove certain practices from

its sphere on the grounds that they are not aberrant but only atypical (and perhaps not even markedly so: it was Kinsey who remarked that if law-enforcement agencies were as efficient as they are supposed to be, a majority of young men would be convicted sex offenders. He also reported that sado-masochistic narratives were arousing to one in five of his male subjects and one in eight of his female ones.)

It is this style of quantitative, non-judgemental or even '*laissez faire*' sexology that has led to the attitude mocked by Robert Stoller as 'explaining necrophilia as merely a statistic at the outer reaches of a bell-curve'. In fact, the problem with it is arguably that it makes no attempt to explain anything (though common-sense biologistic notions of what is 'natural' are often waiting in the wings, as it were). Description and quantification become ends in themselves. For an alternative approach we have to look to psychoanalysis, in which the development and meaning of sexuality occupies a central theoretical position. Psychoanalytically oriented writers and therapists have contributed a great deal to the modern literature on the sadistic sexual killer.

Psychoanalysis

Psychoanalysis and sexology are in many respects worlds apart, but on one point at least, Freud and Krafft-Ebing are agreed: that sadism has been with us from the dawn of time, finding fertile ground in the naturally (i.e., biologically) aggressive sexuality of men. Freud remarks,

> The sexuality of most male human beings contains an element of *aggressiveness* — a desire to subjugate; the biological significance of it seems to lie in the need for overcoming the resistance of the sexual object by means other than . . . wooing. Thus sadism would correspond to an aggressive component of the sexual instinct which has become independent and exaggerated and, by displacement, has usurped the leading position.[50]

Freudian discourse on sexual sadism cannot get away from the idea that it is founded on something natural and inborn: but biology in itself is not enough to explain sadism, or indeed to produce it in any given individual. To understand it therefore, we must move on from biology and explore the autonomous organization of psychic life.

To understand Freud's views on sexual perversity, or any other psychoanalytic view, it is necessary to know something about his theory of sexuality. We may summarize the most important points of this, very briefly, as follows.

There is for Freud no 'natural' form of sexuality: our sexual drive or libido is extremely plastic both in its object (who we desire) and aim (how desire is expressed). Genital reproductive heterosexuality is desirable for the maintenance and ordering of society; but it is not innate. Perversions arise precisely because the path to socially valued 'normal' heterosexuality is a tricky one, offering many opportunities for deviation.

In Freudian theory it is taken as axiomatic (the original insight deriving from early clinical work) that the path to adult sexuality begins in early childhood. Sexual development is mediated through the family, and in particular, through the child's relations with its parents. For all children, the earliest love-object is the mother (and specifically, her breast, from which the first sexual pleasure is forthcoming along with physical nourishment). Children thus desire their mother's body. But they have to learn they cannot possess it, and that the mother—child relationship is not the only one: there is also the father, who thus becomes a rival and object of hatred.

This picture is complicated by the child's discovery of sexual difference. For boys, the Oedipal desire for the mother is resolved by the 'castration complex'. Learning that some people (women, girls) do not have a penis, the boy becomes anxious that he might lose his own: he fantasizes that the rival father will punish him by castrating him. He comes to understand that if he renounces desire for the mother this fate can be avoided; eventually he will become like his father and have a substitute for his mother. The little girl, by contrast, must realize she is *already* castrated, transfer her desire from the mother to the father and from him to the men who will be her future partners. It has often been said that the castration complex resolves the Oedipal conflict in boys and precipitates it in girls.

Given this complex developmental process, it is hardly surprising that things can go awry. Traumatic experiences at crucial points in development can cause the anxiety and guilt which are inevitably present (since fear of castration is bound to cause anxiety and harbouring death-wishes against your parents tends to make you feel guilty) to escalate into serious conflict, against which defences must somehow be mounted. The cost of defensive measures is that they may return to plague you in the form of neurotic symptoms such as psychosomatic illness or compulsive behaviour. Alternatively, they may show up in some form of sexual perversion.

For Freudians, as for Ellis, sadism and masochism represent facets of a single perverse impulse (masochism is regarded by psychoanalysts as the turning of sadistic desires against the self). This impulse itself is a defence against castration anxiety. For the sadist, it works by reassuring him that 'I am the castrator, not the castrated one.' In other words, the sadist believes he will be punished or harmed and to ward off that anxiety he is compelled to harm others.

Most writers on this subject have noted, of course, that sadists tend to be men and not women. The author of a widely read textbook of 'psychosexual disorders' has asserted, 'Heterosexual sadism, though fairly common in the male rarely occurs in the female. . . . No woman of the Peter Kürten type seems to have been recorded in history and we may be fairly sure none ever existed.'[51] As we have seen, such explicit recognition of the gender-specificity of sexual murder is unusual: the psychoanalytic literature is untypically rich in speculation as to why sadism is a masculine trait and it is interesting to consider the most common lines of argument.

First of all, there are some writers who resort to mere biologism in the style of Krafft-Ebing. Men have stronger aggressive drives and a stronger libido (the better to 'overcome the resistance of the sexual object'). We have already explained why this sort of proposal is quite unsatisfactory on every possible level. An elegant and peculiarly Freudian variation of biologism is provided by the idea that women do not suffer from castration anxiety to the same degree as men and therefore do not need the defensive strategy represented by sadism — the reason for this being that women do not in fact possess a penis to be cut off and anxiety about a fantasized object cannot be as intense as anxiety about a real one.

Then there is the very popular idea, fitting neatly with prevalent sexual stereotypes in our culture, that women do become perverse, but in their case it takes the form of masochism, not sadism. This again can be seen to have biologistic underpinnings, since no other level of explanation for a sex-differentiated outcome of perverse impulses is offered: it is simply assumed that since men are aggressive they are likely to become sadists, while since women are passive they are likely to become masochists. This explanation is incompatible with the first one, since it asserts that women *do* become perverse, whereas the other claims they do not; but both explanations rest on the premiss of women's natural, innate passivity.

A certain amount of empirical cold water is thrown on the female masochism theory by the observation that what is *called* female masochism seems not to be a sexual perversion at all; it is certainly not what male masochists practise. Whereas a male masochist will seek out partners to whip him and tie him up, exhibiting a desire for (carefully controlled) domination in the specific domain of his sexual life, analogous female masochists are rare. As one expert says, masochism in women is 'a behaviour problem rather than a neurosis'.[52] This observation crassly overlooks the social determinants of women's so-called 'masochism' (i.e., doormat-like behaviour, self-hatred etc.), but it does acknowledge that perverse sexual practices, whether sadistic or masochistic, are a mostly male preserve.

One further explanation of why men and not women are sadists deserves our attention. This explanation locates the phenomenon not so much in castration anxiety as in the differing relation of boys and girls to their mothers and by extension in later life, to women. For most children, the relationship with the mother is their first and most intense bond, emotionally and physically. All deeply felt emotions are directed at her, which means not only love, but also hatred and rage against a figure who appears to the child as all-powerful. This is the case for children of both sexes, but two important differences between boys and girls will emerge, with possible consequences in later years.

The first of these is that to develop as a male, the boy will need to separate himself from his early identification with the mother to a degree that will not be necessary for the girl. As a consequence, the girl will have a stable core of gender identity: the boy's, less constant, is much more precarious and he is much more likely to feel anxious about it. Secondly, whereas the girl will desire male sexual objects who will therefore *not* evoke the deeply ambivalent feelings she has for her mother, the boy will mix up his intense childhood emotions with his future desire for other women. The net result of these two factors is that male heterosexuality is more likely than female to contain strong elements of fear and envy, fantasies of role reversal and revenge against women.

The idea that perversion, including sadism, has something to do with gender identity, has been developed by Robert Stoller in a book entitled *Perversion, the Erotic Form of Hatred*. Stoller is a scientist familiar with current debates, but he dismisses the pretensions of positivistic science to have anything useful to say about perversity and turns his face equally against 'liberationist' currents which would object to his calling behaviour 'perverse'. He takes the Freudian view that certain 'variations' — in fact, those traditionally regarded as perverse — are forms of 'blighted heterosexuality' and arise as 'a way of coping with threats to one's gender identity'. What they have in common is the element of hostility or hatred, rendered erotic by the imagination. They are not inherited, nor organically based, they are not conditioned responses or statistically atypical variations: they are *meaningful*, as can readily be inferred from the pre-eminent role of fantasy in the formation of perverse desires. Stoller mocks those currents of research which deny the meaningful quality of aberration:

> Will someone please explain pedophilia in geneticists' terms? Or shoe fetishism as the product of a brain mechanism constant through evolutionary development? Or penile exhibitionism as a hormonal defect? Or the need to rape old women as the effect of conditioning? Or necrophilia as merely a statistic at the outer reaches of a bell-curve?[53]

What is being symbolized, both in the fantasies and the actions of the perverse individual, is the turning of childhood humiliation into triumph. 'Perverse sexual behaviour has sprinkled through its remnants, ruins and other indications of the past history of one's libidinal development.'[54]

So why are men and not women, perverse? According to Stoller, because men are compelled to renounce their original identification with their mothers: they feel rage at the loss of this pleasurable state, fear that they will never accomplish separation and a desire to be revenged on the mother for putting them into this position. It is revenge which comes to the fore in perversion: a 'fantasized act of revenge' which reassures the pervert that he is safe and powerful and that his always-threatened masculinity is intact. Of all forms of perverse behaviour, sexual murder disguises its motivation the least. It is an act of gross hatred against one's desired sexual object, and ultimately against one's mother.

Not only Stoller, but many psychoanalytically oriented writers on sexual killing believe mother-hatred to be at the bottom of it and this allegedly explains why so many murderers mutilate the genitals and breasts of their victims. One author claims, 'The sadist wishes to injure the breasts (symbolic of the mother and her relation to the young child) and so, equating the breasts with the genitalia, finally the genitalia.'[55] This author, incidentally, explains homosexual murder by saying it is a transformation of mother-hatred: men are equated with mothers and buttocks with breasts. It is at moments like this that one begins to suspect there is no eventuality which the mother-hatred thesis could not be stretched to cover; there is an unsatisfactory arbitrariness about it to which we will need to return.

First, however, we want to raise the question whether psychoanalytic theory, which is surely the best-developed account of sex murder we have examined so far in this section, has any utility in explaining, *post hoc*, a recorded case history. Although we know of no case where a sexual killer has been analysed — Otto Fenichel lamented this omission in 1945 and as far as we know it has never been made good — one detailed, psychoanalytically informed study of a murderer has recently appeared: Flora Rheta Schreiber's *The Shoemaker*, which deals with the career of North American murderer Joseph Kallinger. Schreiber is not an analyst, but she is a Freudian in her approach to Kallinger and her access to interaction with the killer and his family gives her unusually full knowledge of his childhood circumstances, mediated through a variety of differing accounts and perspectives.

The Shoemaker

Flora Rheta Schreiber insists that Joseph Kallinger is not a sexual killer nor a psychopath, but a schizophrenic who was driven to kill by psychotic delusions. Nevertheless, the crimes for which he was tried in 1975 — burglaries, sexual assaults and the murder of a woman because she refused to chew off a man's penis at his (Kallinger's) request — provide ample evidence of the same conflation of sexuality and aggression which characterizes the sexual murderer. Further evidence can be drawn from Kallinger's fantasy life: he was often impotent unless he held a knife in his hand during sexual encounters and he imagined 'cutting open a woman's stomach or cutting off her breasts . . . sticking her with pins and . . . burning her with a cigarette or a hot iron'.[56] He did not rape his woman victim, Maria Fasching, but he later told Schreiber he had an orgasm while stabbing her.

How did Kallinger's abnormality come about, and why did it take the specific form it did? Schreiber explains it with reference to two traumatic incidents in his childhood. The first stemmed from the general mental and physical cruelty which young Joseph underwent at the hands of his adoptive parents. When he was six, he was operated on for a hernia and when he returned from hospital his parents, who had been worried by signs of sexual curiosity in Joseph, told him that the doctor had excised the 'demon' from his 'bird' (their euphemism for penis) so it would always be small and soft. Just afterwards, he had a realistic day-dream of his penis resting on the blade of a large knife his father used for cutting shoe soles. The combination of this symbolic castration by his parents, the vision of the knife and the real pain and trauma of the operation formed a basis for subsequent delusions. The second incident came two years later, when a group of boys forced Joe to submit at knife-point to having fellatio performed on him.

These events can be fitted in with what Kallinger later did, and with the notion that he was defending himself against castration anxiety, as well as revenging himself on his parents who had castrated him. As an adult, Joe wanted to kill by chewing off a man's penis — 'I am the castrator, not the castrated one' — and his sexual assaults took the form of forcing women to perform fellatio on him, which could be interpreted as 'turning childhood humiliation into triumph', since he re-enacted the scene in which he originally was the victim, but this time taking the part of the initiator and terrifying someone as he had once been terrified. It is also evident that the history of Kallinger's libidinal development contained precedents for the later association of sex and knives.

There are, however, several comments to be made on the general utility of Schreiber's approach in the Kallinger case. One of these is that Schreiber pays no attention whatever to the question of gender. For example, given that Kallinger's own sexual abusers were boys, why did his re-enactment of the scene feature *women* as victims? Moreover, it is interesting to note that Schreiber has also written a book, *Sybil*, about a woman who became abnormal as a result of childhood sexual abuse. Sybil, however, developed multiple personality: she did not become a sadist or commit sexual crimes.[57] Schreiber has nothing to say about this striking difference. Of course, we recognize that psychoanalysis does not usually claim to be a predictive science which tells us how people are going to behave by associating invariant causes and effects. Freudian explanations are *post hoc* and tied up with individual life histories. But about the social determinants of those histories, far too little is said.

Freudian thought has always had a tendency to elide the particular even as it probes it, resolving individual and cultural differences in terms of a myth — the Oedipal drama — which is treated as a timeless and immutable universal. So the two important concepts in the Freudian account of sexual murder, castration anxiety and mother-hatred, are not usually related to the patriarchal power structure which must surely underlie them both. It is this power structure which produces the sexual division of labour whereby children are looked after in their early years by women; it is this power structure, if anything, that makes possible the extreme phallocentrism of Freud's universe (and without this, where would we get castration anxiety?).

Psychoanalytic writing is full of puzzling circularities, which result from an inability to decide whether psychic life is determined by family structures, or vice versa. Thus for example the therapist Susanne Schad-Somers, in a book on the aetiology and treatment of sado-masochism, identifies the sexual divisions of our society as a way of dealing with what she calls the 'sadomasochistic substratum', and observes that 'sexism represents a culturally-valued sadomasochistic arrangement . . . in evidence in all known societies.'[58] By this she seems to mean that 'society' conveniently deals with innate sadistic impulses by allotting them in their other-directed (sadistic) form to men and in their self-directed (masochistic) form to women — so that, presumably, everybody's happy! Yet at the same time she would hold that the nuclear family, where this gendered 'arrangement' is most obviously institutionalized, is itself the *source* of sado-masochistic impulses, particularly for the male with his precarious sexuality.

Once we start to think about the way social arrangements must determine psychic life, it might well seem as if complex psychoanalytic accounts of the latter are superfluous in discussions of sadistic sexual murder. For there are plenty of practices and representations available in our culture which might lead men to hate and despise femininity and to express their sexuality in overtly sadistic ways. We do not have to posit that men hate women because women remind them of the all-powerful mother; it would be equally true to say men learn to hate their mothers because their mothers are women, the powerless Other; men want to be masculine, with all that implies within a given society.

The idea that sexual murder has socio-cultural roots is certainly one to which we would subscribe. It leads us away from psychoanalysis and the other discourses we have examined so far, and towards the more sociological criminologies, with their stress on behaviour as learnt and constructed. Can sociology, and particularly the sociology of deviance, throw light on the actions of sexual killers?

SOCIAL EXPLANATIONS OF SEX MURDER

In contrast to all the theories we have examined so far, sociology is committed to explaining the actions of individuals by reference to events and conditions occurring in the society or in the culture. The direction of explanation is from society to the individual and not from deep inside the individual to her or his acts. It will be clear that in our view, sociology represents an improvement on biologistic and psychologistic accounts and in what follows we are going to examine several sociological treatments of crime and deviance.

So far we have been using the terms 'crime' and 'criminal' as if they were more or less self-evidently appropriate descriptions of reality. This is because we have been presenting the various competing explanations of sexual murder in their own terms. Of course, we have had to point out from time to time how naive the use of categories like 'crime' can be, and how this undermines the validity of some criminological research findings. The idea of the 'criminal', similarly, does not simply refer to a pre-existing category, but is a concept which imposes upon us a particular way of understanding the world. It also has the effect of making 'criminality' a pathological condition of individuals and sending the searchers after causes burrowing into the heart of the individual himself.

But in the second half of the twentieth century, sociologists have seriously, and at great length, challenged the whole project of 'criminology', bringing its fundamental concepts and assumptions into question. We want now to trace the development of their critique, which renames its subject-matter 'the sociology of deviance'; and we are concerned in particular with the challenge of 'radical criminology'. It must of course be borne in mind that our ultimate interest is in the explanation of sexual murder, and this dictates our selective coverage of the literature: we make no claim to give a full account of how the various traditions and schools interconnect, nor to cover all the philosophical, methodological and empirical debates that have gone on, and continue to go on, in their work.[59]

Before moving on to the sociology of deviance, however, we must examine a body of literature which seems to take a promisingly social approach, but turns out to have more in common with the mainstream criminology we considered earlier — victimology.

Victimology

Victimology asks — or has the potential to ask — why members of some groups tend to be killed or assaulted by members of others. Potentially, therefore, it is anti-individualistic: it concerns itself not with criminal pathology, but with the wider social context of criminal actions.

Unfortunately, feminists know only too well how an emphasis on the victim can be used to support existing prejudices and ultimately, the social status quo. We are familiar with this in discussions of rape, where the fact that women as a group are attacked by men as a group has issued in a constant preoccupation with the behaviour and characteristics of raped women, which effectively renders male violence invisible. The application of victimology to homicide results in a parallel distortion.

Admittedly, some forms of victimology are less obnoxious in this respect than others. For instance, that many crimes of violence are committed in self-defence against someone who has initiated the incident, is an unexceptionable (if hardly novel) conclusion. Marvin Wolfgang, an American expert, carried out a study of 'victim precipitated homicide', defined by the United States courts as homicide in the heat of passion resulting from adequate provocation.[60] He reported that the largest single category of such killings were carried out by women against violent men.

But if we go back to the original work which victimologists acknowledge as the source of their analytic framework, we find that von Hentig, the pioneer in the field, tends to focus exclusively on the shortcomings of victims, shortcomings which go far beyond merely initiating the violence that leads to their death.[61] A glance at his headings for 'typical victims' gives a depressing picture of von Hentig's social analysis: the dull, immigrants, females, minorities, the old, etc. And though these are presented as social categories, in fact von Hentig retreats to a highly individualistic and even biologistic perspective on the behavioural disorders, ignorance and general inadequacy to be found among members of certain groups.

Considering the importance of the cultural perception that some people 'ask for it' (one work in the field is actually titled *They Asked For Death*) the literature on victimology is surprisingly small. The idea behind it has had tremendous impact on the institutions of criminal control and justice. This makes victimology rather different from many other strands of sociology, which as we shall see, have been ignored by the authorities. Its influence can be seen in the remarks of judges, the attitudes of police officers and the outpourings of antifeminists. There is a tendency to be very uncritical about what constitutes provocation: in practice it can be constituted by a woman accepting a lift from a man (taken as a signal that she consents to have sex with him) or in the case of murder, working as a prostitute, which is construed, as we pointed out in the introduction, as openly 'asking for' violent death. It is obvious that such actions do not initiate violence in the same way as, say, drawing a gun, but at its worst victimology conflates these very different behaviours.

It is not surprising, however, that an academic discipline which resonates so well with popular prejudice should have become influential in the institutions of the law. And the result of this influence is to blunt any critical edge victimology might have had — since after all, it would be possible for victimologists to ask how accepting a lift can reasonably be taken as consenting to sex. It is ironic, too, that the significance of one group of homicide victims — violent men whose wives kill them in self-defence — is always eclipsed by the cultural salience of another group, namely women who walk alone at night and thereby force men to assault, rape and kill them.

The response to the Yorkshire Ripper murders in the 1970s makes it very clear that it begs important questions to construct certain groups as 'natural' murder victims. Feminists pointed out at the time how the deaths of prostitutes were deemed worthy of very little attention from the police or the press; Sir Michael Havers, prosecuting Peter Sutcliffe for the killings, remarked that the real tragedy was that some of his victims were *not* prostitutes.

There was also a rather bizarre contest at the trial between the prosecution and defence psychiatrists. The psychiatrists for the defence claimed that Sutcliffe believed he had been called by God to rid the world of prostitutes: he was therefore a paranoid schizophrenic. The prosecution contended that on the contrary he was 'just plain evil', a typical sex beast. The premiss of this contest appears to be that although actually *killing* prostitutes is extreme, wanting to stamp them out is quite comprehensible and not 'plain evil'. That study after study in victimology should find this unremarkable is very worrying.

If victimologists were to focus on the social and cultural conditions which cause the prostitute to be categorized as a 'natural' victim of sexual murder, they might be doing a useful job. As it is, however, they send us back to the pathological individual as a focus for research and attempt to explain the behaviour of prostitutes instead of the desires that lead men to want to kill them.

Victimology thus has the ludicrous effect of recommending that victims reform or change their behaviour, or educate themselves, or alter their attitudes, without at the same time having anything to say about the political and cultural structures that constitute groups as victims and simultaneously (though this corollary is never discussed) constitute other groups as aggressors. Victimology leaves intact poverty and food-shortage, implying that people should stop themselves starving; it leaves male violence intact and demands that women prevent themselves becoming victims of rape and murder.

Learning theory

When we discussed psychologistic approaches earlier in this chapter, we remarked that their more sophisticated exponents were aware of the importance of learning and learned behaviour in determining, along with a multiplicity of other factors, whether or not someone would become a criminal. Learning can attenuate the effect of genes and hormones; it can mediate between personality and behaviour; it can intervene in the causal chain from body type to crime. Feldman, for example, puts biogenetic factors into the context of learning, and Craft is convinced psychopathy is learned behaviour.[62] Here we consider further the question of learning.

Science's understanding of the phenomenon of learning is still fairly primitive: it is not possible to explain, for instance, why two children learn at different rates, or different things, in a similar situation. But in any case, research on learning suffers, from our point of view, from a serious flaw. Because, once again, it is focused on the individual (and sometimes on her or his immediate family) the question of what is actually available to be learned — which is obviously a more broadly *cultural* matter — is neglected or ignored, or else taken for granted (which amounts to the same thing). Thus accounts of how a young boy has grown up to be a sex-murderer have the same arbitrary and bewildering quality we noted in the psycho-analytic literature: without some analysis of the kind of culture and power structure we live in, how are we to make sense of someone who is terrorized by a brutal father and therefore grows up to kill *women?*

Precisely this question came up recently in relation to the case of the 'M4 Killer', John Steed, who was sentenced to life imprisonment in November 1986 for the murder of a prostitute and the rape of three other women. *The London Standard* of 10 November reported as follows: 'The brutal childhood that turned M4 rapist John Steed into a woman-hating killer was revealed in court today. At the age of five he saw his father rape his mother and his whole attitude towards women became warped, said his solicitor, Mr Robert Flach.' The solicitor's account is presented here as simple common sense, yet we do not find it quite so obviously compelling. In particular, it seems odd to us that this childhood incident, traumatic as it was, should have warped John Steed's attitude specifically to *women*. On the face of things it would be less surprising if Steed had developed an aversion to his father, or men in general, and gone around assaulting rapists. If this alternative course of action is unthinkable — if Steed in fact resolved the trauma in the only possible way, by identifying with the father — this is surely not to be explained in purely psychological terms. The acquisition of masculinity and the identification with male role-models is a cultural prescription, its content culturally determined by the norms of patriarchy. To understand why a boy grows up seeing women as objects of hatred and conflating aggression with masculine sexuality, it is necessary to go beyond his immediate environment, concentrating on the meanings and concepts cherished by the society, which inevitably permeate all our lives.

Subculture theory

An approach which gets rather nearer to this ideal is subculture theory, which examines the place of 'crime' and 'violence' in the values of certain groups or subcultures. The concept of a 'subculture' has developed over the last few decades. Initially subcultures were seen in relation to *the* stable, ascendant, dominant culture, which in the sociology of the United States and Britain was taken to be white Anglo-Saxon Protestant, achievement-oriented and middle class.[63] The large number of young people, newcomers to the society, who are destined to failure as measured against dominant values, construct alternative values of their own, norms of conduct in terms of which they can be counted successful. These norms and values then become a positive constraint on behaviour; living in accordance with them becomes a way of life. Later work on subcultures modifies this slightly, casting doubt on the appropriateness of the concept of a dominant culture and emphasizing instead the plurality of cultures in any society, which form distinct 'social worlds', each with its own rules and norms.

The subcultural approach has been taken up by criminologists. Wolfgang and Ferracuti, for example, propose that there are 'subcultures of violence' and that these subcultures in turn may *explain* violence.[64] Their thesis stresses learning and socialization processes and they illustrate it with examples of cultures such as that of the central mountain area in Sardinia, where ritual (but very real) violence in the form of the *vendetta barbariana* is a way of life: anyone who refuses to participate and behave in the prescribed way will be stigmatized.

Henry Lundsgaarde's book *Murder in Space City* is an extended study of the kind of subculture Wolfgang and Ferracuti discuss.[65] He explains the particular pattern of homicide in Houston, Texas, in terms of a residual 'frontier mentality' and the transmission of highly localized cultural values such as a man's right to defend himself and his property in the 'traditional way'. Houston is high in the world homicide league and also has a high acquittal rate, since juries on the whole share the values of those who kill.

The 'classic' studies in subcultural theory dealt with communities on the margins of cities, where the resort to crime can be viewed as a solution to the dilemmas of exclusion and powerlessness: a rational response to a crazy situation.[66] The Chicago school of sociology redefined delinquency in this way — delinquents are not pathological cases, but people carrying on what is their normal way of life. It is from this kind of perspective that we get our common notion of hippies, punks, gays, feminist separatists, rockers, lesbians, jazz musicians and so on — groups who are not necessarily isolated geographically — as forming subcultures. This idea in turn has spawned vast amounts of sociological research which testifies to the fact that many groups do have highly normative standards of conduct, into which their members have to be socialized.[67] Throughout this sort of work we find plenty of evidence that in many subcultures, male violence and sexism, including violence against women, are bound up with masculine consciousness.[68] This evidence is generally treated as incidental, not requiring explicit discussion; recent feminist work has done something to redress this balance, but any real attention to male violence *per se* within subculture theory is still at an early stage.

Obviously, sex-murderers are not members of a subculture, either in the sense of living together in one location or in the sense of hanging out together and sharing an identity, as feminists or punks do. As a matter of fact, both Wolfgang and Ferracuti and Lundsgaarde specifically omit 'abnormal murderers' from their analysis, implying that an individualistic and probably biological explanation is more appropriate in their case. Nevertheless, we can see considerable potential in subculture research on the construction and acting-out of masculinity and the transmission of masculine values, in explaining how the desires of the sexual killer are conceived.

Labelling theory

According to the perspective of labelling theory, the sociology of deviance should explore the ways in which certain behaviours or classes of acts become defined as deviant or are *criminalized*. It is naive, in this view, to take any act as criminal a priori, and the traditional conception of the relation between deviance and control is inverted. As Lemert observes, 'Older sociology . . . tended to rest heavily upon the idea that deviance leads to social control. I have come to believe that the reverse idea, i.e. social control leads to deviance, is equally tenable, and the potentially richer premise for studying deviance in modern society.'[69] What he means by this is that only when the agencies of control, such as the law, the psychiatric profession or the police, start to concern themselves with something does that something become visible as a problem. Control actually *creates* the deviant behaviour that supposedly justifies its existence. Thus for instance there was no 'problem' of 'maternal deprivation' until child psychologists, educationalists, social workers and so on started to talk about it. By attempting to control the behaviour of mothers, these controllers immediately redefined that behaviour as deviant and wrong.

This view eliminates some of traditional criminology's more glaring absurdities. For example, we have noted time and again that criminologists have an inadequate notion of crime and that their naive acceptance of the idea that a class of objectively criminal acts exists leads them to ignore the cultural processes whereby different behaviours, at different times and places, are defined as 'normal' or 'deviant'. By saying that crime is a *relative* concept, we challenge the whole project of searching for invariant biological characteristics that mark out the criminal individual.

The 'relative' concept of crime also has a political pay-off. Criminology has tended to take the correlation of crime and social class to indicate either that poverty causes crime or that something else causes both. But in self-report studies where subjects are asked if they have ever broken the law, upper-class and rich people are found to be frequent law-breakers. The fact that they are not *criminalized* has led sociologists such as Stephen Box to argue that social control is disproportionately aimed at the poor, who are a priori labelled deviant. This line of argument brings together labelling theory and 'controlology'.

A strong labelling thesis would hold that there is no crime unless it is labelled as such: the undiscovered sex-murderer is not a criminal until he is caught. Although this does not reflect the common-sense viewpoint (and let it be said here that we feel it would be absurd to argue sex murder is an 'arbitrary' crime like marijuana smoking; *any* society worth the name should criminalize it) it is a subtle analysis, and captures the extent to which upper-class crimes like tax evasion and fraud are part of everyday life, unremarked unless and until social control is directed at them. A slightly weaker thesis might also take into account *self*-labelling: acts can be defined as deviant if the perpetrators themselves take them to be so. Thus someone who habitually smashes milk bottles may do it precisely in order to flout social norms, and it may not affect her concept of what she is doing whether or not she is actually caught and labelled criminal. Here again, it is notable that upper-class individuals typically reject the label of 'deviant'.

What about sex-murderers? As far as we can tell, they do not accept the label 'deviant' in the ways described by research on self-labelling. Some of them appear to be motivated by the pleasure of transgression and enjoy the contest with the police (cf. Jack the Ripper): their deviant status is certainly part of their role as cultural heroes. For others, the fact that they are 'law-breakers' is the last thing on their minds. And indeed it might be argued that the sex-killer always knows, or believes, that he is transgressing something far more fundamental than the letter of the law.

One body of work which might well be relevant to sex-murderers, and is somewhat akin to labelling theory, is *role theory*, though its exponents have not concerned themselves with crime and deviance as such.[71] Role theory postulates the existence of already constructed 'scripts' which provide guidelines on how social actors should behave in a given situation. Typically, members of a society can slip into the role of, say, 'shop assistant' or 'secretary' because it is part of cultural common knowledge how such persons behave. Someone who took a job as a shop assistant and then proved *not* to know how to behave and failed to be suitably polite or attentive to customers, for example, would be considered a social oddity. No one expects to have to overtly *teach* members of our society how a shop assistant acts.

A dramatic demonstration of the power of roles and scripts to shape people's behaviour is given in a famous experiment by Haney and his colleagues.[72] A group of ordinary United States male college students took part in a simulation in which some students played the part of prisoners and were denied human rights (they were kept prisoner and had to wear prison clothes) while others played warders. The experiment was designed to last two weeks, but had to be abandoned after five days because the 'warders' were treating their 'prisoners' so badly: physically abusing them and punishing them by withholding food, and so on. It was an alarming illustration of the ease with which 'ordinary' young men could slip into enjoying brutality, and of the

power of a *role* behind which individuals could purport to hide
themselves, their behaviour and actions being apparently dictated by
the script.

That experiment was an example of role-giving: a sex-murderer, by
contrast, is a role-*taker*. What is striking, though, is that there is a very
clear role for men to take if they want to. Sex-killers have a culturally
given repertoire of accounts of themselves and their actions (from 'I
don't know what came over me' to 'I was cleaning up the streets'); they
can conceive of themselves as sex-murderers and they know the sorts
of things such people do.

Role theory is open to criticism for conjuring up a picture of the
social actor as a 'cultural dope', a behavioural robot who does not
exercise free will. But whether we think a label is accepted, and the
appropriate behaviour then pursued, or that a ready-made 'role' is
slipped into and played, we should not forget or underestimate the
extent to which this is a *decision*, an act initiated by the indivudual.
Consider for instance the diary of Ronald Frank Cooper which we
quoted in the preface: before going on to demonstrate his detailed
acquaintance with the role of the sexual killer, Cooper wrote: 'I have
decided . . . I should become a homosexual murderer'. To draw
attention to the existence of a 'sex-murderer' role in the culture is by
no means to explain why any specific social actor takes it up.

What the sociological theories we have been discussing here fail to
explore is the constraints which social structures and divisions impose
on actors' selection of available roles and labels. Perhaps there is no
ultimate explanation of why Ronald Frank Cooper, of all people,
became a sex-murderer, but it does need to be pointed out that there is
no script for a putative female counterpart, no model of how she
would behave, or why. It is no coincidence that Myra Hindley, the
only plausible candidate for a female sex-killer ever recorded, has
never given any real account of herself. We cannot imagine a woman
sitting down and writing as Cooper did, 'I have decided [to] become a
homosexual murderer.' As things stand, labelling theory and role
theory are unable to explain that fact.

Radical criminology

The radical criminologists of the mid-1970s were reacting both to the gradualism of the 'becoming deviant' school of sociology and to the institutional ascendancy of bourgeois positivist criminology, which had remained unmoved by new concepts of deviance.[73] Radical criminology intended to succeed where labelling theory had lamentably failed, and challenge the mainstream on its own terms, inverting the causal arrows to point from society to the individual, instead of the other way.

The radical criminologists insistently emphasize the interconnections of 'crime' and capitalism. Instead of beating about the bush with 'labels' and 'cultures', the radicals wanted to say that if the working classes are criminal, capitalist society makes them so. Similarly, they have been at pains to write back into the record the crimes of the rich and powerful and name them for the wicked acts they are; they show how being a good agent of capitalism and being a criminal — an embezzler, a killer, an exploiter and breaker of contracts — are separated by only the finest of fine lines. Again, the notions of labelling and control can be used to explain why the crimes of the powerful are not seen or named: why we are sensitized to the existence of lower-class 'muggers' and 'hooligans', but hear nothing of corporate crime, avoidable killing or government-sponsored genocide.[74]

One problem with all this from a feminist viewpoint is that it represents 'crime' as an arena in which the state and the ruling class do battle with a criminalized proletariat — the power dimension of *gender* is overlooked (indeed there are some on the Left who feel it is an embarrassment when the sisters are tactless enough to point the finger at working-class men and their violence against women). Under pressure from feminism, however, there have been moves in the direction of remedying this defect. Stephen Box's book *Power, Crime and Mystification* includes a chapter on rape and sexual assault, defining these as crimes of the powerful, along with corporate crime and crimes of the police. This bears witness to the way in which feminism does make some small advances in changing the terms of political/academic debate, since Box is obviously challenging the monopoly of class analysis in radical criminology. He is followed in this by Matthews and Young in their recent book *Confronting Crime*, which includes a chapter on the sentencing of rapists.[75]

There is also, of course, a new feminist criminology, whose main concern is with the effects of gender difference and male power on the process of criminalization and the experiences of women in the courts and in prison. Feminists are also active in the sociology of law, with family law receiving particular attention.

What is the radical position on sexual murder? The answer is that radical criminology has not concerned itself with the subject at all. Given the increasing interest in rape and sexual assault, this requires explanation: why is there a silence on sexual killing? We would attribute it to several factors.

First, we believe there is general (if grudging) acceptance among radicals of the feminist argument that rapists are not abnormal, but the product of a sexist culture. But many people are extremely reluctant to accept that this could also be the case with murderers. Their reluctance is intensified by the ingrained, common-sense belief in the sex beast who is seriously mentally disturbed, a sufferer from some individual pathological condition. The beast, moreover, is extremely rare: not only does this support the idea that he is abnormal rather than being part of the culture, it also makes many researchers feel that their time would be better spent considering those crimes from which ordinary people are constantly at risk.

A number of counter-arguments occur to us. One is theoretical: to be content with an individual, pathological account of sex-killers when no such account would be tolerated elsewhere is a retreat to essentialism and should be deplored by any radical. However distasteful it is to admit it, there are many indications that sexual killing is as much a cultural phenomenon as rape. Indeed it is similar to rape in a number of ways: it has the same gender-specificity (i.e., men do it, usually to women); it is a staple ingredient of cultural representations, particularly pornographic ones; and it has generated a similar kind of discourse to rape, in which biologistic explanations are sought, or the victims are blamed, or the perpetrators are labelled subhuman, 'animals'. If rape has been dealt with by radical criminologists, so could sexual murder be dealt with.

Another argument is more pragmatic. If we are reluctant to bother with the sexual murderer because he is at a extreme and very rare, it is worth bearing in mind that his position in the culture is nevertheless not a marginal one. By this we mean that awareness of sexual murder — the fear of it — looms just as large, if not more so, in the lives of women and parents of young children, especially girls, as does the fear of rape — even though rape is statistically more likely.

Furthermore, the very fact that the sex-murderer is extreme makes him potentially an interesting case-study of masculinity as a general phenomenon (on the principle that the abnormal often highlights the normal more clearly). If we accept that sex-killers are products of their culture, albeit untypical and exaggerated products, we can hope to learn from their very excesses what is usually hidden in male sexuality. And if things are to be changed, this seems an eminently necessary step.

CONCLUSION

Explanations of the murderer as deviant have taken many forms in the past hundred years. The murderer is deficient in body, or in mind; he has an inadequate personality; he was traumatized in childhood; or perhaps he has learnt his antisocial behaviour; maybe he belongs to a subculture which rewards it; maybe he is self-consciously playing a role.

Obviously, some of these accounts are more relevant than others to the particular type of murderer we are considering in this book. Some are more plausible and more promising than others. But although they are a heterogeneous collection, they have in common at least one thing: a lack of any serious attention to the question of why the sexual killer is male rather than female. As an empirical generalization, of course, many of them do record this point, frequently in the form of an unsupported statement that female sexual killers are 'unusual' or 'rare'.[76] None of them, however, can explain it satisfactorily; many consider it so obvious, so 'natural', they do not even attempt an explanation, while those who accept that deviance is social rather than natural nevertheless have very little to say about the effects of patriarchal power structures on deviant behaviour.

It is almost time for us to put forward an explicit analysis of sexual murder and its origins in a certain form of patriarchal culture. But before we reach the conclusion of this book, we must round off our account of existing discourses by examining the ways in which their ideas have been taken up in relation to a number of specific case histories. By considering particular instances of sexual murder, we will show how the 'hero' and the 'deviant' come together: how the abstract analyses of the previous chapters apply to real persons and concrete events.

The Murderer Personified

At the end of the last chapter, we explained what we hoped to achieve by looking at case histories: a demonstration of how various ideas and kinds of discourses have been applied in specific concrete instances. This general declaration of intent must be qualified at once, since things are not usually as simple as it suggests. It is not a matter of ideas 'existing' and then being 'applied' to events as they come along: more often, ideas emerge along with events and subsequently turn into general theories whose particular origins disappear from view.

For example, it is obvious to anyone familiar with the literature that practically everything said about the 'sadistic sex-killer' in post-war psychiatric textbooks is actually based on just a handful of examples, whose case histories are recycled until they become elevated into abstract 'types'. The figure of Peter Kürten, the Düsseldorf mass-killer, looms especially large in a vast array of writings, not because he is somehow a typical example, but because in 1938, Dr Karl Berg published a study, *The Sadist*, based on detailed conversations with him.[1] Since Kürten had spent a lot of time thinking about his own desires and behaviour, he produced for Dr Berg a remarkably full and interesting account, which made *The Sadist* a rather unusual document. It has been cited so often by subsequent writers, the effect has been to make Kürten a yardstick against whom all past and future sadists are measured. And yet the impression is frequently given that Kürten himself is just a good example of a general, pre-existing clinical category. In fact, he shows how influential a well-received case history can be in shaping our responses to murder.

Berg's work, of course, is a 'clinical' case history — of a genre which seems to have become outmoded. Today's case history of a notorious murderer, perhaps because of the influence of detective fiction and true-crime writing, is more of a 'dossier', often written by a journalist with a journalist's interest in disclosing the 'full facts'. In many cases, this has the effect of downgrading the actual killer's importance: Ludovic Kennedy's *Ten Rillington Place*, which told the story of the necrophile, Christie, was written to expose a miscarriage of justice (Christie's neighbour, Timothy Evans, was wrongly hanged for the murder of his wife and child who were actually murdered by Christie), rather than to explain why Christie acted as he did, while Gerold Frank's study, *The Boston Strangler*, was designed not as a biography of Albert de Salvo but as a portrait of a city in the grip of terror.[2]

Journalistic case histories of this type vary in their pretensions to serious analysis, ranging from sensational 'quickie' books to much weightier treatments. There is also, of course, a more 'literary' tradition of intellectuals writing about murder in such a way as to throw light on the society in which it occurs. In her autobiography, Simone de Beauvoir mentions the interest she and her circle took in various *causes célèbres* of the day, on the grounds that

> Gide, the surrealists and Freud himself had all convinced us that in every person there lurks . . . an indestructible kernel of darkness, something that cannot break up social conventions . . . but does, now and then, burst out in a peculiarly scandalous fashion. Every time one of these explosions took place, we believed, some truth was always revealed, and those which brought about an access of freedom we found especially impressive. . . . Trials no less than crimes drew our attention; the grimmer sort raised the question of individual and collective responsibility.[3]

We have already commented on the attitude of de Beauvoir and her associates to murder as a source of 'freedom' and an aspect of the human condition (see chapter 2). But the last sentence quoted above suggests they regarded murder as revealing not only the heart of darkness that 'lurks in every person', but also and perhaps more importantly, the social order, which has made individual killers what they are and in some sense determined the form of their crimes. We may not all be murderers, but we are all implicated in the society that produces them.

This sociological attitude to murder, with its challenge to any analysis that focuses exclusively on the individual, is much less ingrained in the English-speaking countries than it is on the continent (though there are partial exceptions such as Orwell's essay 'Decline of the English Murder' and Capote's *In Cold Blood*). Especially in Britain, murder tends to be treated as a peg on which to hang discussion of other issues (prostitution and slum-clearance in the case of Jack the Ripper; cheque-book journalism and police incompetence in the Yorkshire Ripper case; the vulnerability of homeless young gay men in the case of Dennis Nilsen and so on). It is not thought to hold any profound significance of its own, or to be of interest to intellectuals. (It has been remarked that despite the abundance of popular true-crime writing, Britain has been unable to sustain any less lurid literature: attempts at a notable trials series comparable to the French *Causes Célèbres* have foundered several times and there are no serious magazines dealing with crime.) One consequence of this is a total lack of any social or political analysis of murder cases, informed by a knowledge of Marxism and/or feminism: even the recent studies of Sutcliffe and Nilsen by the journalists Gordon Burn and Brian Masters, which have found so much favour among British literati, are completely untheoretical and individualistic.[4] Feminist comment on the Sutcliffe case exists, but is confined to surprisingly few (and brief) articles, plus a single book — by a French feminist writer.[5]

To sum up, then, writing in English about sex murder is meagre in quantity, patchy in quality and does not provide the kind of explanation which we as feminists are looking for. What it does do, however, is provide good examples of the kinds of discourses we have been discussing in this book, skilfully integrating a whole range of concepts so they form a detailed picture of a single case. In this chapter, we pick out a number of murderers and by using various sources, from the ephemeral (newspapers) to the would-be weighty (full-length biographies and studies), we dissect out the various strands to be found in discussion of them: themes and approaches which we have talked about before, in relation to the two images of the 'hero' and the 'deviant'.

RIPPERS: A CENTURY OF PROSTITUTE-KILLING

I am down on whores and I shant quit ripping them till I do get buckled.

('Jack the Ripper', letter to the police, 1888.)

I were just cleaning up streets.

(Peter Sutcliffe, comment to his brother, 1981.)

We want to demonstrate both change and continuity in writing about Jack the Ripper and the Yorkshire Ripper, Peter Sutcliffe, two prostitute-killers separated by almost a hundred years. We particularly want to pick out common themes in discussion of the two cases: the conflict between discourses of sickness and sin, the construction of prostitutes as 'natural' victims and the obfuscation of gender and male sexuality.

Serious writing about Jack the Ripper is untypical of the biographical/ case history approach. Because his identity was never established, 'Jack' has attained the status of a popular folk-devil, rather like Dracula or Frankenstein's monster. One imagines him stealing down foggy London streets, with a top hat and swirling black cloak, tapping his cane.

The bare facts known about the Ripper's career give little license for such imaginings. Briefly, he committed some half-dozen murders between August and November of 1888 in the Whitechapel district of London's East End. The victims were all women living in poverty, who engaged in prostitution, habitually or occasionally, to supplement earnings from casual labour or the meagre relief the authorities provided. The Ripper's trademark was extensive mutilation of his victims' bodies. Some idea of the extent of this is given by the following account, from the *Pall Mall Gazette* of 10 November 1888, of the discovery of the body of Mary Jane Kelly. This graphic description, which would nowadays be suppressed to stop 'copy-cat' killers from complicating matters, is a useful, if harrowing reminder of the realities of sex-killing.

The woman lay on her back on the bed, entirely naked. Her throat was cut from ear to ear, right down to the spinal column. The ears and nose had been cut clean off. The breasts had also been cleanly cut off and placed on a table which was by the side of the bed. The stomach and abdomen had been ripped open while the face was all slashed about, so that the features of the poor creature were beyond all recognition. The kidneys and heart had also been removed from the body and placed on the table by the side of the breasts. The liver had likewise been removed and laid on the right thigh . . . the thighs had been cut.[6]

The killer was never caught, and despite much later speculation he has never been conclusively identified either. He has, however, been mythologized: he features in stories, books, plays, operas, films and even in children's games and rhymes. He has generated a large and peculiar literature, a cross between the lurid and the downright crankish, most of it concerned with the question of who he might have been.[7]

Almost a hundred years after the Whitechapel murders, there occurred a series of (mainly) prostitute-killings in several towns in the north of England. Thirteen women died between 1975 and 1980 and several more survived attempts on their lives. As in the earlier case, victims were mutilated, this time by multiple stab wounds in the breasts, abdomen and vagina; as in the earlier case, the police received communications from a man who called himself 'Jack the Ripper' — though in fact the notorious 'Ripper tape' was not produced by the real killer.

Peter Sutcliffe went on trial for the 'Yorkshire Ripper' murders in May 1981. A plea of diminished responsibility was rejected and he was sentenced to a prison term of at least thirty years. After episodes of mental disturbance in prison, he was eventually transferred to a special hospital.

Given the power of the Jack the Ripper myth, and the extent to which it permeates the national consciousness, it is hardly surprising that the Yorkshire killings were read as they were, with Sutcliffe construed as a latter-day 'Jack', the so-called 'Yorkshire Ripper'. Although he was not responsible for the cassette received by Yorkshire police, Peter Sutcliffe may well have made the connection himself: we know Jack the Ripper was a prominent exhibit at the Victorian wax museum he frequented at Morecambe.[8] Yet the similarities were not *just* read in, and this is reflected in contemporary discussions. For anyone familiar with the Yorkshire Ripper case, reading the newspapers of 1888 produces very strong feelings of *déjà vu*. It becomes clear that commentators on the crimes of Peter Sutcliffe in many ways merely re-enacted debates which had their first airing a hundred years before. We can best demonstrate this continuity between the two

Rippers by picking out important themes their cases have in common. We begin with the ideas of sickness and sin.

The opposing discourses of sin and sickness as explanations for sexual murder organize writings about the two Rippers in more complex ways than we might want to think. Looking at various contemporary accounts, we cannot simply postulate a historical progression from the notion of sin (in the case of Jack the Ripper) to the idea of sickness (in the case of Peter Sutcliffe). The two ideas coexisted in each case: Jack the Ripper was pronounced to be 'a victim' of 'mania' by adherents of the emerging scientific study of sex; Sutcliffe was said to be 'just plain evil' at a trial which proved popular tradition's tenacity by going entirely against the clinical grain. Without denying the many historical differences, it has to be said that there are striking similarities.

One undeniable difference between them was, as you might expect, that the concept of sexual murder *per se* was taken more for granted in the later case. The London newspapers in 1888 printed a selection of theories about Jack the Ripper's motives which would never have been entertained in the 1970s, from the 'Burke and Hare' theory that the killer removed sexual and reproductive organs to sell for medical and scientific purposes, to the 'scientific sociologist' theory that he was outraged by conditions in the London slums and was deliberately trying to galvanize the authorities into action.

On the other hand, as we have seen already, the ideas of sex crime and sexual murder were already available by 1888 and it was accepted by many people that the Ripper had a sexual motive. Indeed this suggestion was frequently couched in the all too familiar language of the 'sex beast'. In 1888, however, this language had a number of features which are far less important in today's discussions: the picture of the beast entertained by the Victorians was riddled with racism and overt class prejudice, so that even serious analysis of the Ripper was informed by xenophobic and anti-Semitic stereotypes. One quite popular theory was that the Ripper was Jewish and was following an allegedly Talmudic injunction that men should atone for having sex with a Christian by killing her immediately after the act. The East End was of course inhabited by many Jews in the 1880s and serious newspapers like the *Pall Mall Gazette* were extremely anxious to see this theory discredited. Nevertheless, the *Gazette* was not above invoking the bestiality of other races and peoples: at one point, for instance, it remarked that 'We should have to go to the wilds of Hungary or search the records of French lower peasant life before a more sickening and revolting tragedy could be told.'⁹ A different commentator confidently asserted, 'In France the murdering of prostitutes has long been practised, and has been considered to be almost peculiarly a French crime.'¹⁰

References to 'peasants' and the lower classes were as persistent as references to sinister foreigners. In fact the evil propensities of working-class 'savages' were sometimes linked explicitly with conditions in the slums: 'The Savage of Civilisation whom we are raising by the hundred in our slums is quite as capable of bathing his hands in blood as any Sioux who ever scalped a foe.'¹¹

Ideas like these and in particular the depiction of the killer as a 'Savage', received theoretical support from the positivistic criminology of Lombroso, with its contention that criminals are atavistic throw-backs to earlier stages of human evolution and therefore comparable with 'uncivilized' or 'primitive' peoples. The Mr Hyde in all of us could similarly be theorized as a throw-back, and his existence, it was suggested, might place inherent limits on a society's capacity to be civilized and humane. As the *Gazette* remarked about one of the murders,

> This renewed reminder of the potentialities of revolting barbarity which lie latent in man will administer a salutory shock to the complacent optimism which assumes that the progress of civilisation has rendered unnecessary the bolts and bars, social, moral and legal, which keep the Mr Hyde of humanity from assuming visible shape among us.¹²

As we have pointed out, both the pessimism and the biologism of this view retain their centrality in discussions of sex murder.

The *Gazette*'s reference to the 'Mr Hyde of humanity' is an interesting example of the importance of the Jekyll and Hyde myth in writing about Jack the Ripper: a stage play based on Stevenson's story was actually produced during the 'autumn of terror', and it provided a neat and convenient framework for understanding contemporary events. Through the fiction of the 'dual personality', in particular, commentators were able to voice the alarming possibility that the killer might be neither 'slum-bred' nor foreign. Indeed the Ripper's more ritualistic activities were sometimes taken as evidence for a certain aristocratic finesse: 'He did his bloody work with the lust it is true of the savage, but with the skill of the savant.'[13] This 'savant', of course, had a real-life prototype in the Marquis de Sade (labelled, tabloid-style, 'the maniac marquis'). Except in the sense that class ensures respectability, Sade seems a strange choice of Jekyll-and-Hyde: his life and writings were all Hyde and no Jekyll. Nevertheless, he occupies a crucial position in the whole debate about sin and sickness, since both camps felt able to claim him for their own.

Occasional passages in the *Pall Mall Gazette* point up the contradiction between the two discourses. Take for example the following comment:

> The murderer is a victim of some erotic mania, which often takes
> the awful shape of an uncontrollable lust for blood. Sadism, as it
> is termed from the maniac marquis . . . is happily so strange to
> the majority of our people that they find it difficult to credit the
> possibility of mere debauchery bearing such awful fruitage.[14]

This remark draws an implicit distinction between the majority conception of sadism as 'mere debauchery' (the *Gazette* itself had two days earlier explained Sade's blood-lust as a result of 'the unbridled indulgence of the worst passions' — i.e., mere debauchery) and a quasi-scientific or medical way of conceiving it, as an abnormal mental condition or 'mania'; something 'uncontrollable' of which the killer himself is 'a victim'. In the case of Jack the Ripper, we are seeing the definition of sexual murder at an early and relatively confused stage; the criminal is in a state of transition as educated people assimilate recent scientific developments.

One of the most uncompromisingly clinical assessments of Jack the Ripper was made by Dr Thomas Bond, who wrote a report on one of the murders after examining the victim's body. Dr Bond characterized the killer as 'a man subject to periodical attacks of Homicidal and Erotic mania. The character of the mutilations indicate that the man may be in a condition sexually that may be called Satyriasis'.[15] This medicalization of Mr Hyde and the concomitant discarding of his spiritual dimension, is one of the most important points of resemblance between the case of Jack the Ripper and that of Peter Sutcliffe.

In a round-up of theories ('Who is the Murderer and How May he be Caught? — An Epitome of the Suggestions of the Public') the *Pall Mall Gazette* of 2 October 1888 printed the speculation that the murderer might feel he had 'a mission from above to extirpate vice by assassination'. The piece's author labelled this speculation 'aimless and absurd'. Nevertheless, in the case of Peter Sutcliffe, the same suggestion surfaced again. This time, it served a rather different purpose: Peter Sutcliffe's claim that he heard a voice from God telling him to go out and rid the streets of prostitutes was used not as a defence in itself, but as the means to a defence of diminished responsibility. The jury considered not whether God *had* spoken to Sutcliffe — that possibility was not on the agenda — but whether Sutcliffe sincerely believed God had spoken, in which case, clearly, he was schizophrenic.

Sutcliffe's trial and the discussion of his case revolved around the question, was he mad or just plain bad? Just as much as in the time of Jack the Ripper, the alternatives posed were either sinfulness or sickness. Indeed Sutcliffe posed the question much more starkly, since on it hung the verdict — guilty of murder or manslaughter. Much of the press coverage took the view that the psychiatrists, not Sutcliffe, were really on trial.

It might be thought that in the sophisticated 1980s, the madness of someone who had done what Sutcliffe did would be a foregone conclusion; yet this was not the case. Particularly it was not the case where the general public was concerned: dissent was expressed through a number of channels, from petitions calling for the Ripper to be hanged, to posters (paid for by a Yorkshire businessman) which bore the legend 'The Ripper is a Coward.' Striking also were the statements of the murdered women's relatives, which slipped very easily into sex beast rhetoric. The mother of Jayne MacDonald, for instance, the first victim not to be a prostitute, said on television in November 1980 'I think you are the devil himself. You are a coward. You are not a man, you are a beast.' Sutcliffe himself used the same sort of language: 'They are all in my brain, reminding me of the beast I am. Just thinking of them all reminds me of what a monster I am.'[16]

But was Sutcliffe a monster of conscious depravity, or was he turned into a monster by the delusions of psychosis in the same way the powders turned Jekyll into Hyde? Since he had pleaded diminished responsibility under section two of the Homicide Act, it was precisely this question which the court addressed. Two alternative answers were put forward: the prosecution contended that the man in the dock was a sexual sadist who had killed for his own pleasure, while the defence maintained that the killings were not sexual, but part of a moral crusade inspired by the voice of God telling Sutcliffe to rid the world of prostitutes.

It reveals a great deal about our everyday assumptions that this opposition between 'sadism' and 'cleaning up the streets' was almost universally regarded as quite logical. Yet the underlying premises without which it would be senseless are open to a number of important criticisms.

For instance, it seems to have been accepted without question that the court should concern itself only with the issue of whether or not Sutcliffe suffered from delusions and not with the actual content of his delusions. It is part of everyday knowledge that delusions are irrational and this leads to an assumption that they are also meaningless, neither needing nor permitting of any real explanation. But irrational behaviour is not necessarily meaningless: Sutcliffe's in particular is perfectly interpretable, and moreover its meaning is the same whether or not it was 'caused' by a delusion. As the feminist Wendy Hollway wrote soon after the trial, 'The explanation that it was a delusion does not show *why* the voice told Sutcliffe to kill women. Whether it was God's voice, the devil's voice or the projected voice of Sutcliffe's own hatred makes no difference: the content derives from a generalised, taken for granted misogyny.'[17] Hollway goes on to point out that by arguing only about whether Sutcliffe heard a voice, and refusing to attend to what the voice in fact *said*, the discourse of psychiatry obscured the extent to which the 'abnormal' Sutcliffe resembled other, normal men.

As well as ignoring the meaning of Sutcliffe's alleged delusions, his defence counsel and psychiatrists resolutely ignored the meaning of what he actually did to his victims. This is a persistent feature of 'Ripper' killings generally: from Jack the Ripper on there is always an argument available to the effect that a prostitute-killer is not a sex beast but someone who believes he is 'doing the world a favour' by being 'down on whores'. Thus at Sutcliffe's trial it was claimed by the defence that the killings had no sexual significance at all. They were simply part of a street-cleaning mission, and the fact that Sutcliffe raped Helen Rytka as she died, rammed a wooden plank up Emily Jackson's vagina and stabbed Josephine Whitaker's repeatedly with a screwdriver signalled only the blunted sensitivity of the schizophrenic, not the concerns of the sexual sadist.

In questioning this account, the prosecution did not make the response which seems so obvious to us, namely that sexual sadism is not incompatible with a pathological hatred of, and mission to kill, prostitutes. Instead they insisted that Sutcliffe's behaviour could only be interpreted as that of a sex beast, and left the way open for the psychiatrists to dispute what the clinical picture of a sex beast really is. Dr Terence Kay argued on behalf of the defence that Sutcliffe did not fit the sex beast diagnosis because,

> A sadist killer can very rarely relate to adult women and therefore is very rarely married; secondly, he has a rich sexual fantasy life, dreams about sex and is usually . . . very anxious to discuss his fantasies; thirdly, such people would stimulate their fantasy with pornography and would be interested in torture, whips and female underwear.[18]

It is worth pointing out that Dr Kay's remarks are absurd even in their own scientific/empirical terms, inasmuch as it is difficult to call to mind a single heterosexual mass-killer from the modern pantheon who was single at the time he committed his offences (Kürten, Christie and DeSalvo all had wives; Brady had Hindley; Neville Heath was divorced and re-engaged) and even more difficult to prove 'scientifically' that Sutcliffe did not have a 'rich sexual fantasy life'. As for the 'torture, whips and female underwear', it seems Dr Kay has succumbed to a bad case of what we might call 'Dr Robert Brittain syndrome': a tendency to take several arbitrary findings from clinical practice, assume a causal link between them and sex murder and on these grounds make conformity to the findings themselves a part of the actual definition of sex murder!

From a feminist perspective, none of the distinctions made at the trial stands up to scrutiny. A feminist cannot see any contradiction between sadistic sexual murder and a mad crusade against prostitutes; in fact, she tends to view these things as stemming from the same root of Western Christianity and its approach to sexuality. The Christian tradition equates sexuality with sin *and* pleasure: lust may delight the body but it endangers the soul. In a patriarchal culture where Man has been able to make himself the universal subject, has had the power of representing himself and the world, the ambivalent feelings evoked by sexuality — pleasure and danger, desire and disgust — are projected onto a female figure, the prostitute who is simultaneously an object of desire and an object of contempt. The prostitute here functions as an archetype: she represents the sexual aspect of all women. So the ambivalent responses the prostitute calls forth are part of men's feelings about women in general. The desire to kill prostitutes is thus not sharply distinct from sadism: it is another outcome of the same conflation of sex, transgression, hatred and death.

If we attend to the Christian echoes from deep below the surface of cultural consciousness, it becomes less puzzling that the 'sick or sinful' dilemma came out as it did in the Sutcliffe trial. If Sutcliffe got pleasure from killing thirteen women, he was committing a sin, the sin of lust and impurity, for which a certain form of retribution would seem appropriate. But if he was trying to stamp out sin himself — sin, that is, personified by the figure of the Whore — then he was suffering rather from delusions of grandeur. Stamping out sin is God's prerogative, and a man who usurps it reveals himself as mad. The whole edifice of the trial was built on the equation of sex with sinfulness and women with sex; equations so utterly familiar, so ancient, it was well-nigh impossible to call them into question.

Our analysis may be starting to sound like the old libertarian cry that all the world's evils are due to 'repression', especially the Christian repression of sex. So let us make it clear that we do not take that line. We are not saying that if sex were 'set free', if the streams of authentic desire flowed unchecked, then sexual murder would vanish from the scene. Christianity does entail a particular construction of sexuality as a source of guilt and shame, something longed-for and yet vile; this is clearly a significant influence on the sadistic and murderous desires we have discussed. But once again, we must pay attention to *gender*: the construction of *women* as repositories of sex, and thus of the vileness which sex represents, is not a consequence of Christianity itself, but of the more fundamental historical fact that Christian cultures are patriarchal and misogynist. This is also a fact about non-Christian cultures, and we therefore find sadistic and murderous desires elsewhere, though expressed in slightly different forms reflecting the dominant images of other traditions.

It is precisely because they are aware of this point that feminists have been unenthusiastic on the whole about the modern so-called

'liberation' of desire. This may have broken to some extent through
the restraints of Christian traditional attitudes, but it has not freed us
from the patriarchal structures which are even more important
determinants of our sexualities and desires. This is a very important
point, to which we shall return several times in the remainder of this
book.

In Sutcliffe's case, the issue of 'sin or sickness' was used to obscure
the deep meaning of prostitute-killing. That the prostitute symbolizes
female sexuality, which our culture hates and fears and which it feels a
need to punish, may seem quite obvious in feminist circles; commentators in the public arena, however, were painfully obtuse on this
crucial point. They took hatred of prostitutes completely for granted,
while ignoring its significance as an indicator of misogyny.

In both the Yorkshire and the Whitechapel murders, the fact that
the victims and targets were prostitutes profoundly affected the course
of public discussions, and again was used to obscure the issue of
misogyny. One notable effect was a widespread indifference and even
hostility to the women who were killed. The prosecuting counsel in
the Yorkshire Ripper case made a typical assessment of the worth of a
prostitute when he remarked that 'some of the victims were prostitutes,
but perhaps the saddest part of this case is that some were not.'[19] But
the main effect in both cases was to draw attention away from the
agents of sexual murder, and their desires, while turning the spotlight
on the behaviour of the victims, and on the 'moral' question of
prostitution.

We have already observed in previous sections that the killing of
prostitutes is often regarded as a classically 'victim-precipitated' crime.
Victimology is the twentieth-century social scientist's codification of
this view, which existed much earlier in common-sense discourse and
in the public discussion of the Jack the Ripper murders. The police
chief in charge of the case, Charles Warren, told the press in October
1888, 'The police can do nothing as long as the victims unwittingly
connive at their own destruction. They take the murderer to some
retired spot, and place themselves in such a position that they can be
slaughtered without a sound being heard.'[20]

By the 1970s, talk was not so much about prostitutes conniving at
their own destruction as about the tragedy of the killer's inability to
confine himself to prostitutes. Concern about the Yorkshire murders

escalated dramatically when the Ripper killed Jayne MacDonald, a 'respectable' young woman. Just after this happened, an open letter in the *Yorkshire Evening Post* addressed the killer thus: 'How did you feel yesterday when you learned your bloodstained crusade had gone so horribly wrong? That your vengeful knife had found so innocent a target?'[21] Condemnation of prostitutes as natural and deserving victims was if anything far more unanimous in popular discourse in the later case than at the time of Jack the Ripper. This probably reflects the fact that the Victorians could draw on an alternative discourse about prostitution, a set of ideas which, as it happened, reached a peak in the 1880s around the time of the Whitechapel murders. We refer to the discourse on the 'fallen woman', the prostitute produced by a combination of her own moral weakness and the poverty and brutality of the city slums. This figure was the object of bourgeois concern and of practical attempts to redeem her by philanthropy. She was discussed *ad nauseam* by writers about the Ripper and we will therefore give some attention to the variety of ways in which they represented her.

The nature and extent of prostitution in Victorian London has been documented by historians, including some feminists.[22] It is worth noting that the issue of prostitution was a live one for feminist and other reform movements of the 1880s and was well to the forefront of public awareness when the Jack the Ripper killings occurred. Only three years before, a piece of scandal journalism, the 'Maiden Tribute of Modern Babylon', had 'revealed' in the pages of the *Pall Mall Gazette* how working-class girls were sold into prostitution for the benefit of aristocratic rakes. The decade had also seen the culmination of campaigns against the Contagious Diseases Acts (laws which gave the state powers to regulate prostitutes and alleged prostitutes living in garrison towns). There was thus considerable concern about the fate of women at the mercy of male (especially upper-class male) lust.

As Judith Walkowitz has pointed out, this kind of concern can always cut two ways. Feminists (for instance Josephine Butler) tried to use it as a weapon in the struggle for women's emancipation, pointing to women's economic oppression and their political impotence (to be remedied by the Vote), and campaigning for single standards of sexual morality. But this more progressive line always had to compete with a male-dominated and reactionary initiative to 'protect' vulnerable women, strengthening the family and men's power within it. From this perspective, prostitution was seen not as oppressed sisters responding to economic necessity but as 'fallen women' in need of guidance and protection.

Articles about fallen women abounded in contemporary newspaper coverage of the Whitechapel killings. A typical human-interest piece on the East End and its inhabitants was headed 'Homeless and Friendless'; its author cried, apropos of the prostitutes, 'What wrecks of womanhood, what hopeless, battered remnants of humanity!'[23] Two weeks earlier, the *Pall Mall Gazette* had printed a petition from 'women of the labouring classes' (probably organized in this instance by one of the reforming or religious groups) which referred to 'the lives of those of our sisters who have lost a firm hold on goodness and who are leading sad and degraded lives'.

This kind of sentimental and moralistic writing was not the only kind of discourse about prostitution; as the feminist historian Sheila Jeffreys has demonstrated, there were much more radical feminist analyses too.[24] But the 'fallen woman' had much wider currency and certainly more effect on discussion of the Ripper murders. Its effect was by no means a positive one, either, since not only did it misrepresent the nature of prostitution, it also implied that the problem in Whitechapel was not so much the existence of a Ripper as the existence of prostitutes themselves; as if sexual killers merely responded to prevailing mores instead of being a part and product of them; as if, had the prostitutes and the slums been cleared away, the Ripper's lust to kill would have evaporated like dew.

It was the absence of male violence, as opposed to fallen women, from the centre of debate which was criticized by feminists, both in the Yorkshire and the Whitechapel cases: though the habits of thought behind 'fallen women' rhetoric were and are so ingrained that any feminist response made only the tiniest, most limited impression. If we examine the public utterances of feminists, once again we discover very striking similarities between 1888 and the late 1970s.

The women who spoke out in the Yorkshire Ripper case were drawing attention to the continuity between Sutcliffe's behaviour and 'normal' male fantasies expressed in pornography, literature and art. They protested against the woman-blaming distinction between 'innocent' victims and prostitutes and they pointed out the general unwillingness of society to take male violence against women seriously.

Similar arguments were heard in 1888. It was pointed out that violence against women was all-pervasive and very frequently condoned. In the words of Mrs Fenwick Miller's letter to the *Daily News*,

> Week by week and month by month, women are kicked, beaten, jumped on until they are crushed, chopped, stabbed, seamed with vitriol, bitten, eviscerated with red-hot pokers and deliberately set on fire — and this sort of outrage, if the woman dies, is called 'manslaughter': if she lives, it is a common assault.[25]

The message was the same over ninety years later: our culture is one of unremitting male violence and Ripper-style killings are only to be expected.

So far, we have referred only to the public discourse of the law, psychiatry and newspaper comment. This discourse organizes our abstract concept of 'the Ripper' as a generic figure or type. But what of the private and particular pressures that go to make a Ripper out of this man, not that? With this question we enter the realms of biographical case-history writing. There are various 'biographies' of Jack the Ripper which we do not intend to consider, since no illuminating biography can be written of a subject about whose life and identity we know nothing. We shall, however, consider how Sutcliffe has been treated in biographical accounts of his career.

There are several studies of the Yorkshire Ripper case. Three were written in the wake of the trial, during 1981: Beattie's *The Yorkshire Ripper Story*; Cross's *The Yorkshire Ripper* and Yallop's *Deliver Us from Evil*. Two were written after rather more reflection: Burn's 1984 study, *Somebody's Husband, Somebody's Son* and Nicole Ward Jouve's *The Streetcleaner*, published in 1986 (there was an earlier version in French, titled *Un Homme nommé Zapolski*, but *The Streetcleaner* is a reworking rather than a translation).

We do not propose to say much about the 'quickie' books, since inevitably they were based on hurried research and were designed — in some cases all too obviously — for the 'true-crime' consumers of sensation and moralism (Beattie's book was actually a co-publication of the tabloid *Daily Star*). All devote a lot of space to discussions of police incompetence and all offer familiar accounts of the Ripper himself as a sex beast, using the terms we have already documented in chapter 2. Yallop's title, *Deliver Us from Evil*, sets the tone; he obviously feels he is dealing with a mysterious, inescapable wickedness which cannot be understood by society at large, but should nevertheless have been hunted down with a bit more zeal. The book itself is written from an improbable set of perspectives: part narrated from the killer's own viewpoint, part from Yallop's and part — unforgivably — from that of the student victim Barbara Leach, whose letters are used to full mawkish effect.

Burn and Ward Jouve are more ambitious; both attempt social and psychological analysis of the Sutcliffe case. Although they employ very different methodologies — Burn's hard-nosed honest-to-goodness journalistic research and Ward Jouve's a linguistic/psychoanalytic analysis using structuralist theory — they come to remarkably similar conclusions. Sutcliffe was alienated from his social milieu and the site of his conflicts was masculine sexuality. *The Streetcleaner*, written by a feminist woman, sees this point in explicitly political terms; yet interestingly, Burn is also forced to take account of feminist ideas. His is in fact the fuller documentation of Sutcliffe's circumstances — Nicole Ward Jouve's book draws heavily on Burn's — and we will therefore take it as our focus in this chapter. The particular — and so far unique — contribution Ward Jouve's study makes is to emphasize the meaning of the case for women and we shall return to her insights later on, in our concluding chapter.

As the title *Somebody's Husband, Somebody's Son* implies, Burn is concerned to make the general point that Sutcliffe was not evil; superficially, he was *ordinary*, indeed rather more attractive than most of his family, friends and workmates. If this approach recalls feminist insistence on male violence as a continuum, appalling acts like Sutcliffe's shading into more 'normal' attitudes to women, it is by no means a coincidence. Gordon Burn may stand on no political soap-boxes, but the influence of the political debates of the 1970s can be seen quite clearly in his selection of material. Burn provides, quite knowingly and deliberately, the kind of detail on which can be built an authentic feminist portrait of a Ripper. That is to say, in his collection and arrangement of illustrative details — anecdotes, quotations, descriptions of events — Burn implicitly pays attention to the fact that Peter Sutcliffe was a man and not a woman.

Burn is at pains to depict working-class Bingley as a social milieu where misogyny is routine. He quotes the sort of remarks to be heard there: 'Women are for frying bacon and screwing.' Peter Sutcliffe grew up in a culture which valued a certain exaggerated form of masculinity and which sanctioned any marked deviations from this. To win the accolade 'a real lad', the men of Sutcliffe's family, his workmates and friends, engaged in activities such as eating offal, body-building, petty crime, hard drinking, fighting and casual sex — including going with prostitutes. Burn suggests that Peter had trouble in presenting the world with a suitably masculine persona. He drank relatively little, he rarely fought, he found it hard to chat up women or be masterful with prostitutes (his demeanour often caused them to say that he was 'useless'). As his father, talking to Burn, expressed it, 'He was a right mother's boy from the word go.'[26]

From these observations, it is possible to infer that Peter Sutcliffe suffered from the sort of anxiety about gender, about masculinity, that Robert Stoller identifies as leading to woman-hatred. But he also suffered from something else as well: a morbid obsession with a set of wax images depicting the loathsomeness of female sexuality.

These images, regularly visited by Sutcliffe, were in an upstairs room at a Morecambe wax museum. Interestingly, they were of Victorian vintage; they were a relic of the prurient interest of that period in decadent or diseased sexuality, where Gothic horror met scientific classification. Gordon Burn describes the wax displays thus:

> The torsos are life-size, headless, legless and female. There are nine of them and the cross-sections cut from their lower abdomens betray their function, which was to illustrate 'the nine stages of pregnancy' to an audience of Victorian lay people. Time, however, has eroded definition and basted the developing foetuses and the glistening ropes of internal organs to a uniform ox-blood colour; the impression is of gaping wounds around the umbilicus, growing progressively bigger, gorier and more congealed.[27]

Pregnancy was not the only 'condition' to be modelled, there were also several display cases devoted to syphilitic organs.

> The chancred lips of a vagina ooze and fester beneath a grey cloud of pubic hair. . . . Four babies' faces are obliterated by the sort of green scabs and horrible running sores that are an insistent theme, filling the room with images of feculence and pus. A

hand is thrust deep into a wound, its fingers closed around a deformed foetus . . . [A] nipple . . . is discoloured and heavily encrusted, and the bare, waxen white breasts are covered in venereal sores and hives.[28]

To one of these lurid tableaux of motherhood defiled was attached a couplet of prophetic significance:

> Vice is a monster of so hideous a mien
> That to be hated needs but to be seen.

Peter Sutcliffe, like the Victorians who made the waxworks popular, was both attracted and repelled by vice, which he saw, according to cultural convention, as a quality belonging to the prostitute woman, with her pox-infested body, a series of gaping wounds.

Of all the types of sexual murders, prostitute-killing is the clearest example of a lust to kill whose main component is misogyny. One of the claims we make in this book, though, is that murderous desires are not *just* misogynistic. The masculinity with which they are associated includes woman-hatred but cannot be reduced to it. What else is involved can be seen more clearly in a different category of sexual killer, the type which we will refer to as the 'sadist'.

SADISTS: THE INIQUITY OF BRADY AND HINDLEY

I didn't think he was cracked, I thought he was intellectual

(David Smith on his relationship with Ian Brady.)

There are some books that are not fit for all people, and some people who are not fit for all books

(Pamela Hansford Johnson, *On Iniquity* (1967).)

In 1966, a young couple went on trial on three counts of murder at Chester assizes. Ian Brady and Myra Hindley had lured at least two children to their Manchester home; photographs of one victim, ten-year-old Lesley Ann Downey, posed clad only in a gag, were produced in evidence along with a tape of her pleading with her captors as they stripped and gagged her. When dead (which person killed them and how was not determined) the children's bodies were buried on the nearby moors: the killers posed for photographs on their unmarked graves, and spent nights drinking wine in the presence of their victims. Brady, in addition, had abused and then slaughtered a seventeen-year-old homosexual boy. He did this in the presence of Myra's brother-in-law, David Smith, who finally reported the incident to the police.

The moors murderers, as they soon came to be known, raised several extremely uncomfortable questions, especially for the liberal thinkers of the period: questions of culture and representation, especially the relation of representation to action. Since we also believe that these topics are crucial, we discuss this aspect of the case in some detail. But for us, it is also a source of great interest because it presents us, uniquely, with a woman who participated in and was convicted of sex murder. Myra Hindley: is she a challenge to our thesis, the exception that proves the rule, or a misleading aberration? Clearly, we need to pay close attention to the role of Hindley and the way she is read.

Culture, representation, action

Ian Brady and Myra Hindley resemble many of the other killers we have looked at in the way they constructed, from existing discourse, a definite identity or murdering role which they reflected back to themselves and one another by producing a new, private discourse of their own. In their case this discourse took a form which the public found peculiarly repellent and which told heavily against them: they tape-recorded and photographed the humiliation of one victim, then recorded their own presence on the two secret graves. Jonathan Goodman has observed that these two 'were voyeurs, *écouteurs* of their own corruption — they derived at least as much satisfaction from the shadow of their deeds as from the deeds themselves'.[29] However unpleasant we find their particular form of self-representation, though, it is analogous to the satisfaction of other killers in more overtly 'acceptable' sorts of discourses: the lengthy confession of Pierre Rivière, the letters to the police sent by Jack the Ripper, the three private diaries of Ronald Frank Cooper, the testimony of Kürten to Berg, Nilsen's poetry — it is in the act of representing his act that the killer lays claim to his position in our culture.

Brady in particular was steeped in the culture of murder as transcendence which we have explored. The key texts in his thinking were Sade's *Justine*, Hitler's *Mein Kampf* and Dostoevsky's *Crime and Punishment*. What these three texts have in common is the theme of the Faust or superman who transcends conventional morality, who kills in the cause of his freedom and power. Thus Brady was a sadist in a more exact sense than many of those to whom the term has been applied. Not only did he eroticize cruelty and killing, he took on board the whole philosophy behind this. As David Marchbanks wrote soon after the trial, 'He was a disciple of the philosophy of amoralism and the absolute right of the individual to indulge in whatever evil he chose, evil being as much part of the instinct and nature of man as good.'[30]

When Brady met the journalist Fred Harrison in 1983, he expanded at length on the significance of Dostoevsky's character Raskolnikov in his life and career as a sadistic murderer. Raskolnikov is the 'Napoleonic' killer of *Crime and Punishment*, who kills an old woman and later accounts for it by saying,

> I wanted to murder, Sonia, to murder without casuistry, to murder for my own satisfaction, for myself alone . . . I had to find out then, and as quickly as possible, whether I was a louse like the rest, or a man. Whether I can step over or not. Whether I can stoop or not. Whether I am some trembling vermin, or whether I have the *right*.[31]

Brady too believed he was a 'man' who had 'the right'.

One of Dostoevsky's motives in writing the novel *Crime and Punishment* was his feeling of unease about the kinds of ideas represented by Raskolnikov, which he referred to as 'half-baked' and which were very fashionable in Russia at the time. It is ironic that the actions of Ian Brady, who regarded himself as a latter-day Raskolnikov, should have awakened a similar unease in Britain about the 'half-baked' ideas of the 1960s.

Public discourse at the time of the murders was centred on the role of the permissive society in fostering crimes such as Brady and Hindley's. Reading certain parts of the transcript of the trial, one is sometimes unsure whether Brady was on trial for murdering children or for reading pornography, for instance in bizarre exchanges like the following:

COUNSEL: This was the diet you were consuming, pornographic books, books on violence and murder?

BRADY: No pornographic books. You can buy them at any bookstall.

COUNSEL: They were dirty books, Brady?

BRADY: It depends on the dirty mind. It depends on your mind.

COUNSEL: Let me give you the name of one or two.

JUDGE: *Uses of the Torture Chamber. Sexual Anomalies and Perversions.*

BRADY: These are written by doctors. They are supposed to be social.

COUNSEL: Was your interest in them on a high medical plane?

BRADY: No, for erotic reasons.

COUNSEL: Of course, this is the atmosphere of your mind. A sink of pornography, was it not?

BRADY: No. There are better collections than that in lords' manors all over the country.[32]

The underlying dispute here is about the relation between represent-ation and action. The court takes the familiar view that reading pornography is bound to lead to the commission of crime; that is why it attempts to establish that Brady's mind was 'a sink of pornography'. But Brady himself rejects this point of view and produces the rather more sophisticated argument that 'it depends on the dirty mind' what a representation means. He also hints at another problem: the elitism of so much that is said on this subject. His reference to literature being 'written by doctors' and collected by members of the aristocracy, makes the point that reading pornography is commonplace — even if the privileged and educated conceal their tastes under alternative labels. Thus Brady rejects the court's crude portrayal of him as either a dupe, corrupted by what he read, or a striking exception in his tastes. (In this connection it is interesting to note how little was made of Dostoevsky's novel at the trial, by comparison with Hitler and Sade. It would clearly have vexed the establishment to have to argue that Brady had been corrupted by the classics!)

The simplistic connection between pornography and murder was made not only by the court, but in public discourse generally. The complicity of society in producing the moors murders was harped on at every opportunity, from an article in the *Sunday Express* headed 'Are Brady and Hindley the only Guilty Ones?' which indicted the lax moral climate of the times, to the 'personal reflections' of Pamela Hansford Johnson, published a year after the trial under the title *On Iniquity*.

Hansford Johnson's book is fairly typical of the deeply conservative political position from which so much comment on the moors murders came. She urges us to face up to the existence of evil — iniquity, which should be named as such and not hidden behind euphemisms like 'pathology' or 'deviance'. Evil desires must be repressed, not encouraged: the permissive and liberal climate of the sixties allowed sadism to flourish and legitimized perversion.

In a famous work of radical criminology, Stuart Hall and his associates' *Policing the Crisis*, the year 1966 is located as the end of consensus and the 'moment of force'. Public hysteria about the moors murders is mentioned as a factor in the swing to "Law and Order"; Hansford Johnson's book is cited, among others, with the dismissive comment that 'the moral backlash had commenced.'[33]

Clearly, the work of Pamela Hansford Johnson and her ilk did represent a moral backlash against the social changes of the 1960s — pornography, permissiveness and social degeneracy, as they were often perceived. But it also embodied a realization which the Left was, and still is, unwilling to voice, that events like the moors murders and people like Brady are not random aberrations but cultural products. At least Hansford Johnson locates the problem in collective attitudes and not individual sickness; *Policing the Crisis*, by its tone and what it does not say, conveys an impression that a few sexual murders are not a legitimate reason for concern about the culture.

This notable reversal of the usual order, with right-wingers claiming a problem is social while the Left takes refuge in individualism (or silence) is not confined to *Policing the Crisis* and we do not want to single out its authors for particular criticism. This spectacle can be witnessed regularly in connection with the topic of 'sexual freedom' and pornography. The Left has been at pains ever since the 1960s to refute the contention of people like Mary Whitehouse, that pornographic representations can *cause* violent acts such as rape and sexual murder. We too are sceptical about this idea of cause, which we have argued is generally inappropriate to the explanation of human action. But this does not imply that sexual murder is not cultural, or that it is unconnected with prevailing forms of representation. On the contrary, without the web of representations of murder and murderers, sexuality and death, which we have analysed in previous chapters, the behaviour of someone like Ian Brady would be unimaginable and incomprehensible. Representations help construct and shape people's desires by offering them certain objects, certain channels, certain meanings. What aspirations and pleasures are available, what practices, identities and dreams are even thinkable is determined to a very large extent by the culture. Our culture has violent, pornographic dreams; it has aspirations to (male) freedom and transcendence. Not coincidentally, it has sadistic sexual murder.

That our desires themselves are social constructs is the very point right-wing analysts miss. For Pamela Hansford Johnson, phenomena like the moors murders and Nazism represent an eternal, immutable 'dark side' to human nature which civilized society must struggle constantly to repress (echoes here of the Hobbesian state of nature). For a feminist, conversely, it is something of an axiom that desires are moulded by social structures, institutions and representations (for example the nuclear family, the division of labour, Enlightenment philosophy, religion, snuff movies, etc.). Since they are constructs, desires can be *re*constructed within different structures, institutions and so on. Repression is not the only plausible strategy for those who can imagine a new world of transformed desire.

Such Utopianism is not open to conservatives, with their static conception of fallen 'human nature'. But strangely, it is also alien to most Marxists, who continue to avoid the issues raised by sexual killing. Twenty years after the moors murders, who do Marxist writers still refrain from any critique of the forms of modern sexual desire?

We suspect this has partly to do with the overwhelming dominance in Anglo-American society of liberal ways of thinking and the resultant focus on individual freedoms, which downplays the whole question of where our desires come from. There is a tendency to assume, as the feminist historian Sheila Jeffreys says, 'that there is an essence of sexuality which, though repressed at times in the past, is gradually fighting its way free of the restrictions placed upon it.'[34] But a number of influential recent Marxist writers have been eager to challenge the concept of an essence of sexuality. They are apt to celebrate instead what has been called 'the new pluralism', a colourful diversity of sexualit*ies* which extend the range of what can be given erotic meaning:

new contexts, new practices, new parts of the body. For them, the 'essence of sexuality' has arguably become Freud's polymorphous perversity (except that the child's unawareness of sexual meanings and boundaries has been replaced by the conscious imposition of eroticism — the child is polymorphous, the new pluralists perverse). Referring in particular to sado-masochistic scenes, Jeffrey Weeks has related this current to the post-Enlightenment search for transcendence: 'At stake here, clearly, is a politics of transgression where desire exists to disrupt order, and where disruption and transgression are the keys to pleasure.'[35] To us this implies that the new pluralism is not radical enough or maybe not radical at all. The lust to kill does not disrupt the social and sexual order; an observation which illustrates the general point that what passes for perversity is polymorphous only within the limits of patriarchal culture. As we will argue in more detail later, all sexuality is deeply marked by the historical realities of gender and power. Thus sexual 'diversity' in the twentieth century is unified by its assumption of a transcendent (i.e., masculine) sexual subject. We do not mean that the sexual subject is biologically male, but that desire itself has been masculinized, made dependent on dichotomies of self and other, subject and object, which presuppose some version of the social/sexual hierarchy, male:female. We say 'some version' because we are aware that some women and feminists today aspire to be transcendent sexual subjects themselves. Those women are reconstructing their own desires, but still within the limits of existing power structures. They are not undertaking any radical reconstruction of Western sexuality in general.

If the Left passed over the moors murders in silence — except to excoriate the moral Right — it is surely the sign of an imaginative failure, an inability to break out of patriarchal ways of thinking. The form of desire that is celebrated still is exactly the same desire gloried in by Sade, portrayed by Dostoevsky and acted out by Ian Brady.

Myra Hindley: it's different for girls

Whenever we have explained the main argument of this book, we have usually been asked 'what about Myra Hindley?' Hindley is the only serious potential counter-example to our proposition that sexual killers are men, and it is in considering a problematic case like hers that we must emphasize the limits of what we can know. We have a trial, a verdict — guilty of two child murders — and a great deal of discourse about Myra Hindley. We do not have much more for her male counterparts, but the lack of any stable cultural codes which could help us make sense of Hindley's motives and her conduct renders her case much more enigmatic than theirs.

Did Myra Hindley have a lust to kill? Did she derive sexual gratification from the couple's joint activities? What exactly was her role in those activities? Did she, like Brady, use sadistic rituals as a way of affirming her transcendent subjectivity? We do not know how she herself would answer these questions, but we do know the answers the culture produced and these in the end are of greater significance. Writings about Hindley make it very clear indeed that her actions did not have the same meaning as Brady's; they were differentiated by the factor of gender, and by the fact that no language existed for speaking of a woman's lust to kill — indeed one still does not exist.

Ever since the moors murders first came to light, there have been two contradictory accounts of Myra Hindley. Both are structured by gender-specific stereotypes and both deny that Hindley, as a woman, could have been the agent of sexual killing in the same way as Brady undoubtedly was.

The first of these accounts, subscribed to by psychiatrists and also, notoriously, the campaigner Lord Longford, claims that Hindley was simply corrupted by Brady — as Fred Harrison puts it, 'He substituted a crazy hotchpotch of evil ideas in place of the workaday attitudes on which Myra had been weaned in Gorton.'[36] She committed her crimes (whatever they were) entirely under the influence of Brady. We could call this the 'Pygmalion theory', after the play by Shaw in which an upper-class professor remakes a Cockney flower-girl in the image he desires. The story behind it is implicitly gendered: it is the tale of a masterful, superior man who fills the otherwise empty mind of his female disciple with ideas which she accepts just because they are his, and not because of any independent assessment.

The Pygmalion theory in relation to Hindley is frequently given a clinical gloss in the assertion that she suffered from *folie à deux*, a condition where one individual's mental illness communicates itself to a lover or close relative. Brady was 'psychopathic', and according to Harrison, '[Myra] came to share Ian's insanity; her character was adapted to blend in with his.'[37] Again, the issue of gender is salient, though discussions of *folie à deux* tend to gloss over it: it seems to us that in male-dominated society, for a woman to adapt her character in order to blend in with that of a man is a common enough outcome of socialization, and of the pressures within heterosexual relationships. So if Myra Hindley came to adopt her boyfriend's ideas, if she changed to accommodate him, that is not, in itself, unusual. The question is rather why most writers have assumed that Brady's ideas would have been alien to Myra *unless* she was under an evil spell.

This whole assumption, it transpires, has its basis in the sexist cliché of 'maternal instinct', which should have ensured that Myra Hindley would be repelled above all by the sexual abuse and murder of children. Fred Harrison's rhetoric is fairly representative: 'How could a woman offend against the protective maternal instinct that was nurtured into the genes in a process of evolution that spanned a period of two million years?'[38] We see now that Myra Hindley's real crime was hubris: she went against the sex role laid down by the gods or nature! But if Harrison's question has any answer at all — and let us keep in mind that this was written in 1986, not 1966 — it must be that Myra Hindley did it for love. Her naturally protective emotions toward children could only have been overcome by devotion to a man. Supporters of the Pygmalion theory take it so much for granted that love makes women fools, they do not bother to ask whether Hindley was actually attracted not only to Brady, but to the ideas he expounded. If she was, it would be interesting to speculate on why, but this discourse forecloses on that line of enquiry.

The second account of Myra Hindley is rather different but equally clichéd, depending once again on the common-sense premiss that a woman who condones, far less takes part in child sex-murder is a wholly unnatural monster of depravity. But rather than attribute her unnatural behaviour to the malign influence of a murderous Svengali, proponents of this theory take it as a sign that the woman is much more profoundly wicked than any man. This 'Lady Macbeth' theory — after the Shakespearean character who urges her husband to kill in pursuit of his ambition — has often been applied to Myra Hindley. The conviction surfaced during the trial and has been steadily growing in strength ever since, that she was in some sense the 'power behind the throne': John Deane Potter, in his 1966 book *The Monsters of the Moors*, said that:

Those who saw Myra in the witness box agree that she was an

intelligent, probably tougher character than her lover. . . . Was
Myra in fact the dominant partner? When she heard his views
and boasts did she, woman-like, say in effect, 'Let's not dream
and indulge in these fantasies. Let's do something about them.
Let's make them real'.[39]

It seems that this is the alternative to depicting women as men's
creatures: showing them as the corruptors who tempt men to evil. The
discourse of our culture — and not just on this topic — casts women in
only those roles which locate them at extremes: they personify spotless
innocence, or else essential wickedness; either Snow White or the
Wicked Queen.

As far as Myra Hindley is concerned, it seems as if the Queen is
taking over from Snow White. If Deane Potter conceptualized her as
the evil genius who persuaded Brady to act out his desires, others
perceive her as an actor in her own right. In a recent interview,
Mrs Ann West, the mother of moors victim Lesley Ann Downey said,
'In my own mind it was Hindley who took my Lesley's life, and if she
were released today, nobody's little girl would be safe.'[40] On the face
of it, this sentiment is somewhat surprising: going entirely against the
cultural grain, it casts Hindley, not Brady, as the insatiable sex beast,
whereas whatever we make of Hindley's behaviour, it is scarcely *more*
likely that she killed the children. Yet Mrs West is not alone in feeling
far more hatred for Hindley than for Brady; since the couple went to
prison more than twenty years ago, it is Hindley who has come to
personify the essence of their evil.

This may well have something to do with Hindley's efforts to obtain
parole and the efforts of Lord Longford on her behalf (Brady has said
he does not wish to be released). But it also owes something to the
sexual double standard by which sadism and monstrous behaviour are
judged. Not only are women judged more harshly than men because
the norms are different and more is expected of them, they are also
liable to become easy targets for the general misogyny which pervades
the whole culture. Ironically, the disproportionate and irrational
loathing with which Myra Hindley is widely regarded may be analysed
as stemming from a similar set of attitudes toward women as those
which we detect in so many sexual killings.

Whatever Myra Hindley may have thought she was doing, playing
Juliette to Ian Brady's Saint-Fond, the fact of her gender placed

inherent limitations on her capacity to realize transcendence and transgression. The point is graphically illustrated, in fact, by the representations she and Brady produced. Though Hindley was not an unwilling victim — unlike the unfortunate Lesley Ann Downey — she was not the *subject* of the photographs either. On the contrary, she, like Lesley Ann, is the object of Brady's gaze and of Brady's desire. In some of the pictures she is posed to display the marks of Brady's whip on her naked body. In these pictures Myra Hindley confirms the masculine transcendence of her sadist lover.

In the end, Myra Hindley is something of an anomaly. Apparently a puzzling exception to the norm, she is actually interpreted through the usual conventions; rather than provoking new concepts of femininity in the style of the 'Sadeian Woman', her existence is used to confirm ancient female archetypes. Instead of defining a new female identity, Myra Hindley raises problems about the limits of women's selfhood which remain intractable twenty years on.

NECROPHILES: DENNIS NILSEN, THE INCURABLE ROMANTIC

'*Peaceful, pale flesh upon the bed*
Real and beautiful — and dead.'

(from *Monochrome Man: Sad Sketches* by Dennis Nilsen.)

Dennis Nilsen strangled to death sixteen young men between 1978 and 1983. He disposed of their bodies as best he could — by burying them in the garden of his London flat, or cutting them up and putting them in refuse sacks, or down the toilet, or boiling them to reduce them to bones. Eventually he was caught because the drains of his house were blocked, with what turned out to be human remains.

Both the necrophiles we discuss in this chapter, Dennis Nilsen and John Christie (who was executed in 1953 having murdered six women whose bodies were subsequently discovered in his house and garden) are different from the prostitute-killers, sadists and serial murderers, because of the significance of the site of their deeds in the popular imagination. Our horror at what they did is measured by the horror of their houses. The appalled fascination of the public, and of the journalists and authors who tell us all about it, is with the perennial questions of how could they bear it, how could they do it? How could you *live* in a house with dead bodies in every nook and cranny?

Both Christie and Nilsen killed to get a body. Christie had sex with his women victims as soon as they were dead. Nilsen had a longer, more intense and complex relationship with the corpses — he kept the body of one boy under the floorboards for about two weeks, periodically taking it up, sitting it in a chair beside him while he watched television, caressing it, bathing it, talking to it and having sex with it. Christie was in fact usually in more of a panic to hide the bodies of his victims, since for the larger part of his murderous career he was living with his wife (he eventually killed her about a year before he was finally arrested). Nilsen's solitary domestic arrangements made his erotic and sensuous relationship with the corpses possible.

But what, apart from these banal facts about their respective domestic lives, can throw light on what these men did? We are going to focus on Nilsen rather than Christie here, because Brian Masters's book, *Killing for Company*, includes long extracts of Nilsen's own writings about himself. While on remand awaiting trial, Nilsen wrote long letters to Masters every day and filled fifty prison notebooks with reminiscences, poetry and other notes, in an attempt to reach some satisfactory account of his actions and emotions. Our information about Christie is much less vivid: it comes mainly from Ludovic Kennedy's book *Ten Rillington Place*, which was written to protest the innocence of Timothy Evans, hanged in 1950 for the murder of his wife and baby who had actually been killed by Christie. Kennedy naturally pays little attention to the meaning of the killings to Christie himself.

Nevertheless, both biographers follow the convention of beginning at the beginning — with their subjects' childhoods. We learn that both Christie and Nilsen had a particular sort of childhood experience, connected with the loss of a beloved grandfather. When Nilsen was five and when Christie was eight, they were shown the bodies of their grandfathers. Christie, who had been rather in awe of his grandfather, experienced a great feeling of serenity and pleasure.[41] Nilsen felt a mysterious excitement and was silently confused by his grandfather's failure to reawaken.[42] Both Kennedy and Masters tell us that these deaths left the little boys to be brought up in households full of dominant women.[43]

Both biographers hedge their bets, though. These childhood traumas are reported, and the ritual comments about 'dominant women' made seemingly wholly because it is conventional to do so. Explanations of enormities like necrophilia more or less *have to* be psychological explanations. But Kennedy's subsequent account takes it for granted that Christie was really a *wicked* man; the key to his behaviour is sin, not sickness; he is possessed of a measure of evil that is beyond the understanding of science.

In an article for *The Observer*, Brian Masters too discusses his worries that Nilsen's evil might be contagious; that he, Masters, might be contaminated. Evil works in ways, we know not how, that are beyond rational knowledge. When Nilsen gave Masters the contents of his flat — the television, kitchen equipment and so on — he wondered, 'Could the proximity of these objects exert some fearful influence? The idea seemed preposterous, yet the reaction in some of my friends proved that it touched a chord somewhere beyond logic. My doctor cannot bear to talk about the subject, so uneasy does it make him.'[44] The scientific monopoly on the explanation of human behaviour is not, in practice, absolute; Freud's axiom that it is the child who is father to the man is in the end considered less than compelling, despite the gestures Kennedy and Masters make towards it. Pre-scientific notions of 'sin' and 'evil' seem to answer the case much more effectively.

The clash between rational science and metaphysical fundamentalism is also evident in Nilsen's writings about himself. Nilsen's struggle to explain himself, to himself and to Masters, demonstrates precisely why our attempts to construct a coherent account of sex murder would not have been made easier by talking directly to sex-murderers themselves. This kind of contact would not have improved the degree of approximation of our account to 'the truth'. For Nilsen just does not have an account of what he was doing and why. This is not only because of the difficulties of recollection, the way our grasp of the past is always suffused with the present (though this is a very real problem for Nilsen. His accounts tend to be peppered with discrepancies of detail — for example, whether the victim was on the bed or on the floor). More significantly, he has real difficulty in remembering *why* on earth he strangled the man in question and this is not simple failure to recall, as we shall see.

Sometimes he describes his motive in terms of compulsion: 'I could feel the power and the struggles of death — a series of impressions — of the absolute compulsion to *do*, at that moment, suddenly' [Nilsen's own emphasis].[45] At other times he rationalizes his acts by implying that he is putting the victims out of their misery, giving them succour and comfort.[46] Sometimes he talks of feeling detached and distant from his actions: 'I seem not to have participated [in the killings], merely stood by and watched them happen — enacted by two other players — like a central camera',[47] or even experiences himself as a split personality, 'I always covered up for that "inner me" that I loved. . . . He just acted and I had to solve all his problems in the cool light of day.'[48] But sometimes he takes complete responsibility for himself. 'It would not do for me to escape just punishment. I am an irresponsible selfish bastard who deserves everything that is coming to him. Society has a right to call me a cold, mad killer. No other category fits my results.'[49] In the search for an account of himself, Dennis Nilsen takes all our culture's categories, attempts to 'fit them to his results' and finds them all ultimately wanting — for it is clear that the last quote is a despairing one: he does *not* experience himself as a 'cold, mad killer' (a psychopath, in other words), but he has to be something and it might as well be that.

In his dilemma, finding that the language cannot adequately describe what he is and utterly failing to make up what the language lacks, Dennis Nilsen graphically illustrates the extent to which our reality is bounded by discourse. For at the same time that none of our categories 'fits my results', so they all do: they all make sense to us, they all give us a way of understanding Nilsen's acts. The culture has a multiplicity of clichés which can order Nilsen's experience: the split personality, the man driven by an irresistible impulse, the watcher, the man with a mission, the cold, mad killer. Nilsen is bewildered by this array of concepts in a way that Ian Brady, for example, was not: Brady had constructed himself to fit a category, he had chosen a role, learnt his part and performed according to the script. Nilsen was not a self-conscious role-player in this sense, but nevertheless he is a fully-fledged member of our culture, a master of its language and when he 'looks into himself' and tries to contemplate what he has done, he has recourse to *all* and *only these* cultural categories.

All members of our culture have these concepts at our disposal; we generally use them unthinkingly, but nevertheless, when we contemplate our future acts we have to do it through the 'spectacles' of these concepts; when we attempt to interpret what other people are doing we only have these categories to use as a framework; when we look into our pasts we can only organize them into the patterns given by our culture. Of course such categories are not fixed for all time: new ones can come into being (feminism for example has recently introduced new ways of seeing the world). Our intellectual commitments, prejudices and dogmas give us tools for deciding which category is 'the best'. Judging by the sum of his writing, Nilsen did not seriously accept that he was a psychopath, a cold, mad killer. On the other hand, there is one set of organizing categories which is very dominant in his writing, and which has also been identified by us as having particular salience and being particularly helpful in casting light on sex-killing. These organizing categories are the ideas of transcendence and the aesthetic standards which have come down to us via the Romantic and existential movements. They particularly stress the significance of the *gaze*. For us, the most significant of Nilsen's accounts of himself is the account of himself as the one who looks.

We have called Dennis Nilsen 'the incurable romantic'. We intend this in two senses: first, the contemporary sense of the genre of romantic fiction, mostly aimed at women but which permeates all sorts of cultural forms. This genre prizes monogamy; Nilsen suffered from the terrible fear (or knowledge) that his lovers would not stay with him and seems to have had a genuine longing for a steady relationship. 'I remember thinking that because it was morning he would wake up and leave me . . . I remember thinking that I wanted him to stay with me over the New Year whether he wanted to or not.'[50] Nilsen's attachment to the corpses of his victims and especially his descriptions of these relationships, contain many of the motifs of romanticism in this sense: the emphasis on physical beauty, the sensuous sexuality. Just like the hero in a woman's magazine, Nilsen is thrilled to have full ownership and control of a beautiful body.[51] As in a Mills and Boon novel, he sometimes feels that the body is 'far too perfect and beautiful for the pathetic ritual of commonplace sex'; but often his passion gets the better of him.[52]

Secondly, of course, Nilsen's adoration of the *dead* body irresistibly reminds us of the Romantic tradition of the aesthetic value of death and the thrill of the Horrid. 'I worshipped *the art* and the act of death, over and over', he writes (our emphasis).[53] Nilsen had long obtained sexual stimulation from contemplating a depiction of deathly beauty. Before he ever killed, he would use talcum powder, charcoal and pale-blue cosmetics to make his body look like a corpse; he would use cochineal for blood; he would contemplate his death-like figure in a mirror as he lay on his bed; he would fantasize that he was indeed a corpse and that a man digs him up from his grave and masturbates over him.[54] His treatment of real corpses was very like this fantasy — taking the body up from under the floorboards, masturbating. Nilsen would also bathe, powder and make up the bodies, then gaze at them both, Nilsen made up like death beside a real example of death, in the mirror.

Nilsen's own words license us to interpret these acts as acts of self-affirmation: 'I only thought of the sublime pleasure these feelings gave me',[55] or, 'I cared enough about them to kill them. . . . I was engaged primarily in self-destruction . . . I was killing myself only but it was always the bystander who died'[56] and then:

> I did it all for me. Purely selfishly . . . I worshipped the art and
> the act of death, over and over. It's as simple as that . . . I was
> honouring myself . . . I killed them as I would like to be killed
> myself . . . enjoying the extremity of the death act itself. If I did it
> to myself I could only experience it once. If I did it to others I
> could experience the death act over and over again.[57]

Remember Sade's sexual universe in which the objects of desire must be consumed totally, in which 'all passions require victims.' For Sade and his existentialist followers the erotic is transgressive and transgression is erotic. Nilsen the necrophile is the transgressor *par excellence*.

But this is not all Nilsen is; and many of the motifs of sadism are absent from Nilsen's acts (for instance, the abuse of the live person was not central to his pleasure). Nilsen certainly is a transcendent subject by virtue of killing the object of his desire, but further, his subjectivity is affirmed *when he gazes at it*. Nilsen's fantasy life, and later his acts of murder, were not only acts: as he himself says, they were *art*. To begin with, Nilsen contemplated himself as an object, as a representation, using mirrors. Later he powdered and beautified the bodies of his victims, and gazed. He made another representation — himself and the corpse, reflected in the mirror. He took photographs of the corpses with a polaroid camera, and made drawings of them, some of which are reproduced in Masters's book.

Many readers will protest that this only shows how unfortunate it is that some people, like Nilsen, cannot keep fantasy and reality distinct. This is Brian Masters's view.[58] Representations should not and in the normal course of events do not, have anything to do with 'reality'. From this it follows that criticism of representations (for example, feminist criticisms of pornography) are misguided and irrelevant, as well as tending unacceptably toward censorship and judgements about what people may or may not read and see. But Susanne Kappeler has recently argued that 'reality' and 'representations' are not as easily distinguishable as this sort of argument implies.[59] We want to explore this argument in relation to Nilsen and other sex-murderers now.

Kappeler argues that far from being 'nothing to do with reality' representations are *produced* and that production is a human activity which takes place in the social world, the realm of reality. We can take an example that has nothing to do with the pornography/censorship debate: it comes from John Berger's classic *Ways of Seeing*. Berger points out that the production of a portrait in oils in the eighteenth century, which might typically 'represent' a bourgeois or aristocratic man with his wife, children, livestock, *objets d'art* and land, *both* relies on the prior existence of a certain social structure — a certain distribution of wealth and valorization of particular life-styles — before it can be understood, *and* confirms that social structure, distribution and evaluation.[60]

A contemporary pornographer, in order to produce a photograph for a magazine, must already be in a certain working relationship with a model (payer/payee, director/directed). This unequal relationship is presupposed in the production process, just as any manufacturer is able to act on the material of his trade. But then, the product itself, the pornographic image, the manufactured article serves to confirm that relationship between producer and produced, man and woman, subject and object.

In this sense, Nilsen is like the producer. When his gaze rests on the bathed and powdered corpse of a boy it is resting on an image which he has manufactured. This image is part of reality in exactly the same way as the mirror-image of himself and the corpse lying on the bed (another image on which Nilsen's gaze rested often). Are these more real than the polaroid photograph he might gaze at later? Clearly not, if we take into account the process by which that image is produced. The production of the body, the mirror-image and the photograph all presuppose a social relationship, namely that between murderer and murdered, producer and produced, subject and object.

In his sexual life, Nilsen is the Subject of the gaze, he is the looker.

Whatever he looks at has been constructed by him; what he looks at is his Object, his fantasy. There is no 'reality' of Dennis Nilsen's sexuality which is distinct from his 'fantasy': he didn't slip, by accident, from one to the other, or merely confuse the two. Rather it is erotic, in Dennis Nilsen's world, to look at an Object, a representation. In looking, one is Master of all one surveys.

Nilsen's aesthetic standards are those of the Gothic, and although this is still highly significant in our culture, it makes him slightly less easy for many of us to understand. But his ideas of the Beautiful are not the point. When Nilsen looks at a mirror-image, or a 'real' dead body, or a photograph, they are all equally representations. (The prostitute on the Bradford street, we might add, is as much a representation as the model in the centre of Peter Sutcliffe's copy of *Mayfair*. The prostitute has been produced, or produced herself, as a saleable commodity, as the sort of thing she knows male punters fantasize about.) Body, mirror-image, photograph. Representations. Objects. Nilsen, the gazer, is in his own words 'near himself and distant/he is the cameo who activates.'[61] The producer of images, the Subject of representations, is a powerful actor in the real world. And the question is: *who* produces the representations in our culture? Who is the looker? The archetypal gaze is the male gaze, and it is only by paying attention to gender that we can make any sense of what acts like Nilsen's mean.

NORTH AMERICAN SERIAL KILLERS: GETTING THEIR KICKS ON ROUTE 66

If the fate of twentieth century man is to live with death . . . why then the only life-giving answer is to accept the terms of death, to live with death as immediate danger, to divorce oneself from society, to exist without roots, to set out on that uncharted journey into the rebellious imperatives of the self. In short . . . the decision is to encourage the psychopath in oneself, to explore that domain of experience where security is boredom and therefore sickness, and one exists in the present, in that enormous present which is without past or future . . . It is this adoration of the present which contains the affirmation of Hip . . .

(Normal Mailer, 'The White Negro' [1957].)

Once I've done it, I just forget it.

(Henry Lee Lucas, serial killer [1985].)

Around the mid-1970s, police departments in the United States began to be aware of an alarming trend which had either not existed or not been noticed before. This was the rise of the 'serial killer', the man who roams round the vastness of North America raping, killing and torturing people in their scores and even hundreds. Theodore ('Ted') Bundy is thought to have murdered thirty-six women; he himself puts the figure higher, but refuses to reveal it. Henry Lee Lucas has confessed to killing between 200 and 360 people.

Serial killing is an interesting example of a new category being created by discourse about it, since on the face of things, many of the men now referred to as serial killers are not much different from the mass-murderers of the past. Though the spate of books, articles and television documentaries about it stress its 'random' or 'motiveless' quality, closer scrutiny of the phenomenon reveals serial killing to be a variant on sexual murder: all the perpetrators without exception have been men, they have tended to kill their sexual objects (thus a majority of victims have been women, with a sprinkling of men killed by homosexual murderers and a fair number of children of both sexes) and the killings have regularly included such features as sexual assault, rape, torture and mutilation.

Despite the depressing familiarity of this scenario, it is being talked about in North America as if it were something entirely novel. The Federal Bureau of Investigation (FBI) has set up a 'behavioural sciences unit' which constructs personality profiles of the serial killer, profiles that are intended to help police investigations. Predictably, they bear an uncanny resemblance to the sex-murderer stereotypes of the 'hero' and the 'deviant' and are especially interesting as a shining example of the utter vacuity of so-called scientific descriptions in this field.

Very detailed insights into the FBI's practice are provided by a 1984 television documentary entitled 'No Apparent Motive'. The title of this programme emphasizes the apparent random nature of serial killing and the resultant bewilderment of law officers attempting to find a murderer who might be anyone, might be anywhere on the continent and might kill again at any moment. In an attempt to narrow the field, the FBI convene a case conference attended by agents, police and psychiatric assessors. Agent Bob Resler opens the proceedings by explaining the purpose of this kind of meeting: 'Give me a specific case to look at, let me do an assessment of that case and

I'll tell you what category of person would do that kind of crime.' North Carolina police present him with a 'lust murder' case in which the victim's breasts and genitals have been 'assaulted' and a bottle rammed into the vagina. Her body has been dumped a short distance from a dirt road, although a hundred yards further on is a fast-flowing river. Resler begins by 'pinpointing the sort of person they are looking for': 'a person [*sic*] who might have animosity against women in some way'. Unfortunately, his further remarks are singularly unhelpful. He tells the (presumably amazed) local police, 'I think what you're dealing with here is a serial murderer, a man who is to commit a crime like this definitely would have been involved in crimes in the past, and in all probability will be involved in crimes like this in the future.' The dumping of the body by the road tells Resler that:

> What I'm looking at here is perhaps a guy who doesn't care, he doesn't care if the body's found there, furthermore he wants it to be found there, and he's taunting the police. I'm also wondering if our subject, he's one of those people who's well integrated into society, who's respected and er who may be uh not a likely suspect as far as neighbours are concerned. . . . In the case of many of these individuals they lead a kind of secret life, in the sense that they and they alone know what they may be doing and yet they live an apparently rather normal life when they're not doing the criminal activity. . . . A person who commits a series of twenty or thirty murders frequently is going to be a very nice guy, to talk to, to deal with, and they're not gonna be abnormal.

A psychiatrist adds:

> Most of them are very normal and very friendly, uh that you maybe went into a pub to have a drink, an you'd sit there and talk to him and he'd all of a sudden become one of your good friends, you can't look at him and tell that this is something strange about him, they're very normal.

Under the guise of telling us something *scientific* ('these psychological profiles which often prove to be right on target') this FBI case conference merely restates the clichés with which it began, namely that serial murderers could be anyone at all and are quite indistinguishable from ordinary people.

The FBI clearly recognizes, despite the language of 'persons', that serial killers are *men*, but the discourse of serial murder downplays the gender factor, perhaps because commentators prefer to stress the meaninglessness of the crime, relating this to what is seen as the increasing alienation of the individual from society, especially modern North American society.

The serial killer is definitely an all-American phenomenon. This is not just because other cultures have not encountered mass-killing on such a scale, or even because they have not developed a discourse about it (as we have said, many serial murderers are highly analogous to mass-murderers of the familiar kind: an often-cited example, the 'Green River Killer' is actually a 'Ripper' with a tally of victims not much larger than Sutcliffe's). The real reason why the concept of serial murder has arisen in North America and not elsewhere is its dependence on a certain representation of North America itself, its culture, its symbols, its heroes. The serial killer, as we shall shortly argue, is the American counterpart of Genet's or Wilson's existential rebel.

Many criminologists and sociologists have attempted to link serial murder with the culture in which it occurs, but they usually overlook the question of the representations that culture makes available, concentrating instead on more material factors. One thing that is often mentioned is the sheer size of the United States and the geographical mobility of its population. According to one senior police officer, this is the key to why serial killers are able to kill so many people:

> Let's say you take an early flight from New York to Chicago, pick a stranger off the streets, take another plane to Boston, kill someone else there and then fly back to New York. You could be watching the late show at home before the cops in either of those cities even know that anyone is missing.[62]

But this hardly explains why the killer *wants* to kill so many people. The mere existence of a road as long as Interstate Highway 5 from California to Washington State does not in itself solve the problem of why the 'I-5 Killer', Randall Woodfield, drove tens of thousands of miles up and down that road, deliberately looking for people to murder. The careers of men like Woodfield and Lucas suggest that quantity of victims is important to some serial killers in a way it has not always been to all mass sexual murderers.

In an attempt to answer the question of motivation, some sociologists relate serial killing to the frustrations caused by an open society, where the 'American dream' of success and prosperity is meant to be attainable by anyone who works for it. In fact, the dream is an ideological fiction: North American society is not really open, but the idea it is makes its failures doubly frustrated, with an anger that often turns to destructiveness and violence. Serial killers are trying to 'be someone' — to attain the place in people's esteem that society has denied them. (On the other hand, as Bob Resler would surely tell us, a lot of serial killers are 'well integrated into society'.)

It is also pointed out how 'anomic' North American society is — that is, how it lacks that sense of community which preserves strict norms of conduct. Some serial killers are apparently without any roots in the community at all, merely drifting about on the fringes of society (as are a significant proportion of their victims). Again this would not be true of all those labelled serial killers, but someone like Henry Lee Lucas would fit the theory. Lucas and his partner Otis Toole wandered aimlessly across the United States for some eight years, killing. One could hardly speak of this as these men's 'secret life': for almost a decade it *was* their life, period.

But if serial killing is connected to these conditions of life in the United States — mobility across vast spaces, frustration, anomie — it is also very particularly connected with the manifestation of these conditions and their glorification in certain products of the culture. The aimless odysseys of a Lucas or a Woodfield recall nothing so much as the 'road' narratives of the 1950s 'Beat generation', who expressed their outlook in books, films and music, becoming an attractive and alternative culture, a way of thinking about life in the modern United States. 'Road' fictions celebrate the vast spaces of the continent, being on the move but without any ultimate goal; they also celebrate a masculine ethos of sexual conquest and random violence, rather akin to the ethic and aesthetic of the French existentialists we examined in chapter 2, but with a definite and distinctive American flavour.

It is therefore with the greatest interest that we reread, in the era of the serial killer, a 1957 essay by Norman Mailer, 'The White Negro'. This is a highly articulated expression of a quasi-existentialist 'Hip' philosophy and it overtly celebrates the murderer as a hero and social catalyst. In the remainder of our discussion of serial murder, we want to examine Mailer's essay in some detail.

'The White Negro' is about 'Hip', a 1950s subculture with its roots and its most important characteristic markers (jazz, language, marijuana smoking) in Black American culture. It was, however, adopted by white youth as a style and an outlook; what Mailer advocates in his polemical essay is precisely this rebellion of what he calls 'the white negro'.

Mailer invites us to admire hip for its combination of transcendence and transgression. He argues that the hipster emerged along with the stifling conformity of the post-war period in the United States and for the same reason: because the dual holocaust of the Nazi death-camps and Hiroshima had undermined the certainties of white America and made it aware it was living on the edge of death. But whereas most of the culture retreated into fear, becoming a lumpen, objectified mass, the hipster adopted the way of the Black, and embraced the possibilities of death by courting danger, living in the present, tearing up roots, challenging morality. Choosing, in other words, to *Be*, in the special sense given to that term by existentialism. To be an existentialist, Mailer remarks, 'One must know one's desires, one's rages, one's anguish, one must be aware of the character of one's frustration and know what would satisfy it.'[63]

The hipster, according to Mailer, is just such an existentialist, but he is also akin to the psychopath, the madman whose disorder consists precisely in the fact that he lives entirely in the present and gratifies his desires at whatever violent cost. In his 'search for an orgasm more apocalyptic than the one which preceded it'[64] the psychopath 'knows instinctively that to express a forbidden impulse actively is far more beneficial to him than merely to confess desire in the safety of a doctor's office'.[65] He is like the existentialist but he makes his desires real.

In this argument, Mailer ingeniously marries our two discourses of hero and deviant and not just by using a figure of speech. He is arguing for two connected propositions. The first is that we should regard the psychopathic deviant as a hero, because he dares transgress in the real world. Mailer even goes so far as to defend 'the murder of a candy-store owner by two hoodlums' on this sort of ground:

> One murders not only a weak 50-year old man but an institution as well, one violates private property, one enters into a new relation with the police and introduces a dangerous element into one's life. The hoodlum is therefore daring the unknown, and so no matter how brutal the act, it is not altogether cowardly.[66]

Apparently it is by the criterion of cowardice versus daring that acts of violence are to be judged.

Mailer's second proposition is that when a society is as conformist as the one in which Hip arose, a hero becomes, by definition, a deviant: his heroic qualities are totally abnormal in a community made up of faceless, cringing objects. Only the psychopath/existentialist, the hero, deviant and rebel rolled into one, can possibly save North American society, for he 'extrapolates from his own condition, from the inner certainty that his rebellion is just, a radical view of the universe which thus separates him from the general ignorance, reactionary prejudice and self-doubt of the more conventional psychopath.'[67]

The sort of figure who is celebrated in Mailer's essay — cool, hip and psychopathic — has in fact become a touchstone of American masculinity. He is an up-to-date exemplar of the 'outlaw' tradition which appears in a variety of representations of North America. The serial killer too is a transformation of the traditional loner on his unending journey, a perverse incarnation of the 'Man with no Name'. Traditional North American individualism sorts well with the existentialist theme of the free man's right to transcend ordinary constraints on behaviour. As Norman Collins, killer of seven women in Michigan wrote in a college essay:

> If a person wants something, he alone is the deciding factor of whether or not to take it — regardless of what society thinks may be right or wrong. . . . It's the same if a person holds a gun on somebody — it's up to him to decide whether to take the other's life or not. The point is: it's not society's judgement that's important but the individual's own choice of will and intellect.[68]

It is a mark of the familiarity of this kind of sentiment that the professor who graded the paper in which these words were written, later said that Collins had always seemed 'completely normal'.

Sexual murder has become the practice of surprisingly many 'completely normal' men, raised as they are in a Western culture whose discourse, from the popular to the highly intellectual, urges upon them what Norman Mailer called 'the rebellious imperatives of the self'. How and why has this come to be? Why is the self in question always a male self? What would constitute a feminist critique of the sorts of assumptions in Mailer's essay? These are the questions we take up, finally, in our concluding chapter.

The Murderer as Misogynist?

The power of men is first a metaphysical assertion of self, an I am *that exists a priori, absolute, no embellishment or apology required, indifferent to denial or challenge. . . . This self is not merely subjectively felt. It is protected by laws and customs, proclaimed in art and in literature, documented in history, upheld by the distribution of wealth. This self cannot be eradicated or reduced to nothing. It is. When the subjective sense of self falters, institutions devoted to its maintenance buoy it up.*

The first tenet of male-supremacist ideology is that men have this self and women must, by definition, lack it. Male self . . . is entitled to take what it wants to sustain or improve itself, to have anything, to requite any need at any cost. . . . The self is the conviction, beyond reason or scrutiny, that there is an equation between what one wants and the fact that one is.

(Andrea Dworkin, *Pornography* [1981].)

We have proposed that there are two kinds of discourses about the sexual murderer. There is a 'cultural' discourse in which he is a hero, at the centre of literary and philosophical celebration; and there is a 'scientific' discourse in which he is a deviant. There is a flaw in both these accounts, however: they overlook the highly salient issue of how sexual murder is structured by gender. Sexual murderers are, as it turns out, men who murder the objects of their desire. None of the discourses we have considered have a satisfactory explanation of this and some of them fail to acknowledge it at all.

To a feminist, by contrast, the maleness of sex-killers is immediately visible and highly significant. The last two decades of feminist activity have made available a conceptual framework in which this maleness seems almost inevitable. Its central notion is that of 'male violence' or 'violence against women'.

SEXUAL MURDER AS VIOLENCE AGAINST WOMEN

Male violence against women is defined broadly by feminists to include not just the most obvious abuses — rape, wife-battering and incest for instance — but also and importantly, a range of male behaviours that have often been dismissed as mere routine minor nuisances, like flashing, stealing underwear and making obscene phone-calls. Feminist analysis puts these various things together for two reasons.

First, they all enact very similar assumptions about male sexuality and women's relation to it. They say that men need and feel entitled to have, unrestricted sexual access to women, even — sometimes especially — against women's will. They say that men's sexuality is aggressive and predatory. Superficially, flashing is quite different from rape, yet from the point of view of their function they are surprisingly similar: both are acts which men do in order to reassure themselves of their power and potency; both include, as a crucial factor in that reassurance, the fear and humiliation of the female victims.

Secondly, the myriad manifestations of male violence collectively function as a threat to women's autonomy. They undermine our self-esteem and limit our freedom of action — not only must we all live with the fear of sexual violence, society makes it our own responsibility to prevent it. If the worst does happen we may be blamed, not protected; our suffering will be trivialized, questioned or ignored. Thus a powerful incentive exists for us to police our own behaviour and acquiesce in the idea that men's sexuality is 'naturally' predatory, only to be contained by female circumspection.

These facts have led feminists to locate male violence against women in the realm of the *political*. It expresses not purely individual anger and frustration but a collective, culturally sanctioned misogyny which is important in maintaining the collective power of men. We can extent to all forms of male violence the phrase that is often used specifically about rape: 'an act of sexual terrorism'.

Is sex murder also a form of sexual terrorism? Certainly, we believe it can be given a partial analysis in those terms. It is relatively easy to see killing as male violence taken to its logical extreme, where humiliation becomes annihilation. Death is the ultimate negation of autonomy, and the kind of death inflicted by many sexual killers —

the ripped breasts and genitals, the wombs torn out — is the ultimate violation of the female sex and body.

'Sexual terrorism', moreover, is a very apt description of the effect of sexual murder on the female population. A generalized fear of the lurking sex beast is instilled in women from their early years; it is death we fear, just as much as rape, and sadistic killers haunt our very worst nightmares. When a multiple killer is at large in our communities, we often end up living in a state of siege. Nicole Ward Jouve describes Yorkshire, her home, in the period of Peter Sutcliffe's 'reign of terror': 'Yorkshire Universities organized relays of buses and cars to see all female students home at night, and you didn't dare let your daughter go to the fair or even cross the village street in the dark.'[1] She also describes her feelings as a woman:

> One of the worst things about the panic that had set in was that, instead of feeling self-righteous, as you should have done if the high tone of indignation of the papers was anything to go by, you felt . . . guilty. Apologetic. About going out in the dark. About wearing attractive clothes. Being out in the streets. Almost, about being a woman. Being a woman meant that you were murderable, and it was wrong of you so to be. In order to make up for it, you had to be specially good. Stay indoors. Not wander away from the protective side of a man: your man. For no other was safe and perhaps even he?[2]

These descriptions recall the words of Susan Brownmiller in *Against Our Will*, her study of rape, when she refers to it as a process of intimidation whereby all men keep all women in a state of fear: an institution. All men, because any man could have been the killer. An institution, because not only Sutcliffe but the whole weight of the culture colluded in the terror that affected women's existence in the North of England: the police who insisted we stay off the streets, the commentators who so callously devalued the lives of prostitutes, the football crowds who chanted and made jokes about the Ripper, those men, who under cover of protecting frightened women found a golden opportunity to threaten and assault us. The killer even invaded our private thoughts and dreams, as Nicole Ward Jouve makes clear in her account of her own nightmares:

A few nights later I saw him again. He was with a group of people I was quite happily going to join. He could not move, that is, he could not leave them. As soon as I saw he was there I tried to retrace my steps, creep out unnoticed, but before I was far enough, he turned his eyes and looked at me. His glance was terrifyingly blue. I woke up bathed in sweat.[3]

Terrorism: the rule of fear. Violence against women: the law of misogyny. No account of sexual murder could possibly be adequate which did not point out how perfectly the lust to kill exemplifies both.

Yet it is equally true that no account of sex murder could possibly be adequate if it ended there. There is more to sexual killing than misogyny and terror; and if this seems like a rather unorthodox conclusion, we can only reply that in the course of our research we were forced, despite initial resistance, to draw it.

SEXUAL MURDER AS MASCULINE TRANSCENDENCE

Feminists have written little specifically about sexual murder and what they have written tends to focus on specific cases; as far as we know, there is no other feminist study of sexual killing as a general phenomenon. And this is probably an important reason why feminists tend to identify sex murder as another, extreme form of violence against women, motivated (like rape, only more so) by misogyny. We have already explained that we agree with this view — but only up to a point. It can only be a partial, incomplete account, for if one examines sexual killers *as a group*, it is evident misogyny is not their only motive and indeed that not all are engaged in violence *against women*. Let us take these two points one at a time.

To begin with, the point that many sexual killers have desires and motivations that cannot be analysed as merely or exclusively misogynistic. This takes us back to the quest for transcendence and the way in which murder has been used as an act of self-affirmation. To be sure, this may be mixed up with hatred for the victim, but often 'transcendence' is the dominant theme. We have cited a number of instances already: the 'Napoleonic' complex of Ian Brady, the quest for identity of Ronald Frank Cooper, the conscious experimentation of Kürten, the desire for fame of the serial killer. None of these examples can be analysed convincingly as expressions of woman-hatred pure and simple.

Some of them, moreover, as not easily analysed as expressions of misogyny at all, for the simple reason that their victims were not women. From the start of our research we have had to take seriously the existence of killers whose victims are *men*. We did initially consider the possibility that such killers were a totally different breed, but this idea did not stand up to scrutiny, since we found that men who murdered other men or boys were quite strikingly similar to those who murdered women. Furthermore, they fitted neatly into our definition of sex-killers as men who murder their objects of desire — the only difference being that their desires were homosexual ones.

Does homosexual murder present special problems for our thesis? Certainly, it does not challenge the generalization that sex-killers are male (like other women, lesbians have killed for motives of jealousy and revenge, but there has never been a lesbian Nilsen or Cooper). But it does challenge any simple equation of sex murder with violence against women.

If in this last remark we seem to be stating the obvious, it must be borne in mind that for many psychoanalytically oriented writers, homosexual sex murder *is* directed against a woman. Like all sexual murder, it is really an act of revenge against the mother and male victims must therefore be analysed as symbolic woman-substitutes. We find this line of argument less than compelling, deriving as it does from an unquestioned assumption that homosexuality is nothing more than a distorted or pathological heterosexuality and that all sexual objects are by definition 'female'.

We can surely accommodate the striking resemblance between heterosexual and homosexual sex-murderers without pretending they are one and the same. Rather, what we need is a 'common denominator' which connects sexual killings of women and of men. Instead of focusing on the gender of the victim, we must look at what does not vary — the gender of the *killer*. The common denominator is not misogyny, it is a shared construction of masculine sexuality, or even more broadly, masculinity in general. It is under the banner of masculinity that all the main themes of sexual killing come together: misogyny, transcendence, sadistic sexuality, the basic ingredients of the lust to kill.

What is it, then, about masculinity that permits the emergence of these fatal themes? We believe the answer lies in the combination of two factors: first, the way that men have historically been defined as social and sexual subjects, and secondly, the particular notion of subjectivity that has been developed in Western culture. Let us take each of these factors in turn.

That Western thought has defined men as Subjects is often asserted, but it needs to be explained. After all, a philosophically-minded sceptic might enquire, are not all human beings by definition subjects? Is this not the measure of what being human *is*? If so, surely women too possess subjectivity; it cannot be part of masculinity *per se*. In one sense the sceptic would be perfectly correct, for women like men are conscious actors in the world. Nevertheless, gender does make a difference. Although both men and women may be subjects in virtue of their shared humanity, culturally it is men who stand at the centre of the universe. As Andrea Dworkin observes, the male subject is 'protected in laws and customs, proclaimed in art and in literature, documented in history, upheld in the distribution of wealth . . . when the subjective sense of self falters, institutions devoted to its maintenance buoy it up'.[4] Lacking these supports in social institutions and representations, women's subjectivity can easily slip away. Furthermore, in order to protect the centrality of the male subject, the not-male, the female, are defined by the culture as Other, objects. Thus subjectivity is at the heart of men's existence, whereas women's subject status is constantly being negated. Being treated as an object is a threat to male being in a way it can never be a threat to female.

Andrea Dworkin also points out that the importance of male self is part of male power. It is hard to challenge what she refers to as 'an *I am* that exists a priori, absolute', inscribed in every corner, every aspect of the culture.[5]

If the subject of Western culture is male, how has this male subjectivity been defined? In chapter 2 'The Murderer as Hero', we explored some constructions of male subjectivity in philosophy and literature from the eighteenth century onward. We picked out in particular the theme of man's *transcendence*, the struggle to free oneself, by a conscious act of will, from the material constraints which normally determine human destiny.

In fact, this theme has always been important in the Western philosophical tradition. 'Man' has been seen as a subject engaged in a struggle to master and subdue his object, nature, to know and act upon it (upon *her*, of course, in traditional parlance). This view is reflected in many ancient myths: the story of Prometheus who stole fire from the gods, of Faust and Satan, the overreachers, of quest narratives like the romance of the Holy Grail. Interestingly, myths about female seekers after knowledge, such as Eve and Pandora, have a different significance. Rather than being admired as tragic heroes and admitted to the category of transcendent subjects, these women are depicted as wicked or stupid, their feminine curiosity bringing nothing but trouble.

In the eighteenth century, however — the age of 'enlightenment' — Western philosophy came to understand man himself as an object, a part of nature and a proper object for scientific study. But this recognition of man's objectivity brought into sharper focus his striving for subjectivity. Many philosophers grappled with the problem of subjectivity. David Hume, the empiricist and sceptic, concluded that the 'self' was only an illusion.[6] Immanuel Kant insistently wrote the self back in, arguing that we cannot have objectivity without subjectivity and vice versa.[7] With Hegel and Nietzsche, transcendence of the body and bodily consciousness becomes a matter of overcoming the other — the overcoming of objectivity and the attainment of freedom and power. But one thing all these thinkers have in common is their conflation of the Subject with the masculine subject, 'Man'. Transcendence has therefore come to be seen both as the project of the masculine and the sign of masculinity.[8]

Since sexuality does not stand apart from the rest of culture, these themes have been echoed in erotic practice and in the definition of masculine sexuality. The motifs of that sexuality are *performance, penetration, conquest.* In the writings of Sade and his later admirers, the quest for transcendence is explicitly eroticized. Sexual acts and desires that transgress social or religious norms are redefined as inherently forms of transcendence, thus becoming the source of both power and pleasure, and paving the way for that male sexual sadism which becomes, at its most extreme, the lust to kill.

According to this argument, the lust to kill arose as part of a particular historical process, a transformation of sexual desire. In the remainder of this concluding chapter, we want to focus on the possibilities for further transformation of our culture's sexual practice. Sexual murder once did not exist: will there be a time when it no longer exists? How can feminists intervene effectively in the cause of a different, less destructive desire? Should this, in fact, be a goal of feminism?

We are asking these questions at a time when sexual practice is a highly contested topic among feminists; at a time, indeed, when the ideas we have been talking about, the ideas of transcendent subjectivity and sexuality, are entering a new phase as they come into contact with feminist analysis and feminist practice.

FEMINISM, THE SUBJECT AND SEXUALITY

As we have pointed out elsewhere in this book, one of modern feminism's crucial assertions is that women under patriarchy are denied their subjectivity. Men are the subjects, women the objects. Simone de Beauvoir, in her ground-breaking *The Second Sex*, declared that for women to become fully human we would need to attain the transcendent subjectivity which has been the historical prerogative of men.[9] Her analysis is echoed by feminists today, especially the influential Lacanian tendency. Many of these theorists argue that transcendence and subjecthood are not inherently masculine characteristics: it is language and culture that lead us to think so, but this error of 'essentialism' must be 'deconstructed'. Then, we can aspire to the transcendent subjectivity which makes us men's equals as full human beings.

The struggle to be subject is played out in many fields, but readers will not be surprised to learn that one key site of struggle is the field of sexuality. Sexuality has been a major issue for the Women's Liberation Movement since its inception and has recently assumed a new importance and urgency. We have alluded several times to the feminist critique of male sexual violence, well established and familiar now for more than a decade. But it must also be said that in certain areas — the most obvious controversy being about pornography — the critique has not gone uncontested by feminists. Against the contention that heterosexual practice is abusive and misogynist, certain feminists have posed the awkward question, 'Yes, but what about the pleasure we get from it? What about our desire for sexual expression?' This question implicitly raises the whole issue of women's aspirations to sexual subjecthood.

Various writers, lesbian as well as heterosexual, have pointed out that women's desires are not automatically for egalitarian 'caring' sexual relationships: female fantasies are not all sexual sweetness and light. Recently, women have begun to speak out frankly about the connection many make between 'pleasure and danger' (which is, incidentally, the title of an anthology from a conference on sexuality at Barnard University in 1982).[10] Among the topics debated and polemicized are pornography, sado-masochism (especially lesbian S/M), butch/femme roles among lesbians and adult—child sex. Willingness to support and engage in these practices is sometimes referred to as being 'pro-pleasure' and we will use that term for a particular current in present-day feminism (despite our own resistance to the obvious implication that those who disagree are in some sense 'anti-pleasure').

'Pro-pleasure' feminists argue that women have been denied their 'right' to an autonomous sexuality. We must stress again that this idea is by no means peculiar to them, it is pretty much an axiom of the modern Women's Liberation Movement and the right to express one's sexuality freely was one of the British movement's seven demands. The underlying analysis is a variant on Simone de Beauvoir's general thesis: under patriarchy, women's sexuality has only been permitted very limited expression, in accordance with male desire and not women's own. Rather than being autonomous *subjects*, women have been defined and treated as sexual *objects*; insofar as our desires were given any attention they were constructed essentially as masochistic and passive. One of feminism's projects, therefore, is to reclaim for women an *active* sexuality, defined autonomously by women's own desires and making women into sexual subjects. In our culture, one outcome is the emergence of female *sadists* and this requires us to pursue the 'pro-pleasure' argument further.

Sexual subjecthood and freedom for women is usually taken by 'pro-pleasure' feminists as involving not the construction of *new* desires, but the exploration of desires that are already there and have merely been suppressed by patriarchal imperatives, or moulded into acceptable forms (such as masochism and passivity). This gives an extra dimension to the argument that things like pornography and sado-masochism are valid: not only do they tend to the attainment of transcendence, they are in the final analysis, *natural*.

In the writings of the more thoughtful 'pro-pleasure' theorists the rationale for this naturalness claim is often couched in psychoanalytic terms. A much-cited example is Jessica Benjamin's article 'Master and Slave: The Fantasy of Erotic Domination',[11] an analysis of the pornographic fiction *The Story of O*. Benjamin believes that this fiction is erotic for both sexes because it resonates with sado-masochistic fantasies that develop in infancy and are common to all of us. We all have an erotic relationship with our first love-object, the mother, which incorporates two contradictory elements, each of them represented in fantasy. As Rosalind Coward explains:

> One is a fantasy of the all-powerful mother who will do everything for the child, control it and never let go. Should this 'really' happen the child would in effect be destroyed since it would never become autonomous. The other fantasy is of the child's omnipotence. It can demand everything of the mother, get everything from her, abolish the separation between them. Again, if this should actually succeed it would be disastrous since the mother would metaphorically disappear and the child would feel abandoned.[12]

Thus the child both rages against the mother, fantasizes about destroying her and desires to be controlled by the mother, to the point where the child's own identity is destroyed. The adult reflexes of these fantasies, acted out in sexual practice, are sadism and masochism. Men, through pornography and other practices, are able to explore both these elements in their psyche; women are permitted to explore only their masochism, but if female sexuality is 'given its head', sadistic tendencies will also emerge — and when explored in a 'consensual' sexual scenario, these will surely be a force for the liberation of women.

Marion Bower, in an article called 'Daring to Speak its Name: The Relationship of Women to Pornography' puts a Kleinian gloss on Benjamin's argument and is dedicated to the proposition that 'female sexual sadism exists in its own right'.[13] Melanie Klein believed that babies' sadistic fantasies are products of the death instinct turned defensively on the Other (in infancy therefore, inevitably on the mother). In Klein's young patients these fantasies took oral and anal, as well as genital, forms: children in analysis fantasized about biting or scooping out the mother's breasts, or attacking the mother with corrosive urine and exploding faeces. Bower points out that these infantile fantasies are re-enacted in pornography with extraordinary literalness: not only are excreta and breast-biting common themes, there are also many instances of women being tortured with corrosive liquids, or having their body contents scooped out. She suggests that women reading pornography *recognize* these scenes and are aroused by them, because they draw on a unisex infantile heritage.

So far, then, we have two connected propositions, both increasingly important in feminist debate: that women should pursue an autonomous sexual subjectivity as part of our liberation and secondly, that this entails the acknowledgement and exploration of the suppressed sado-masochism which is present in us all.

We shall have more to say about each of these arguments, since it seems to us that they are seriously flawed in their refusal to consider in sufficient depth the culturally constructed aspects of sexual desire and practice. But before we move on to a critique of the 'pro-pleasure' position, we want to point out that it converges neatly with another very influential discourse of our time. We mean the discourse of 'sexual liberation', spearheaded by libertarian and (mostly male) gay liberation activists and recently gathered under the banner of the 'New Pluralism'. This 'pluralism' is a celebration of all the possibilities for the individual pursuit of pleasure and like 'pro-pleasure' feminism, it believes sexual desire and the pursuit of unfettered transcendence to be natural and liberating. Its adherents have referred to the mushrooming of sexual subcultures as 'a refusal to refuse the body any more',[14] which implies that the body has unchanging desires which however have long clamoured in vain to be heard.

The convergence of these currents, 'pro-pleasure' feminism and sexual liberationist 'pluralism' has produced a formidable lobby on sexuality. Yet we insist that its twin motifs of pluralism and transcendence and the project of sexual liberation it has developed, are highly problematic because they appeal to 'desire' as a bottom line — the analysis begins with existing desires and thereby takes them to be 'natural', immutable and ultimately valid. For feminists, especially, this is a very strange position to take — no feminist would *dream* of saying that women's desire for heterosexual romantic love was natural and valid. On the contrary, feminism takes the individual's sexual and other desires to be constructed socially, and thus susceptible to social revolution.

In modern Western culture sexual desire and practice are socially constructed according to the imperatives of what feminists have called *compulsory heterosexuality*. Radical feminists have two connected lines of attack on the institution of heterosexuality. First, we criticize the ways in which it is enforced: the rewards accruing to the heterosexual — cornucopias of money, jobs, status, public celebrations and religious festivals, and perhaps above all, the knowledge that one is 'normal'. The sanctions preventing lesbianism and homosexuality, on the other hand, are draconian — a lack of all the above, plus physical violence, legal punishment and even death. Secondly, radical feminists point to the ways in which heterosexuality structures a particular sort of society, based on the sexual division of labour, which benefits men as a class far more than it benefits women. The difficulty of breaking out of the heterosexist norm can be seen in the fact that homosexual subcultures do so often feature 'masculine' and 'feminine' role-play, that is, there are pressures for all forms of sexuality to be parasitic upon heterosexist forms.

It is true, as we have observed, that psychoanalysis strongly suggests that certain sorts of desires (sadistic and masochistic ones, the desire to destroy and be destroyed) *are* fundamental to the human condition. Theorists like Jessica Benjamin and Marion Bower point to the tension set up in the human baby's psyche as she rages at the mother for being absent, and, at the same time feels overwhelming dependence on, and love for, the mother. Both these writers take this fact about human infancy to constitute an explanation of sado-masochism, and a sufficient account of the pervasive presence of sadistic and masochistic images in pornography, and the way pornography 'speaks to' both men and women, touching them deeply.

However, there seem to us to be two serious flaws in this analysis. The first concerns the blatant unnaturalness of all adult sexual practice. 'Sadism' and 'masochism' are categories of our *language*: like all linguistic signs, they cannot be taken as unproblematic reflections of experience, and especially not of the chaotic emotions of infancy, before language is acquired. A massive work of cultural transformation is needed before these emotions can be labelled 'love', 'hate', 'rage' and so on, let alone translated into the clear symbolic artifice of sado-masochistic paraphernalia (leather, bondage, rubber fetishism, etc.). How is the transformation achieved? We would argue, by means of representations. And here again, we would take issue with Bower, who argues that male and female readers of pornography *identify* with the sadistic (male) actor. With Susanne Kappeler, we believe that a major component in responses to pornography is the pleasure of *looking*. This is somewhat different from *identifying*. Instead of projecting themself into the image, the looker is outside, *controlling* the image. The effect is to confirm the looker's status as Subject and this is a pleasurable experience in itself (though hardly a natural, infantile one). The naturalness and inevitability of sado-masochism is one of those truisms which does not stand up to closer scrutiny: in a different kind of culture the inchoate experience of infants might well be moulded into something quite different.

This leads us to our second objection. Psychoanalysis notoriously overlooks the extent to which childrearing practices themselves are culturally and historically specific. Infant psychic states — not to mention the interpretation society makes of them — might be very different in a culture with different arrangements (for instance, if more than one person fed and tended the baby).

Feminists must concur with the Freudian notion of the plasticity of the sex drive, even while we criticize Freud for his failure to follow through the social implications of this. But if desires for 'transcendence' and 'pluralism' are not natural and inevitable, we need to ask the question, in what sense might they be *desirable*? Against the sexual liberationists we would answer this question very firmly, 'in *no* sense', for two reasons.

First, transcendent sexuality intrinsically requires unequal relationships. The subject needs an object, the Self needs an Other, the Master needs a Slave. It could, of course, be argued (and is, interminably), that these are merely roles which could be taken on at will by partners in a consensual, erotic situation. But this argument overlooks a second difficulty. Given that we live in a power structure where men are dominant and women are subordinate, which has produced two-thousand years' worth of representations in which this point is hammered home, it hardly seems as if the choice of roles will be freely made by equal partners. On the contrary, who will do what to whom under the new pluralism is depressingly predictable. Many of those involved in current S/M scenes lament the great shortage of female sadists; according to a classic article by Paul Gebhart such women are 'highly prized' in S/M culture.[15] We do not think this is just a coincidence! Without major changes in the power structure, and new possibilities encoded in the culture, 'pluralism' can only mean more of the same.

We ignore the implications of inequality at great cost. Susanne Kappeler takes issue with women and men who argue that what is needed is for women to treat men as sex objects too.[16] She quotes Gloria Leonard, publisher of the soft-core pornographic magazine *High Society*: 'I do a lot for feminism. I show women, and men too, that it's all right to be a sex object. That's part of what being a whole person is all about.' Kappeler comments:

> Under the glorious banner of Equal Opportunities we are likely to finally lose sight of what the critique of patriarchy, of sexism, of the objectification of women in representation is about. . . . Gloria Leonard of *High Society* (an Equal Opportunities Employer) is showing us that it's alright to be a sex object since, look, the men over there are learning to be sex objects too. In the midst of these waves of progress it might be well to go back to the question of what it means to turn a person into an object.[17]

What turning persons into objects is all about, in our culture, is, in the final analysis, killing them. If women do attain this sort of subjectivity then perhaps it will not be many years before this book is hopelessly out of date. The female sex-murderer may well have emerged. She may have killed a male sex-object — although we would be much more prepared to bet that she will have killed a *woman*, as we don't believe that two thousand years of male subjectivity is as easy to undo as Gloria Leonard imagines.

To pluralists and would-be transcendents who say 'I have discovered these desires in myself — you cannot ask me to repress them' we reply, therefore, 'not repress, but question'. Elizabeth Carola, a member of Lesbians Against Sado-Masochism, insists that all of us must challenge and question our own sado-masochism.[18] She does not pretend, as some of the 'pro-pleasure' lobby have misrepresented feminist opponents of pornography and sado-masochism as pretending, that there are some 'right-on' feminists who are *untouched* by either sadistic or masochistic desires. But, she does insist that we look at the social consequences of acting out such desires.

We insist that there can be a vision of the future in which desire will be reconstructed totally. This involves being critical of our sado-masochistic tendencies. We must be suspicious of 'pluralisms' which leave masochism and sadism untransformed; above all, we must be critical of the whole project of transcendence and the subject—object, self—other dichotomies it entails. It also involves, as we have already hinted, a struggle to once and for all overthrow the structures of male power and masculinity, on which transcendence has always in fact been based. In other words, the struggle must go on, but we must add to it an imaginative concern with the future of women and men in our culture. We must aspire to an equal and feminist future in which murder is no longer a metaphor for freedom, in which transcendence is not the only possible self-affirmation and in which the lust to kill has no place.

Appendix
Sex-murderers referred to in the text

Note

We have compiled this appendix for two main reasons. First, we feel there should be some record here of the reality of sex murder, however painful: on one hand, it is easy for academic writing, which is concerned to be properly theoretical and unsensational, to skate over the details of what has actually happened; while on the other, it is commonplace for the popular memory to embroider the details of *causes célèbres* to the point where they become grotesque caricatures. The accounts which follow attempt to set out plainly the known facts of the careers of a number of murderers. The exercise of collating these facts has a function for feminists beyond the mere avoidance of exaggeration and half-truth: it prevents us from forgetting or 'writing out' the victims, both the fact of their suffering and what exactly they have suffered.

Of course, we have had to be selective in our coverage: however desirable it might be to record every instance of sexual murder, to do so would require a volume twice the size of this one. We have therefore confined ourselves to the cases referred to in the text. And this gives our appendix a second function as a reference system, providing concise details of unfamiliar murders.

In the accounts that follow, the date in parentheses refers to the year of the killer's conviction.

Brady, Ian (1966)

One of the two 'moors murderers', convicted of killing two children and a youth. The children were buried on Saddleworth Moor. Pornographic photographs were found, and a tape of one victim pleading with Brady and Hindley to let her go. Few details are known of the children's deaths since the killers have never revealed the full facts. Brady was sentenced to life imprisonment, and at the time of writing has been transferred to a special hospital because of severe mental disturbance.

Bundy, Theodore ('Ted') (1979)

Celebrated North American serial killer thought to have killed at least thirty-six women between 1974 and 1979. His victims were beaten, bitten, raped and strangled. Before he embarked on his career of murder Bundy read violent pornography obsessively and indulged in 'peeping Tom' activities. He denied responsibility for the murders, claiming that they had been committed by an 'entity' inside him; nevertheless he was sentenced to death, but as we write has won an indefinite stay of execution.

Christie, John Reginald Halliday (1953)

Killer and necrophile who murdered seven women, including his own wife, in his flat in Notting Hill, London, during the late 1940s and early 1950s. He would find a pretext to get his intended victim to inhale carbon monoxide, strangle her and have intercourse immediately afterwards. He was executed in 1953.

Collins, Norman (1969)

Killer of seven women in Michigan, United States. His victims, mostly students, were tied up, sexually assaulted, raped, flogged, stabbed and mutilated. Collins, who was also a student at the time of the killings, was sentenced to twenty years with hard labour.

Collop, Anthony (1961)

Homosexual killer of a thirteen-year-old boy, cited in Morris and Blom-Cooper's comprehensive *Calendar of Murder*. Collop claimed the boy had repulsed his sexual advances and he had therefore strangled him. He was found guilty of manslaughter by reason of diminished responsibility and sentenced to life imprisonment.

Cooper, Ronald Frank (1977)

Homosexual South African child-killer who fantasized about killing both boys and women in a series of diaries. He strangled, and attempted unsuccessfully to rape, a twelve-year-old boy. He was caught when another boy, whom he had previously threatened at gunpoint but then allowed to go, recognized him at a cinema and alerted the police. He was executed in 1978.

De Salvo, Albert (1967)

The 'Boston Strangler', killer of thirteen women who also confessed to around one-thousand sexual assaults and rapes in his guises as the 'measuring man' (who pretended to be from a modelling agency so he could measure women's bodies and touch them up) and the 'Green Man' who broke into women's apartments and raped or assaulted them. His trade mark as the Strangler was to tie a ligature round the victim's neck in a grotesque bow; he also left victims with their legs spread wide and sometimes put objects such as broom handles into their vaginas. He was sentenced to life imprisonment in 1967 and killed by a fellow inmate in 1973.

'Green River killer'

So far uncaptured prostitute-killer in and around Seattle, United States. His activities were first noted in 1982 when several corpses were discovered in the Green River, and he is thought to have murdered between thirteen and twenty-one women since, most of them aged less than twenty. The distinctive method used by this killer in some cases has been kept secret to maximize chances of catching him and to deter copy-cat killers.

Heath, Neville (1946)

Sadistic killer of two women. One was whipped (the lash marks were so clear and distinctive, Heath was eventually arrested on the strength of the whip found in his possession), her breasts were bitten and she was finally suffocated; the other had been beaten about the head, slashed with a knife, her nipple had been bitten off and her throat had been cut. Both women in addition had had their vaginas split by a heavy blow with a blunt instrument. Heath had a history of sadistic encounters which went well beyond consensual sado-masochistic activity. He was executed in 1946.

Hindley, Myra (1966)

One of the 'moors murderers', convicted with her lover, Ian Brady, of the murders of two children, and also of being an accessory to the murder of a youth by Brady. Sentenced to life imprisonment in 1966 and still refused parole at the time of writing, twenty years later. In 1986 police initiated a new search of Saddleworth Moor, for the bodies of two more young people whom Hindley admitted had been killed by Brady.

'Jack the Ripper'

Unidentified killer of six prostitutes in London's East End during the Autumn of 1888. The killer sent two letters to police, claiming to be 'down on whores', but his identity was not discovered (despite much speculation, it never has been) by the time the murders ceased. 'Jack' was not the first 'Ripper' nor the first multiple killer of prostitutes (the 1880s produced a spate of cases, including two which predated Jack — in Paris and Moscow) but he is often considered as the 'Father' of a gruesome tradition. Several later killers have been called after him, for example the 'Black-out Ripper' who murdered several London prostitutes during the Second World War; 'Jack the Stripper' who was never caught (so called because he left his victims naked and with traces of spray-paint) and of course, the 'Yorkshire Ripper', Peter Sutcliffe.

Jones, Arthur Albert (1961)

Child-rapist and killer with a particular penchant for Girl Guides. After raping one and allowing her to go, he sexually assaulted and then strangled a second. He was sentenced to life imprisonment.

Kallinger, Joseph (1975)

North American psychotic killer who stabbed a woman to death when she refused to chew off the penis of a man also being held at gunpoint by Kallinger. He believed he had a mission to kill by removing genitals; as well as the killing, he committed several sexual assaults and fantasized about mutilating and cutting up women's bodies. He was sentenced to up to eighty years in prison.

Kemper, Edmund (1973)

The 'Co-ed Killer' who terrorized the campus of the University of California at Santa Cruz between 1971 and 1973, killing at least half-a-dozen women students. A sadistic child who fantasized about torture and death, and tortured animals, he killed both his grandparents in 1964 when he was sixteen, repeatedly stabbing his grandmother's body with a knife. He spent five years in a mental hospital, but shortly after returning home to live with his mother, he began killing students (usually picking them up when they were hitch-hiking). A necrophile, Kemper would use the bodies of his victims sexually, would decapitate them, and confessed also to cannibalism. He finally killed, decapitated and sexually violated his mother; after this he gave himself up and was sentenced to life imprisonment.

Kinley, Charles (1961)

Kinley was diagnosed as psychopathic and sentenced to life imprisonment for manslaughter. He had at least seven assaults recorded against him, including an attempt to strangle his wife. He strangled and then stripped a woman in her home.

Kürten, Peter (1930)

The Düsseldorf sadist. Kürten engaged in sexual experiments from an early age, discovering that he was stimulated sexually by throttling and by cutting women's abdomens to produce a flow of blood. He was also an arsonist. He made various attacks in which he attempted to strangle women and actually murdered nine people (including a man and some children). He stabbed his victims ferociously. He was convicted on nine counts of murder in 1930 and sentenced to death nine times. It is said that before his execution in 1931, he asked the executioner whether he would be able to experience the flow of blood as his own head was severed.

Lucas, Henry Lee (1984)

North American serial killer who wandered around the United States with a partner, Otis Toole and claims to have killed up to 360 people during an eight-year period, most of them women and children. Lucas also killed his mother, for which he spent time in prison and in addition he strangled the first girl he ever had sex with, when he was fourteen years old.

Nilsen, Dennis (1983)

Homosexual necrophile and killer of sixteen young men. The bodies were kept in his London flat where he engaged in various rituals, sexual and aesthetic, with them. He was sentenced to life imprisonment in 1983.

Rais, Gilles de (1440)

Early example of a man who killed for pleasure: sex-killing as such was not a meaningful category in his time. He is reputed to have murdered 200 boys, inspired by his acquaintance with the doings of the Roman Emperors. He was executed in 1440 and interest in him was revived by Sade and then by a series of 'biographical' essays from 1886 on.

Rix, Peter (1963)

Fifteen-year-old killer of a twelve-year-old girl. Had a history of uncontrollable behaviour, and is cited by Craft as a typical psychopath.

Sims, Edwin (1961)

'Courting couple' killer who murdered and dismembered a woman and a man. He was convicted of manslaughter under section two of the 1957 Homicide Act.

Steed, John (1986)

The 'M4 Killer'/'M4 Rapist'. He forced a woman's car off the motorway, drove her to London and raped her repeatedly. A few days later he shot and killed a prostitute who was travelling with him in his car in central London, and pushed her out of the car door. At his trial the defence explained that he had been forced as a child to witness the rape of his mother, and this had warped his attitude to women.

Straffen, John (1951)

Child-killer who strangled three young girls and threatened another. He was only an adolescent at the time. He was considered severely mentally disturbed and sent to Broadmoor.

Sutcliffe, Peter (1981)

The 'Yorkshire Ripper', killer of thirteen women in the North of England between 1975 and 1981. Most victims were prostitutes. Sutcliffe hit his victims on the head with a hammer and stabbed them repeatedly with a sharpened screwdriver in the breasts and abdomen. In one case he raped the woman as she was unconscious and dying; in another he went back to the body after a period of time and tried to saw the head off. Sutcliffe claimed he had a divine mission to cleanse the streets of prostitutes, but the court that tried him rejected this defence of diminished responsibility owing to delusions, finding him guilty of murder. He was sentenced to thirty years imprisonment and has since become so disturbed that he has been transferred to a special hospital.

Sutton, George (1961)

Prostitute killer.

Verzeni, Vincent (1873)

Nineteenth-century Italian sex-killer and 'Vampire' reported by Lombroso and discussed by Krafft-Ebing. He throttled, mutilated and disembowelled several women and is also believed to have eaten parts of their bodies. Verzeni described the pleasures of killing as 'much greater than I experienced while masturbating'.

Wills, Alan (1961)

Assaulted, raped and murdered a six-year-old girl.

Notes

Preface

1 Genette Tate is one of the many young girls in the United Kingdom who are missing, believed murdered, but whose fate remains a mystery.
2 A. Sheridan, *Foucault, the Will to Truth* (Tavistock, London, 1980), pp. 133–4.
3 *True Detective* (January 1979).
4 Ibid.

Chapter 1   Introduction: In Search of the Murderer

1 For example Ann Jones, *Women Who Kill* (Fawcett Columbine, New York, 1980); Mary S. Hartman, *Victorian Murderesses* (Robson Books, London, 1985).
2 Terence Morris and Louis Blom-Cooper, *A Calendar of Murder* (Michael Joseph, London, 1964), p. vii.
3 *Criminal Statistics, England and Wales* (HMSO, publ. annually); E. Gibson and S. Klein, *Murder 1957–1968* (HMSO, London, 1969); E. Gibson, *Homicide in England and Wales 1967–1971* (HMSO, London, 1975).
4 Cf. C. Wilson and D. Seaman, *Encyclopaedia of Modern Murder* (Arthur Barker Ltd, London, 1983); S. Dell, *Murder into Manslaughter* (Oxford University Press, Oxford, 1984), which was compiled with full access to Home Office records.
5 Nagging was allowed as a defence in the case of Nicholas Boyce (1985) who was sentenced to five years; infidelity was at issue in the case of Peter Hogg (1985) who got six years; and sexual unorthodoxy was taken as a mitigating circumstance in the case of Peter Wood, who killed his feminist lover Mary Bristow. For comment on this case, see E. Wilson, *What is to be Done About Violence Against Women?* (Penguin, Harmondsworth, 1981) and A. Karpf, 'Crimes of Passion', *Cosmopolitan* (March 1985).
6 Dell, *Murder into Manslaughter*.
7 H. Lundsgaarde, *Murder in Space City* (Oxford University Press, New York, 1977).
8 Morris and Blom-Cooper, *Calendar of Murder*, p. 280.

9 Ibid.
10 Gibson and Klein, *Murder 1957—1968*, p. 61.
11 A. Karpf, 'It's Still Safe to Go out to Work', *Cosmopolitan* (October 1986).
12 J. S. Cockburn, *Crime in England 1500—1800* (Methuen, London, 1977), p. 57.
13 Quoted in Jones, *Women Who Kill*, p. 311.
14 *The Guardian* (27 June 1981).
15 Morris and Blom-Cooper, *Calendar of Murder*, p. 333.
16 Wilson and Seaman, *Encyclopaedia of Modern Murder*, p. 217.
17 R. von Krafft-Ebing, *Psychopathia Sexualis*, 10th edn (Aberdeen University Press, Aberdeen, 1901), p. 89.
18 Cf. Colin Wilson's introduction to D. Rumbelow, *The Complete Jack the Ripper* (W. H. Allen, London, 1975).
19 Cockburn, *Crime in England*, p. 56.
20 Wilson and Seaman, *Encyclopaedia of Modern Murder*, p. 31.
21 P. Jacobson, 'Rise of the Random Killers', *Sunday Times* (2 September 1985).
22 Sujata Gothoskat — an interview on feminist action against violence in India, *Trouble and Strife*, 8 (Spring 1986).
23 Christine Delphy, *Close to Home* (Hutchinson, London, 1984), p. 152.
24 P. Highsmith, 'Fallen Women', *London Review of Books* (21 June 1984).
25 M. Wolfgang, *Patterns in Criminal Homicide* (University of Pennsylvania Press, Philadelphia, 1958); Lundsgaarde, *Murder in Space City*. For an example of feminist criminology see F. Heidensohn, *Women and Crime* (Macmillan, London, 1985).
26 Jones, *Women Who Kill*, p. 11.
27 K. Simpson, *Forty Years of Murder* (Granada, London, 1978), p. 203.
28 Morris and Blom-Cooper, *Calendar of Murder*, pp. 276, 323.
29 Ibid., p. 276.
30 G. Burn, *Somebody's Husband, Somebody's Son* (Heinemann/Pan Books, London, 1984).

Chapter 2   The Murderer as Hero

1 All broadsides quoted here come from the Bodleian Law Library and the John Johnson Collection. Very many of these are undated, though it is clear that the vast majority are from the nineteenth century. We give the dates in the text when we know them.
2 Quoted in Michèle Barrett and Rosalind Coward, 'Don't Talk to Strangers', *New Socialist* (November 1985). And cf. the remark of a recent victim's father about the man who strangled his daughter in her own bed: 'He's a creature masquerading as a human being.'
3 *News of the World* (1 December 1985).
4 This is a major change in crime literature, which originally had the criminal as its hero but later replaced him with the detective. For a

Marxist discussion of the transition, see Ernest Mandel, *Delightful Murder* (W. W. Norton, New York, 1984).

5   See Ann Rule, *The Stranger Beside Me* (W. W. Norton, New York, 1980) on Ted Bundy, and Sandy Fawkes, *Killing Time* (Peter Owen Ltd, London, 1977) on Paul John Knowles.

6   Robert Louis Stevenson, *Dr Jekyll and Mr Hyde and Other Stories* ed. Jenni Calder (Penguin, Harmondsworth, 1979), pp. 83–4.

7   Colin Wilson, 'The Ripper Revealed', *Time Out* (19–25 April 1984).

8   Our analysis of true-crime monthlies was facilitated by the editor of British *True Detective*, who kindly permitted us access to the archive and who answered our questions about the production of the titles. We are also indebted to Argus Publications Ltd for information on circulation and readership of the magazines.

9   *True Detective* (January 1986).

10   Ibid., (January 1986).

11   Ibid., (February 1979).

12   Ibid., (April 1979).

13   Ibid., (January 1986).

14   Michel Foucault, *Discipline and Punish* (Allen Lane, London, 1977), p. 68.

15   Professor John Gunn, of the Institute of Psychiatry, quoted in 'Portrait of a Serial Killer', *The Times* (28 July 1986).

16   Dr Edmund Harvey-Smith, consultant forensic psychiatrist, quoted in 'Portrait', *The Times* 28 July, 1986.

17   Cited by Mario Praz, *The Romantic Agony*, 2nd edn (Fontana, London, 1960), p. 44.

18   E. A. Poe, 'Philosophy of composition', in *Literary Criticism of Edgar Allen Poe*, ed. R. Hough (University of Nebraska Press, Lincoln, 1965).

19   C. Maturin, *Melmoth the Wanderer* (1820), quoted in Praz *The Romantic Agony*, p. 138.

20   E. Burke, *Philosophical Enquiry* (1757), quoted in Mario Praz's introduction to *Three Gothic Novels*, ed. P. Fairclough (1968), p. 10.

21   This is the view of Clifford Allen: in his *A Textbook of Psychosexual disorders*, 2nd edn (Oxford University Press, London, 1969), p. 118 he says that 'sadistic behaviour is a murder in miniature . . . murder is the ultimate sadism.'

22   M. Foucault, *Madness and Civilisation*, tr. R. Howard (Pantheon/Tavistock, New York and London, 1965), p. 210.

23   Full accounts of the contents of Sade's major works can be found in A. Carter, *The Sadeian Woman* (Virago, London, 1979).

24   *Justine*, quoted in Praz, *The Romantic Agony* (our translation) p. 122.

25   *Juliette*, quoted in Praz, ibid., pp. 116–17.

26   *Juliette*, quoted in Praz, ibid., p. 124.

27   S. de Beauvoir, *Force of Circumstance*, tr. R. Howard (Penguin, Harmondsworth, 1968), p. 255.

28   The aesthetic of murder in surrealism is usefully discussed by D. Macey, 'Fragments of an Analysis — Lacan in Context', *Radical Philosophy*, 37 (1984).

29 Two recent best sellers illustrate this: Peter Ackroyd's *Hawksmoor* (Hamish Hamilton, London, 1985) and Patrick Süskind's *Perfume* (Hamish Hamilton, London, 1986). (The protagonist of *Hawksmoor* is not a sex-killer — the book is set in the period of transition to Enlightenment ways of thinking — but the hero of *Perfume* is a variant on the lust murderer.) We could also cite many writers of 'modern Gothic' who have made a murderer their central figure.

30 S. de Beauvoir, *The Prime of Life*, tr. P. Green (André Deutsch, London, 1962), p. 129.

31 A. Gide, *Les Caves du Vatican*, quoted in R. Coe, *The Vision of Jean Genet* (Peter Owen Ltd, London, 1968), p. 181.

32 Coe, *The Vision of Jean Genet*, p. 181.

33 Ibid., p. 125.

34 Ibid., p. 41.

35 Carter, *Sadeian Woman*, p. 99.

36 Ibid., p. 86.

37 G. Lloyd, *The Man of Reason* (Methuen, London, 1984), p. 101.

38 Ibid., p. 102.

39 Ibid., p. 98.

40 C. Wilson, 'The Study of Murder', in *Encyclopaedia of Murder*, eds C. Wilson and P. Pitman (Arthur Barker Ltd, London, 1961), p. 21.

41 Ibid., p. 25.

42 C. Wilson, *Order of Assassins* (Rupert Hart-Davis, 1972), p. 28.

43 Ibid., p. 33.

44 C. Wilson, 'The Age of Murder', in Wilson and Seaman, eds *Encyclopaedia of Modern Murder*, p. xxi.

45 Ibid., p. xiv.

46 Wilson, *Order of Assassins*, p. 55.

47 *The Guardian* (14 January 1986).

Chapter 3   The Murderer as Deviant

1 Robert Brittain, 'The Sadistic Murderer', *Medicine, Science and the Law*, 10, 4 (1970).

2 Foucault quotes the nineteenth-century criminologist, Garofolo: 'Criminal law knew only two terms, the offence and the penalty. The new criminology recognises three, the crime, the criminal and the means of repression.' See Michel Foucault 'About the Concept of the Dangerous Individual in Nineteenth-Century Legal Psychiatry', *International Journal of Law and Psychiatry*, 1, (1978), pp. 5—6.

3 Sue Titus Reid, *Crime and Criminology*, 3rd edn (CBS College Publishing, New York, 1982). See chapter 4 for a full discussion of the development of the scientific study of crime.

4 H. Havelock Ellis, *The Criminal*, 3rd edn (Walter Scott, London, 1901), p. 21.

5   Cesare Lombroso, *Crime, its Causes and Remedies* (Heinemann, London, 1911).

6   Ellis, *The Criminal*, pp. 248—9.

7   Ibid., p. 251.

8   Ibid., p. 256.

9   Ibid., pp. 17—25.

10 Earnest Hooton, *Crime and the Man* (Harvard University Press, Cambridge, MA, 1939), p. 393.

11 William Sheldon, *The Varieties of Human Physique: An Introduction to Constitutional Psychology* (Harper and Row, New York, 1940).

12 William Sheldon, *Varieties of Delinquent Youth: An Introduction to Constitutional Psychiatry* (Harper and Row, New York, 1949).

13 Eleanor Glueck and Sheldon Glueck, *Physique and Delinquency* (Harper and Row, New York, 1956).

14 Boyd R. McCanless et al., 'Perceived Opportunities, Delinquency, Race and Body Build among Delinquent Youth', *Journal of Consulting and Clinical Psychiatry*, 38 (1972).

15 Emil M. Hartl, Monnelly, Edward P. and Elderkin, Roland D., *Physique and Delinquent Behaviour* (Academic Press, New York, 1982).

16 D. Hill and D. A. Pond, 'Reflections of 100 Capital Cases Submitted to Electroencephalography', *Journal of Mental Science*, 98 (1952).

17 T. C. Gibbens et al., 'A Follow-Up Study of Criminal Psychopaths', *Journal of Mental Science*, 105 (1959).

18 Kenneth Moyer, 'What is the Potential of Biological Violence Control?' in *Biology and Crime*, ed. C. R. Jeffery (Sage Publications, Beverley Hills, 1979), p. 23.

19 Ibid., p. 24.

20 See, for example, Rom Harré, *Personal Being* (Basil Blackwell, Oxford, 1983), chs 4 and 5, which includes a bibliography on the topic.

21 See David R. Owen 'The 47 XYY Male: A Review', *Psychological Bulletin*, 78 (1972), for a full discussion.

22 M. D. Casey et al., 'Patients with Chromosome Abnormality in two Special Hospitals', *Special Hospitals Research Report*, 2 (1971).

23 Casey et al., 'Patients with Chromosome Abnormality', see Summary.

24 Owen, 'The 47 XYY Male'.

25 For example, Moyer, 'Potential of Biological Violence Control', pp. 28—30, and A. Mednick Sarnoff et al., 'Biology and Violence', in *Criminal Violence*, eds M. E. Wolfgang and Neil Alan Weiner (Sage Publications, London, 1982), pp. 30—1.

26 J. A. Gray and A. W. H. Baffery, 'Sex Differences in Emotional Behaviour in Mammals including Man — Adaptive and Neural Basis', *Acta Psychologica*, 35 (1971); J. A. Gray, 'Sex Differences in Emotional Behaviour in Mammals including Man — Endocrine Basis', *Acta Psychologica*, 35 (1971).

27 David P. Farrington and John Gunn, *Aggression and Dangerousness* (John Wiley and Sons, Chichester, 1985), p. 30.

28 Peter Achinstein, *The Nature of Explanation* (Oxford University Press, Oxford and New York, 1983), ch. 4.

29 H. J. Eysenck, *Crime and Personality* (Routledge and Kegan Paul, London, 1964).

30 The example is M. Phillip Feldman's, see *Criminal Behaviour — a Psychological Analysis* (John Wiley and Sons, London, 1977), p. 172.

31 Harré, *Personal Being*.

32 Feldman, *Criminal Behaviour*, p. 140.

33 D. J. West, ed. *Psychopathic Offenders* (Cambridge Institute of Criminology, Cambridge, 1968), p. 8.

34 Michael Craft, ed. *Psychopathic Disorders and their Assessment* (Pergamon, Oxford, 1966), p. 2.

35 Ibid., p. 5.

36 Feldman, *Criminal Behaviour*, pp. 170—1.

37 Cathy Spatz Widom, 'A Methodology for Studying Non-Institutionalised Psychopaths', in *Psychopathic Behaviour: Approaches to Research*, ed. R. D. Hare (John Wiley and Sons London, 1978).

38 West, *Psychopathic Offenders*, p. 7.

39 Peter Clyne, *Guilty but Insane: Anglo-American Attitudes to Insanity and Criminal Guilt* (Thos. Nelson and Sons, London, 1973), p. 149.

40 Kenneth Robinson 'The Law and Practice of Psychopathic Disorder in England and Wales', in Craft, ed. *Psychopathic Disorders*, p. 28.

41 Craft, ed. *Psychopathic Disorders*, p. 6—12.

42 Foucault, 'About the Concept of the Dangerous Individual', p. 3.

43 Ibid., p. 3.

44 Emil Kraepelin, *Lectures on Clinical Psychiatry*, 2nd edn (Bailliere, Tindall and Cox, London, 1905).

45 R. von Krafft-Ebing, *Psychopathia Sexualis*, 10th edn (Aberdeen University Press, Aberdeen, 1901), p. 501.

46 Ibid., p. 112.

47 H. Havelock Ellis, *Studies in the Psychology of Sex* (Random House, New York, 1942), vol. I, p. 160.

48 See T. Weinberg and G. W. Levi-Kamel, *S & M: Studies in Sadomasochism* (Prometheus Books, Buffalo, NY, 1983).

49 Alfred Kinsey, Pomeroy, W. B. and Martin, Clyde E., *Sexual Behaviour in the Human Male* (W. B. Saunders, Philadelphia, 1948), p. 202.

50 Sigmund Freud, *Three Essays on Sexuality*, in *The Essentials of Psychoanalysis*, selected by Anna Freud, (Pelican, Harmondsworth, 1986), p. 301.

51 Clifford Allen, *A Textbook of Psychosexual Disorders*, 2nd edn (Oxford University Press, London, 1969), p. 134.

52 Ibid., p. 165.

53 Robert Stoller, *Perversion, the Erotic Form of Hatred* (Harvester, Hassocks, 1976), p. 32.

54 Ibid., p. xiv.

55 Allen, *Textbook of Psychosexual Disorders*, p. 120.

56 Flora Rheta Schreiber, *The Shoemaker* (Penguin, Harmondsworth, 1983), p. 168.

57 Flora Rheta Schreiber, *Sybil* (Penguin, Harmondsworth, 1975).

58 Susanne Schad-Somers, *Sadomasochism, Etiology and Treatment* (Human Sciences Press, New York, 1982), p. 15.

59 For an excellent, accessible guide to the literature see David Downes and Paul Rock, *Understanding Deviance: A Guide to the Sociology of Crime and Rule-Breaking* (Clarendon Press, Oxford, 1982).

60 Marvin E. Wolfgang 'Victim-Precipitated Homicide', in *The Sociology of Crime and Delinquency*, eds M. E. Wolfgang, Savitz, Leonard and Johnson, Norman (John Wiley and Sons, New York, 1970).

61 Hans von Hentig, *The Criminal and his Victim* (Yale University Press, New Haven, 1948).

62 Feldman, *Criminal Behaviour*; Craft, *Psychopathic Disorders*.

63 Downes and Rock, *Understanding Deviance*, pp. 115—16.

64 M. E. Wolfgang and F. Ferracuti, *The Subculture of Violence* (Sage Publications, Beverley Hills, 1982).

65 H. Lundsgaarde, *Murder in Space City* (Oxford University Press, New York, 1977).

66 Downes and Rock, *Understanding Deviance*, p. 67.

67 See, for example, H. Becker, 'Marijuana Users and Social Control', in *Outsiders*, H. Becker (Collier-Macmillan, London, 1963).

68 Cf. P. Willis, *Profane Culture* (Routledge and Kegan Paul, London, 1978); W. Whyte, *Street Corner Society* (Chicago University Press, Chicago, 1965).

69 E. M. Lemert, *Human Deviance, Social Problems and Social Control* (Prentice-Hall, Englewood Cliffs, NJ, 1967), p. v.

70 D. Matza, *Delinquency and Drift* (John Wiley and Sons, New York, 1964); *Becoming Deviant* (Prentice-Hall, Englewood Cliffs, NJ, 1969).

71 See, for example, the work of Erving Goffman, especially *The Presentation of Self in Everyday Life* (University of Edinburgh Social Sciences Research Centre, Edinburgh, 1956).

72 C. Haney, Banks, C. and Zimbardo, P., 'Interpersonal Dynamics in a Simulated Prison', *International Journal of Criminology and Penology*, 1 (1973).

73 Downes and Rock, *Understanding Deviance*, pp. 203—4.

74 S. Box, *Power, Crime and Mystification* (Tavistock, London, 1983), p. 12.

75 J. Young, 'The Failure of Criminology: The Need for a Radical Realism', in *Confronting Crime*, R. Matthews and J. Young (Sage Publications, London, 1986).

76 We are intrigued by those authors — such as Brittain, Krafft-Ebing, Masters and Lea — who will authoritatively state that female sexual killers are 'rare', without in fact citing a single instance of a female sexual killer. Only Allen, *Textbook of Psychosexual Disorders*, goes so far as to say that such women just do not exist.

Chapter 4   The Murderer Personified

1 K. Berg, *The Sadist* (Acorn Press, London, 1938).

2 L. Kennedy, *Ten Rillington Place* (Panther, London, 1971); G. Frank, *The Boston Strangler* (Pan Books, London, 1967).

3 S. de Beauvoir, *The Prime of Life*, tr. P. Green (André Deutsch, London, 1962), p. 129.

4 Gordon Burn, *Somebody's Husband, Somebody's Son* (Heinemann/Pan Books, London, 1984); B. Masters, *Killing for Company* (Coronet, London, 1986).

5 N. Ward Jouve, *The Streetcleaner* (Marion Boyars, London and New York, 1986) — originally published in a different version as *Un Homme nommé Zapolski* (Des Femmes, Paris, 1983).

6 *Pall Mall Gazette* (10 November 1888). Because of its particularly detailed coverage, the *Gazette* is our main source for contemporary comment on Jack the Ripper. Not only did it take a special interest in the case, it also commented on and in some instances actually reprinted the coverage of the morning papers (the *Gazette* itself was a London evening newspaper, known for its campaigning stance and for its opposition to the [Tory] government).

7 For speculation on this question see (among many others) T. A. Cullen, *Autumn of Terror* (Bodley Head, London, 1965); D. Rumbelow, *The Complete Jack the Ripper* (W. H. Allen, London, 1975).

8 Burn, *Somebody's Husband*, pp. 155—7.

9 *Pall Mall Gazette* (8 September 1888).

10 *Pall Mall Gazette* (1 December 1888).

11 *Pall Mall Gazette* (8 September 1888).

12 Ibid.

13 *Pall Mall Gazette* (14 September 1888).

14 *Pall Mall Gazette* (10 September 1888).

15 Rumbelow, *Complete Jack the Ripper*, p. 155.

16 Burn, *Somebody's Husband*, p. 293.

17 W. Hollway, '"I Just Wanted to Kill a Woman". Why? The Ripper and Male Sexuality', in *Sweeping Statements: Writings from the Women's Liberation Movement, 1981—3*, eds H. Kanter et al. (Women's Press, London, 1984), p. 17.

18 Quoted in Burn, *Somebody's Husband*, p. 346.

19 Quoted in Hollway, 'I Just Wanted to Kill a Woman', p. 21.

20 *Pall Mall Gazette* (4 October 1888).

21 Quoted in Burn, *Somebody's Husband*, p. 181.

22 See especially Judith Walkowitz, *Prostitution and Victorian Society* (Cambridge University Press, New York, 1980); and 'Male Vice and Female Virtue', in Snitow, Stansell and Thompson, eds *Desire*.

23 *Pall Mall Gazette* (15 November 1888).

24 S. Jeffreys, *The Spinster and her Enemies* (Pandora, London, 1985).

25 Reported by the *Pall Mall Gazette* (2 October 1888).

26 Burn, *Somebody's Husband*, p. 99.

27 Ibid., p. 158.

28 Ibid., pp. 158—9.

29 J. Goodman, *The Trial of Ian Brady and Myra Hindley* (David and Charles, Newton Abbot, 1973), p. 10.
30 D. Marchbanks, *The Moor Murders* (Leslie Frewin, London, 1966), p. 41.
31 F. Dostoevsky, *Crime and Punishment* tr. D. Magarshack (Penguin, Harmondsworth, 1951), pp. 432–3.
32 Goodman, *Trial of Brady and Hindley*, p. 191.
33 S. Hall et al., *Policing the Crisis* (Macmillan, London, 1978), p. 239.
34 Jeffreys, *The Spinster and her Enemies*, p. 2.
35 J. Weeks, *Sexuality and its Discontents* (Routledge and Kegan Paul, London, 1985), p. 216.
36 F. Harrison, *Brady and Hindley: Genesis of the Moors Murders* (Ashgrove Press, Bath, 1986), p. 58.
37 Ibid.
38 Ibid., p. 17.
39 J. Deane Potter, *The Monsters of the Moors* (Elek Press, London, 1966), p. 226.
40 'Why We Can Never Forgive', interview with Ann West, *Woman's Own* (9 August 1986).
41 Kennedy, *Ten Rillington Place*, p. 31.
42 Masters, *Killing for Company*, p. 45.
43 Ibid., p. 49; Kennedy, *Ten Rillington Place*, p. 45.
44 B. Masters, 'Is Evil Contagious?', *The Observer* (3 March 1985).
45 Masters, *Killing for Company*, p. 133.
46 Ibid.
47 Ibid., p. 144.
48 Ibid., p. 289.
49 Ibid., p. 188.
50 Ibid., p. 110.
51 Ibid., p. 125.
52 Ibid., p. 130.
53 Ibid., p. 277.
54 Ibid., pp. 105–6.
55 Ibid., p. 260.
56 Ibid., p. 264.
57 Ibid., p. 277.
58 Ibid., p. 259.
59 S. Kappeler, *The Pornography of Representation* (Polity Press, Cambridge, 1986).
60 J. Berger, *Ways of Seeing* (BBC/Penguin, London, 1972).
61 D. Nilsen, 'Monochrome Man', repr. in Masters, *Killing for Company*, pp. 303–16.
62 P. Jacobson, 'Rise of the Random Killers', *Sunday Times* (2 September 1985).
63 N. Mailer, 'The White Negro', in his *Advertisements for Myself* (Panther, London, 1968), p. 273.
64 Ibid., p. 279.

65 Ibid., p. 278.
66 Ibid., p. 279.
67 Ibid., p. 275.
68 Quoted by C. Wilson and D. Seaman, *Encyclopaedia of Modern Murder* (Arthur Barker Ltd, London, 1983), p. 88.

Chapter 5   The Murderer as Misogynist?

1 N. Ward Jouve, *The Streetcleaner* (Marion Boyars, London and New York, 1986), p. 17.
2 Ibid., p. 25.
3 Ibid., p. 27.
4 A. Dworkin, *Pornography* (Women's Press, London, 1981), pp. 13—14.
5 Ibid., p. 13.
6 D. Hume, *A Treatise on Human Nature*, ed. D. C. McNabb (William Collins, London, 1962), book I, section 6.
7 I. Kant, *Critique of Pure Reason*, tr. N. Kemp Smith (St Martin's Press, New York, 1965).
8 See G. Lloyd, *The Man of Reason* (Methuen, London, 1984).
9 S. de Beauvoir, *The Second Sex* tr. H. M. Parshley (Jonathan Cape, London, 1953).
10 C. Vance, ed. *Pleasure and Danger* (Routledge and Kegan Paul, London, 1984).
11 J. Benjamin, 'Master and Slave: The Fantasy of Erotic Domination', in *Desire: The Politics of Sexuality* eds A. Snitow, C. Stansell and Thompson, S. (Virago, London, 1984).
12 R. Coward, 'What's in it for Women?', *New Statesman* (13 June 1986).
13 M. Bower, 'Daring to Speak its Name', *Feminist Review*, 24 (1986).
14 J. Weeks, *Sexuality and its Discontents* (Routledge and Kegan Paul, London, 1985), p. 241.
15 P. Gebhard, 'Sadomasochism and Fetishism', in *Dynamics of Deviant Sexuality* (Grune and Stratton, New York, 1969).
16 S. Kappeler, *The Pornography of Representation* (Polity Press, Cambridge, 1986), p. 49.
17 Ibid.
18 N. Griffith et al., 'Agreeing to Differ? Lesbian Sadomasochism', *Spare Rib* (September 1986).

Bibliography

Abrahamsen, David, *The Psychology of Crime* (Columbia University Press, New York, 1960).

Achinstein, Peter, *The Nature of Explanation* (Oxford University Press, Oxford and New York, 1983).

Ackroyd, Peter, *Hawksmoor* (Hamish Hamilton, London, 1985).

Allen, Clifford, *A Textbook of Psychosexual Disorders*, 2nd edn (Oxford University Press, London, 1969).

Avison, Neville H., 'Victims of Homicide', *International Journal of Criminology and Penology*, 2 (1974).

Barak-Glantz, Israel L. and Huff, C. Ronald, *The Mad, The Bad and The Different* (Lexington, MA, D. C. Heath and Co., 1982).

Barrett, Michèle and Coward, Rosalind, 'Don't Talk to Strangers', *New Socialist* (November 1985).

Beattie, John, *The Yorkshire Ripper Story* (Quartet/Daily Star, London, 1981).

Beauvoir, Simone de, *The Second Sex*, tr. H. M. Parshley (Jonathan Cape, London, 1953).

Beauvoir, Simone de, *The Prime of Life*, tr. Peter Green (André Deutsch, London, 1962).

Beauvoir, Simone de, *Force of Circumstance*, tr. Richard Howard (Penguin, Harmondsworth, 1968).

Becker, Howard, *Outsiders* (Collier-Macmillan, London, 1963).

Benjamin, Jessica, 'Master and Slave: The Fantasy of Erotic Domination', in *Desire: The Politics of Sexuality*, eds Snitow, Ann; Stansell, Christine and Thompson, Sharon (Virago, London, 1984).

Berg, Karl, *The Sadist* (Acorn Press, London, 1938).

Berger, John, *Ways of Seeing* (BBC/Penguin, London, 1972).

Blackburn, R., 'Personality Types among Abnormal Homicides', *British Journal of Criminology*, 11 (1971).

Blackburn, R., 'Personality and the Classification of Psychopathic Disorders', *Special Hospitals Research Report*, 10 (1974).

Bluglass, Robert, 'The Psychiatric Assessment of Homicide', *British Journal of Hospital Medicine* (October 1979).

Blom-Cooper, Louis, *The A6 Murder: Regina V James Hanratty* (Penguin, Harmondsworth, 1963).

Bottomley, Keith, *Criminology in Focus* (Martin Robertson, Oxford, 1979).

Bower, Marion, 'Daring to Speak its Name: The Relationship of Women to Pornography', *Feminist Review*, 24 (1986).

Box, Stephen, *Deviance, Reality and Society* (Holt, Rinehart and Winston, London, 1971).

Box, Stephen, *Power, Crime and Mystification* (Tavistock, London, 1983).

Brittain, Robert P., 'The Sadistic Murderer', *Medicine, Science and the Law*, 10 (1970).

Bromberg, Walter, *Crime and the Mind: A Psychiatric Analysis of Crime and Punishment* (Macmillan, New York, 1965).

Brownmiller, Susan, *Against Our Will: Men, Women and Rape* (Penguin, Harmondsworth, 1976).

Buchholz, Erich, *Socialist Criminology — Theoretical and Methodological Foundations* (D. C. Heath, Farnborough, 1974).

Burn, Gordon, *Somebody's Husband, Somebody's Son: The Story of the Yorkshire Ripper* (Heinemann/Pan Books, London, 1984).

Burton, Frank, 'Questions of Violence in Party-Political Criminology', in *Radical Issues in Criminology*, eds P. Carlen and M. Collison (Martin Robertson, Oxford, 1980).

Capote, Truman, *In Cold Blood: A True Account of Multiple Murder and its Consequences* (Hamish Hamilton, London, 1966).

Carlen, Pat et al., *Criminal Women* (Polity Press, Cambridge, 1985).

Carter, Angela, *The Sadeian Woman, an Exercise in Cultural History* (Virago, London, 1979).

Casey, M. D. et al., 'Patients with Chromosome Abnormality in two Special Hospitals', *Special Hospitals Research Report*, 2 (1971).

Chapman, Jane Roberts and Gates, Margaret, eds *The Victimisation of Women* (Sage Publications, Beverley Hills, 1978).

Chesser, Eustace, *The Human Aspect of Sexual Deviation* (Jarrolds, London, 1971).

Chiswick, Derek, 'Sex Crimes', *British Journal of Psychiatry* (September 1983).

Clark, Tim and Penycate, John, *Psychopath: The Case of Patrick MacKay* (Routledge and Kegan Paul, London, 1976).

Clyne, Peter, *Guilty but Insane — Anglo-American Attitudes to Insanity and Criminal Guilt* (Thos. Nelson and Sons Ltd, London, 1973).

Cockburn, J. S., 'The Nature and Incidence of Crime in England 1559—1625', in *Crime in England 1500—1800* (Methuen, London, 1977).

Coe, Richard, *The Vision of Jean Genet* (Peter Owen, London, 1968).

Coulter, Jeff, *Approaches to Insanity* (Martin Robertson, Oxford, 1980).

Cousins, Mark, 'Men's Rea: A Note on Sexual Difference, Criminology and the Law', in Carlen and Collison, *Radical Issues in Criminology*.

Coward, Rosalind, 'What's in it for Women?', *New Statesman* (13 June 1986).

Craft, Michael, *Ten studies into Psychopathic Personality* (John Wright, Bristol, 1965).

Craft, Michael, *Psychopathic Disorders* (Pergamon, Oxford, 1966).

Criminal Statistics, England and Wales (H.M.S.O., London, published annually).

Cross, J., *The Yorkshire Ripper, the In-Depth Study of a Mass-Killer and his Methods* (Granada, London, 1981).

Cullen, T. A., *Autumn of Terror* (Bodley Head, London, 1965).

Dawkins, Richard, *The Selfish Gene* (Paladin, London, 1976).

Dawkins, Richard, *The Extended Phenotype: The Gene as the Unit of Selection* (W. H. Freeman and Co., Oxford and San Francisco, 1982).

Dell, Susanne, *Murder into Manslaughter: The Diminished Responsibility Defence in Practice* (Maudsley Monographs 27, Oxford University Press, Oxford, 1984).

Delphy, Christine, *Close to Home* (Hutchinson, London, 1984).

DeRivers, J. Paul, *The Sexual Criminal, a Psychoanalytic Study* (Charles C. Thomas, Springfield, Ill., 1956).

Dicks, H. V., *Licensed Mass-Murder: A Socio-Psychological Study of some SS Killers* (Tavistock, London, 1972).

Ditton, Jason, *Contrology: Beyond the New Criminology* (Macmillan, London, 1979).

Dostoevsky, Fyodor M., *Crime and Punishment*, tr. David Magarshack (Penguin, Harmondsworth, 1951).

Downes, David and Rock, Paul, *Understanding Deviance: A Guide to the Sociology of Crime and Rule-Breaking* (Clarendon Press, Oxford, 1982).

Dworkin, Andrea, *Pornography: Men Possessing Women* (Women's Press, London, 1981).

Edelman, Murray, 'Law and Psychiatry as Political Symbolism', *International Journal of Law and Psychiatry* (1980).

Ellis, H. Havelock, *The Criminal*, 3rd edn (Walter Scott, London, 1901).

Ellis, H. Havelock, *Studies in the Psychology of Sex* (Random House, New York, 1942), vol. I.

Ellis, Lee, 'Genetics and Criminal Behaviour', *Criminology*, 20, (1982).

Estep, Rhoda, 'Women's Roles in Crime as Depicted by Television and Newspapers', *Journal of Popular Culture*, 16 (1982).

Eysenck, Hans J., *Crime and Personality* (Routledge and Kegan Paul, London, 1964).

Fairclough, P. (ed.) *Three Gothic Novels* (Penguin, Harmondsworth, 1968).

Farrington, David P. and Gunn, John, *Aggression and Dangerousness* (John Wiley and Sons, Chichester, 1985).

Fawkes, Sandy, *Killing Time* (Peter Owen Ltd, London, 1977).

Feldman, M. Phillip, *Criminal Behaviour, a Psychological Analysis* (John Wiley and Sons, London, 1977).

Fenichel, Otto, *The Psychoanalytic Theory of Neurosis* (W. W. Norton, New York, 1945).

Foucault, Michel, *Madness and Civilisation*, tr. Richard Howard (Pantheon/Tavistock, New York and London, 1965).

Foucault, Michel, *Discipline and Punish*, tr. Alan Sheridan, Allen Lane, London, 1977.

Foucault, Michel, 'About the Concept of the Dangerous Individual in Nineteenth Century Legal Psychiatry', *International Journal of the Law and Psychiatry*, 1 (1978).

Frank, Gerold, *The Boston Strangler* (Pan Books, London, 1967).

Freud, Sigmund, *Three Essays on Sexuality*, repr. in *The Essentials of Psycho-analysis*, selected by Anna Freud (Pelican, Harmondsworth, 1986).

Fulcher, J., 'Murder Reports: Formulaic Narrative and Cultural Context', *Journal of Popular Culture*, 18 (1985).

Gagnon, J. H. and Simon, W., *Sexual Conduct: The Social Sources of Human Sexuality* (Aldine, Chicago, 1973).

Gebhard, Paul, 'Sadomasochism and Fetishism', in *Dynamics of Deviant Sexuality* (Grune and Stratton, New York, 1969).

Gibbens, T. C. et al., 'A Follow-Up Study of Criminal Psychopaths', *Journal of Mental Science* (1959).

Gibson, Evelyn, *Homicide in England and Wales 1967—1971* (HMSO, 1975).

Gibson, Evelyn and Klein, S., *Murder 1957—1968* (HMSO, 1969).

Glueck, Eleanor and Glueck, Sheldon, *Physique and Delinquency* (Harper and Row, New York, 1956).

Goffman, Erving, *The Presentation of Self in Everyday Life* (University of Edinburgh Social Sciences Research Centre, Edinburgh, 1956).

Goffman, Erving, *Where the Action Is* (Penguin, London, 1969).

Goodman, Jonathan, *The Trial of Ian Brady and Myra Hindley* (David Charles, Newton Abbot, 1973).

Goodman, Jonathan, *The Pleasure of Murder* (Allison and Busby, London, 1983).

Goodman, Jonathan, 'The Fictions of Murderous Fact', *Encounter* (January 1984).

Gothoskat, Sujata, 'An Interview on feminist action against violence in India', *Trouble and Strife* 8, (Spring, 1986).

Gray, J. A., 'Sex Differences in Emotional Behaviour in Mammals Including Man — Endocrine Basis', *Acta Psychologica*, 35 (1971).

Gray, J. A. and Baffery, A. W. H., 'Sex Differences in Emotional Behaviour in Mammals Including Man — Adaptive and Neural Basis', *Acta Psychologica*, 35 (1971).

Griffith, Nicola et al., 'Agreeing to differ? Lesbian Sadomasochism', *Spare Rib* (September 1986).

Guttmacher, Manfred S., *The Mind of the Murderer* (Farrar Strauss and Cudahy, New York, 1960).

Hall, Stuart et al., *Policing the Crisis: Mugging, the State and Law and Order* (Macmillan, London, 1978).

Haney, Craig, Banks, Curtis and Zimbardo, Phillip, 'Interpersonal Dynamics in a Simulated Prison', *International Journal of Criminology and Penology*, 1 (1971).

Hare, R. D., ed. *Psychopathic Behaviour: Approaches to Research* (John Wiley and Sons, London, 1978).

Harré, Rom, *Personal Being: A Theory of Individual Psychology* (Basil Blackwell, Oxford, 1983).

Harrison, Fred, *Brady and Hindley: Genesis of the Moors Murders* (Ashgrove Press, Bath, 1986).

Hartl, Emil M., Monnelly, Edward P. and Elderkin, Roland D., *Physique and*

Delinquent Behaviour: A Thirty-Year Follow-Up of William H. Sheldon's 'Varieties of Delinquent Youth' (Academic Press, New York, 1982).

Hartman, Mary S., *Victorian Murderesses: A True History of Thirteen Respectable French and English Women Accused of Unspeakable Crimes* (Robson Books, London, 1985).

Heidensohn, Frances, *Women and Crime* (Macmillan, London, 1985).

Hentig, Hans von, *The Criminal and his Victim* (Yale University Press, New Haven, CT, 1948).

Highsmith, Patricia, 'Fallen Women', *London Review of Books* (21 June 1984).

Hill, D. and Pond, D. A., 'Reflections on 100 Capital Cases Submitted to Electroencephalography', *Journal of Mental Science* (1952).

Hobbes, Thomas, *Leviathan* (J. M. Dent and Sons/Everyman, London, 1973).

Hollway, Wendy, '"I Just Wanted to Kill a Woman". Why? The Ripper and Male Sexuality', in *Sweeping Statements: Writings from the Women's Liberation Movement 1981–3*, eds H. Kanter et al., (Women's Press, London, 1984).

Hooton, Earnest, *Crime and the Man* (Harvard University Press, Cambridge, MA, 1939).

Houts, Marshall, *They Asked for Death* (Cowles Book Co., New York, 1970).

Hume, David, *A Treatise on Human Nature*, ed. D. C. MacNabb (William Collins, London, 1962).

Inciardi, James A., ed. *Radical Criminology: The Coming Crisis* (Sage Publications, Beverley Hills, 1980).

Jacobson, Philip, 'Rise of the Random Killers', *Sunday Times* (2 September 1985).

Jeffery, C. R., ed. *Biology and Crime* (Sage Publications, Beverley Hills, 1979).

Jeffreys, Sheila, *The Spinster and her Enemies: Feminism and Sexuality 1880–1930* (Pandora, London, 1985).

Johnson, Pamela Hansford, *On Iniquity: Some Personal Reflections Arising out of the Moors Murders Trial* (Macmillan, London, 1967).

Jones, Ann, *Women Who Kill* (Fawcett Columbine, New York, 1980).

Kant, Immanuel, *Critique of Pure Reason*, tr. Norman Kemp Smith (St Martin's Press, New York, 1965).

Kappeler, Susanne, *The Pornography of Representation* (Polity Press, Cambridge, 1986).

Karpf, Anne, 'Crimes of Passion', *Cosmopolitan* (March 1985).

Karpf, Anne, 'It's Still Safe to Go Out to Work', *Cosmopolitan* (October 1986).

Kelly, Alexander and Wilson, Colin, *Jack the Ripper* (Association of Assistant Librarians, 1972).

Kelly, J. and Vildman, D. J., 'Delinquency and School Drop-Out Behaviour as a Function of Impulsivity and Non-Dominant Values', *Journal of Abnormal Psychology* (1964).

Kennedy, Ludovic, *Ten Rillington Place* (Panther, London, 1971).

Kinsey, Alfred, Pomeroy, W. B. and Martin, Clyde E., *Sexual Behavior in the Human Male* (W. B. Saunders, Philadelphia, 1948).

Kraepelin, Emil, *Lectures on Clinical Psychiatry*, 2nd edn (Bailliere, Tindall and Cox, London, 1905).

Krafft-Ebing, Richard von, *Psychopathia Sexualis: With Especial Reference to Anti-pathetic Sexual Instinct, a Medico-Forensic Study*, 10th edn (Aberdeen University Press, Aberdeen, 1901).

Lane, Roger, *Violent Death in the City: Suicide, Accident and Murder in Nineteenth-Century Philadelphia* (Harvard University Press, Cambridge, MA, 1979).

Langman, Lauren, 'Law, Psychiatry and the Reproduction of Capitalist Ideology: A Critical View', *International Journal of Law and Psychiatry* (1980).

Lemert, Edwin M., *Human Deviance, Social Problems and Social Control* (Prentice-Hall, Englewood Cliffs, NJ, 1967).

Lloyd Genevieve, *The Man of Reason: 'Male' and 'Female' in Western Philosophy* (Methuen, London, 1984).

Lloyd, Georgina, *One Was Not Enough: True Stories of Multiple Murderers* (Robert Hale, London, 1986).

Lloyd, R. and Williamson, S., *Born to Trouble: Portrait of a Psychopath* (Faber and Faber, London, 1969).

Lombroso, Cesare, *Crime, its Causes and Remedies* (Heinemann, London, 1911).

Lundsgaarde, Henry P., *Murder in Space City: A Cultural History of Houston Homicide Patterns* (Oxford University Press, New York, 1977).

McCanless, Boyd R., Persons, W. Scott III and Roberts, Albert, 'Perceived Oportunities, Delinquency, Race and Body Build among Delinquent Youth', *Journal of Consulting and Clinical Psychology* (1972).

McCord, William and McCord, Joan, *The Psychopath: An Essay on the Criminal Mind* (D. Van Nostrand Co. Inc., Princeton, NJ, 1964).

McGurk, B. J., 'Personality Types among "Normal Homicides"', *British Journal of Criminology*, 18 (1978).

MacNamara, D. E. J. and Sagarin, E., *Sex Crime and the Law* (Free Press, New York, 1977).

McVicar, John, *McVicar by Himself* (Hutchinson, London, 1974).

Macey, David, 'Fragments of an Analysis: Lacan in Context', *Radical Philosophy*, 37 (1984).

Mailer, Norman, 'The White Negro', in his *Advertisements for Myself* (Panther, London, 1968).

Mandel, Ernest, *Delightful Murder* (W. W. Norton, New York, 1984).

Mannheim, H., *Comparative Criminology* (Routledge and Kegan Paul, London, 1965), vols I and II.

Marchbanks, David, *The Moor Murders* (Leslie Frewin, London, 1966).

Masters, Brian, 'Is Evil Contagious?', *The Observer* (3 March 1985).

Masters, Brian, *Killing for Company* (Coronet, London, 1986).

Masters, R. E. L. and Lea, Eduard, *Sex Crimes in History: Evolving Concepts of Sadism, Lust Murder and Necrophilia from Ancient to Modern Times* (Julian Press, Inc., New York, 1963).

Matthews, Roger and Young, Jock, *Confronting Crime* (Sage Publications, London, 1986).

Matza, David, *Delinquency and Drift* (John Wiley and Sons, New York, 1964).

Matza, David, *Becoming Deviant* (Prentice-Hall, Englewood Cliffs, NJ, 1969).

Megargee, Edwin I., 'Psychological Determinants and Correlates of Criminal

Violence', in *Criminal Violence*, eds M. E. Wolfgang and N. A. Weiner (Sage Publications, Beverley Hills and London, 1982).

Michaud, S. G. and Aynesworth, Hugh, *The only Living Witness* (Simon and Schuster, New York, 1983).

Milgram, S., *Obedience to Authority* (Tavistock, London, 1974).

Morris, Terence and Blom-Cooper, Louis, *A Calendar of Murder* (Michael Joseph, London, 1964).

Mowat, R. R., *Morbid Jealousy and Murder: A Psychiatric Study of Morbidly Jealous Murderers at Broadmoor* (Tavistock, London, 1966).

Neustatter, W. Lindesay, *Psychological Disorder and Crime* (Christopher Johnson, London, 1953).

Nozick, Robert, *Anarchy State and Utopia* (Basil Blackwell, Oxford, 1980).

Ortner, Sherry B. and Whitehead, Harriet, *Sexual Meanings: The Cultural Construction of Gender and Sexuality* (Cambridge University Press, Cambridge, 1981).

Orwell, George, 'The Decline of the English Murder' (1946), repr. in his *Collected Essays* (Penguin, Harmondsworth, 1970), vol. 4.

Owen, David R., 'The 47 XYY Male: A Review', *Psychological Bulletin*, 78 (1972).

Poe, Edgar Allen, 'The Philosophy of Composition', in *Literary Criticism of Edgar Allen Poe*, ed. R. L. Hough (University of Nebraska Press, Lincoln, Nebraska, 1965).

Potter, John Deane, *The Monsters of the Moors* (Elek Press, London, 1966).

Praz, Mario, *The Romantic Agony*, 2nd edn (Fontana, London, 1960).

Rayner, J. L. and Crook, G. T., eds *The Complete Newgate Calendar* (Navarre Society Ltd., London, 1926), vols I – III.

Reid, Sue Titus, *Crime and Criminology*, 3rd edn (CBS College Publishing, New York, 1982).

Reuck, A. U. S. de and Porter, Ruth, *The Mentally Abnormal Offender* (Ciba Foundation/J. and A. Churchill Ltd., London, 1968).

Root, Jane, 'The Image of Death', *City Limits* (25 November – 1 December 1983).

Rose, Steven, 'Can the Neurosciences Explain the Mind?', *Trends in Neurosciences*, 3 (1980).

Rosenberg, Alexander, *Sociobiology and the Preemption of Social Science* (Basil Blackwell, Oxford, 1980).

Rousseau, Jean-Jacques, *The Social Contract* and *Discourses*, (J. M. Dent, London, 1973).

Ruggiero, Guido, *The Boundaries of Eros: Sex Crime and Sexuality in Renaissance Venice* (Oxford University Press, New York, 1985).

Rule, Ann, *The Stranger Beside Me* (W. W. Norton, New York, 1980).

Rumbelow, Donald, *The Complete Jack the Ripper* (W. H. Allen, London, 1975).

Ryan, Alan, *The Philosophy of the Social Sciences* (Macmillan, London, 1970).

Ryan, William, 'The Art of Savage Discovery: How to Blame the Victim', in *Victimology*, eds Israel Drapkin and Emilio Viano (D. C. Heath and Co., Lexington, MA, 1974).

Sartre, Jean-Paul, 'On the Fine Arts Considered as Murder', in *Genet: A*

Collection of Critical Essays, eds Peter Brooks and Joseph Halpern (Prentice-Hall, Englewood Cliffs, NJ, 1979).

Schad-Somers, Susanne, *Sadomasochism, Etiology and Treatment* (Human Sciences Press, New York, 1982).

Schreiber, Flora Rheta, *Sybil, the True Story of a Woman Possessed by Sixteen Separate Personalities* (Penguin, Harmondsworth, 1975).

Schreiber, Flora Rheta, *The Shoemaker: Anatomy of a Psychotic* (Penguin, Harmondsworth, 1984).

Schröder, J. et al., 'The Frequency of XYY and XXY Men among Criminal Offenders', *Acta Psychiatrica Scandinavia* (1981).

Sereny, Gitta, *The Case of Mary Bell* (Eyre Methuen, London, 1972).

Sheldon, William, *The Varieties of Human Physique: An Introduction to Constitutional Psychology* (Harper and Row, New York, 1940).

Sheldon, William, *Varieties of Delinquent Youth: An Introduction to Constitutional Psychiatry* (Harper and Row, New York, 1949).

Sheridan, Alan, *Foucault, The Will to Truth* (Tavistock, London, 1980).

Shoham, S. Giora, *Society and the Absurd* (Basil Blackwell, Oxford, 1974).

Simpson, Keith, *Forty Years of Murder* (Granada, London, 1978).

Smart, Carol, *Women, Crime and Criminology* (Routledge and Kegan Paul, London, 1977).

Snitow, Ann, Stansell, Christine and Thompson, Sharon, eds *Desire: The Politics of Sexuality* (Virago, London, 1984).

Spatz Widom, Cathy, 'A Methodology for Studying Non-Institutionalised Psychopaths', in Hare, ed. *Psychopathic Behaviour: Approaches to Research.*

Stevenson, Robert Louis, 'The Strange Case of Dr Jekyll and Mr Hyde', in *Dr Jekyll and Mr Hyde and Other Stories*, ed. Jenni Calder (Penguin, Harmondsworth, 1979).

Stoller, Robert, *Perversion, the Erotic Form of Hatred* (Harvester, Hassocks, Sussex, 1976).

Süskind, Patrick, *Perfume* (Hamish Hamilton, London, 1986).

Taussig, Michael J., *Processes in Pathology* (Basil Blackwell, Oxford, 1979).

Taylor, Ian, Walton, Paul and Young, Jock, *Critical Criminology* (Routledge and Kegan Paul, London, 1975).

Toch, Hans, *Violent Men: An Inquiry into the Psychology of Violence* (Aldine, Chicago, 1969).

Trasler, Gordon, *The Explanation of Criminality* (Routledge and Kegan Paul, London, 1962).

Trigg, Roger, *The Shaping of Man: Philosophical Aspects of Sociobiology* (Basil Blackwell, Oxford, 1982).

Vance, Carole, ed. *Pleasure and Danger: Exploring Female Sexuality* (Routledge and Kegan Paul, London, 1984).

Verborne, T. J., 'Blackburn's Typology of Abnormal Homicides: Additional Data and a Critique', *British Journal of Criminology*, 12 (1972).

Walkowitz, Judith, *Prostitution and Victorian Society* (Cambridge University Press, New York, 1980).

Walkowitz, Judith, 'Jack the Ripper and the Myth of Male Violence', *Feminist Studies*, 8 (1982).

Walkowitz, Judith, 'Male Vice and Female Virtue: Feminism and the Politics of Prostitution in Nineteenth Century Britain', in Snitow, Stansell and Thompson, eds *Desire.*

Ward Jouve, Nicole, *Un Homme nommé Zapolski* (des femmes, Paris, 1983).

Ward Jouve, Nicole, *The Streecleaner: The Yorkshire Ripper Case on Trial* (Marion Boyars, London and New York, 1986).

Weeks, Jeffrey, *Sexuality and its Discontents: Meanings, Myths and Modern Sexualities* (Routledge and Kegan Paul, London, 1985).

Weinberg, T. and Levi-Kamel, G. W., *S & M: Studies in Sadomasochism* (Prometheus Books, Buffalo, NY, 1983).

Wertham, F., *Dark Legend: A Study in Murder* (Gollancz, London, 1947).

West, D. J., *Psychopathic Offenders* (Cambridge Institute of Criminology, Cambridge, 1968).

West, D. J., *Criminological Implications of Chromosome Abnormalities* (Cambridge Institute of Criminology, Cambridge, 1969).

Whyte, William, *Street Corner Society* (Chicago University Press, Chicago, 1965.

Williams, Bernard, 'Pornography and Feminism', *London Review of Books* (17—31 March 1983).

Willis, Paul, *Profane Culture* (Routledge and Kegan Paul, London, 1978).

Wilson, Colin, *Origins of the Sexual Impulse* (Arthur Barker Ltd, London, 1963).

Wilson, Colin, *Order of Assassins* (Rupert Hart-Davis, London, 1972).

Wilson, Colin, *The New Existentialism* (Wildworth House, London, 1980).

Wilson, Colin, 'The Ripper Revealed', *Time Out* (19—25 April 1984).

Wilson, Colin and Pitman, Pat, *Encyclopaedia of Murder* (Arthur Barker Ltd, London, 1961).

Wilson, Colin and Seaman, Donald, *Encyclopaedia of Modern Murder*, (Arthur Barker Ltd, London, 1983).

Wilson, Elizabeth, *What is to be Done about Violence against Women?* (Penguin, Harmondsworth, 1981).

Wolfgang, Marvin E., *Patterns in Criminal Homicide* (University of Pennsylvania Press, Philadelphia, 1958).

Wolfgang, Marvin E., 'Victim-Precipitated Homicide', in *The Sociology of Crime and Delinquency*, eds Wolfgang, Marvin E., Savitz, Leonard and Norman Johnson, 2nd edn (John Wiley and Sons, New York, 1970).

Wolfgang, M. E. and Ferracuti, Franco, *The Subculture of Violence* (Sage Publications, Beverley Hills, 1982).

Wolfgang, M. E. and Weiner, Neil Alan eds *Criminal Violence* (Sage Publications, Beverley Hills and London, 1982).

Wright, E. and Howells, K., 'The Sexual Attitudes of Aggressive Sexual Offenders', *British Journal of Criminology*, 18 (1978).

Yallop, David A., *Deliver Us from Evil* (Macdonald Futura, London, 1981).

Index